Cognitive Therapy for Addiction

Cognitive Therapy for Addiction

Motivation and Change

Frank Ryan

A John Wiley & Sons, Ltd., Publication

This edition first published 2013
© 2013 Frank Ryan

Wiley-Blackwell is an imprint of John Wiley & Sons, formed by the merger of Wiley's global Scientific, Technical and Medical business with Blackwell Publishing.

Registered Office
John Wiley & Sons Ltd, The Atrium, Southern Gate, Chichester, West Sussex, PO19 8SQ, UK

Editorial Offices
350 Main Street, Malden, MA 02148-5020, USA
9600 Garsington Road, Oxford, OX4 2DQ, UK
The Atrium, Southern Gate, Chichester, West Sussex, PO19 8SQ, UK

For details of our global editorial offices, for customer services, and for information about how to apply for permission to reuse the copyright material in this book please see our website at www.wiley.com/wiley-blackwell.

The right of Frank Ryan to be identified as the author of this work has been asserted in accordance with the UK Copyright, Designs and Patents Act 1988.

All rights reserved. No part of this publication may be reproduced, stored in a retrieval system, or transmitted, in any form or by any means, electronic, mechanical, photocopying, recording or otherwise, except as permitted by the UK Copyright, Designs and Patents Act 1988, without the prior permission of the publisher.

Wiley also publishes its books in a variety of electronic formats. Some content that appears in print may not be available in electronic books.

Designations used by companies to distinguish their products are often claimed as trademarks. All brand names and product names used in this book are trade names, service marks, trademarks or registered trademarks of their respective owners. The publisher is not associated with any product or vendor mentioned in this book. This publication is designed to provide accurate and authoritative information in regard to the subject matter covered. It is sold on the understanding that the publisher is not engaged in rendering professional services. If professional advice or other expert assistance is required, the services of a competent professional should be sought.

Library of Congress Cataloging-in-Publication Data
Ryan, Frank, 1944–
  Cognitive therapy for addiction : motivation and change / Frank Ryan.
     p. cm.
  Includes bibliographical references and index.
  ISBN 978-0-470-66996-9 (cloth) – ISBN 978-0-470-66995-2 (pbk.)
 1. Compulsive behavior–Treatment. 2. Substance abuse–Treatment. 3. Cognitive therapy. I. Title.
  RC533.R93 2013
  616.85′227–dc23

2012034393

A catalogue record for this book is available from the British Library.

Cover image: *Die Furbige (The Intercessor)* by Paul Klee, 1929. Photo © Geoffrey Clements / Corbis.

Cover design by Richard Boxall Design Associates

Set in 10.5/13pt Minion by Laserwords Private Limited, Chennai, India.
Printed in Malaysia by Ho Printing (M) Sdn Bhd

1 2013

Contents

About the Author ix
Preface xi

1 The Tenacity of Addiction 1
   Introduction and Overview 1
   Discovering Cognition 5
   Implicit Cognition and Addiction 6
   Neuropsychological Findings 9
   Addictive Behaviour is Primary, Not Compensatory 11
   Changing Habits is the Priority 14
   Diagnostic Criteria 15
   Towards Integration 15
   Equivocal Findings from Research Trials 16
   Time for CHANGE 16
   Evolution, Not Revolution 17
   Something Old, Something New 18

2 Existing Cognitive Behavioural Accounts of Addiction and Substance Misuse 21
   The Evidential Basis of CBT for Addiction 23
   Meta-analytic Findings 23
   Behavioural Approaches 24
   Diverse Treatments Mostly Deliver Equivalent Outcomes 25
   What Are the Mechanisms of Change? 26
   The Missing Variable? 27
   A Dual-Processing Framework 28

3 Core Motivational Processes in Addiction 33
   Is Addiction About Avoiding Pain or Seeking Reward? 33
   How Formulation Can Go Astray 34
   Incentive Theories of Addiction 35
   Learning Mechanisms in Addiction 36

*Distorted Motivation and Aberrant Learning: the Emergence
of Compulsion* 41
'Wanting and Liking' in the Clinic 41
The Role of Secondary Reinforcers 43
Beyond Pleasure and Pain: a Psychoanalytic Perspective 43
Conclusion 44

4 A Cognitive Approach to Understanding the Compulsive
Nature of Addiction 45
Theories of Attention 46
Top-Down Influences Can Be Automatic 47
Automatic Processes Can Be Practically Limitless 48
Motivationally Relevant Cues are Prioritized 48
Biased Competition 50
Attention and Volition 51
Appetitive Cues Usually Win 52
Purposeful Behaviour Can Occur in the Absence of Consciousness 53
Attentional Bias and Craving 54
Cognitive Cycle of Preoccupation 56

5 Vulnerability Factors In Addiction 63
Individual Differences in Addiction Liability 63
Personality Traits 63
The 'Big Five' Personality Factors 65
Personality Disorders 66
Affective Vulnerability Factors 67
Brain-Derived Neurotrophic Factors 69
Neurocognitive Vulnerability 70
Findings from the Addiction Clinic 71
From Research to Practice 72

6 Motivation and Engagement 75
Impaired Insight and the Therapeutic Relationship 75
The Sad Case of Julia 80
Conflicted Motivation is the Key 81
Goal Setting and Maintenance 82
The Importance of Between-Session Change 83
Neurocognitive Perspectives on Motivation 83
Motivational Interviewing in Practice 84
Formulating and Planning the Intervention 88
Attributional Biases: the Blame Game 90
Case Formulation 91
Summary 97

Contents

7	**Managing Impulses**	99
	Introduction and Overview	99
	Structuring the Session	99
	Building Resilience	100
	Impulse Control	102
	Craving and Urge Report	103
	Cognitive Processing and Craving	104
	Cognitive Bias Modification	105
	Attentional Bias in the Context of Addiction	106
	The Alcohol Attention-Control Training Programme	108
	Modifying Implicit Approach Tendencies	110
	Reversing the Bias: Conclusion	112
	Brain Training and Neurocognitive Rehabilitation Approaches	112
	Clinical Implications of Delayed Reward Discounting	117
	Tried and Tested Techniques	119
	The Road to Recovery is Paved with Good Implementation Intentions!	125
	Neurophysiological Techniques	129
	Neuropsychopharmacological Approaches	130
8	**Managing Mood**	135
	The Reciprocal Relationship Between Mood and Addiction	135
	Pre-existing Vulnerability to Emotional Distress	137
	Negative Affect Due To Drug Effects	141
	Stepped Care for Addiction	145
	An Integrated Approach to Addressing Negative Emotion	147
9	**Maintaining Change**	155
	Relapse Prevention Strategies from a Neurocognitive Perspective	155
	The Importance of Goal Maintenance in the Long Term	158
	A Neurocognitive Perspective on Relapse	159
	Twelve-Step Facilitation Therapy	161
	Implicit Denial	162
10	**Future Directions**	171
	Neurocognitive Therapy	171
	Increasing Cognitive Control is the Goal	172
	Do We Know Anything New?	173
	Appendix Self-Help Guide Six Tips – a Pocket Guide to Preventing Relapse	179
	Introduction: Why Six Tips?	179
	1. Don't Always Trust Your Memory!	180
	2. Beware of the 'Booze Bias'!	180

3. Separate Thoughts from Actions   181
4. Learn How to Distract Yourself   181
5. Willpower Is Sometimes Not Enough   182
6. Beware of the Dog that Doesn't Bark...   182

References   185

Index   201

About the Author

Dr Frank Ryan trained as a clinical psychologist at Edinburgh University and works as a consultant in Camden & Islington National Health Service Foundation Trust in London, UK. He practices as a cognitive behaviour therapist with a special interest in addiction and co-occurring disorders. He is an Honorary Senior Lecturer in the Centre for Mental Health, Faculty of Medicine at Imperial College and an Honorary Research Fellow at the School of Psychology, Birkbeck College, University of London. He is a former Chair of the Addiction Faculty of the British Psychological Society's Division of Clinical Psychology. He has also served as consultant in cognitive therapy to the United Nations Office on Drugs and Crime. The focus of his research is behavioural and cognitive processes in addiction and translating research into practice, with particular emphasis on findings derived from cognitive neuroscience.

Preface

The story begins with Bill, who was addicted to alcohol. He was attending a group along with eight other men and women in a specialist clinic in Hammersmith, West London, more than ten years ago. They also had experienced problems associated with their use of alcohol and were trying to abstain or reduce their level of alcohol consumption. As group facilitator, my first task was usually to ask members to 'check in' with an update on how the past week had been for them: the problems, the worries, the cravings, the lapses and the coping. When it was Bill's turn to say something about the week just passed, he froze momentarily. Unlike some in the group, Bill did not experience anxiety in social situations; on the contrary, he was usually a fluent, relaxed speaker. I asked whether he wanted to collect his thoughts and let someone else speak in the interim but he declined. He quickly recovered his composure and said that his pause was due to hearing the word 'binge' uttered by the woman sitting next to him. Bill apparently found this word distracting and he was unable to concentrate on what he had intended to say about his own ups and downs in the preceding week.

I was intrigued by this episode: if the mere mention of an alcohol-related word could be so distracting, how potent could other addiction-related cues be in capturing attention, especially outside the confines of the clinic, where temptation was everywhere? A subsequent literature search revealed just one study of what is termed *attentional bias* in addiction. This investigation (Gross *et al.*, 1993) found that when cigarette smokers were deprived of nicotine for 12 hours they were more likely to be distracted by smoking related cues compared with fellow smokers who did not experience deprivation. Distraction was indexed by the slightly longer time it took the deprived smokers to name the colour used to print smoking-related words such as *tobacco* or *lighter*. Thus, they were slower to correctly respond with 'red' or 'blue' to these words than to neutral words such as *locker* or *man*. It was as if the words associated with cigarette smoking exerted a magnetic effect on the minds of abstinent smokers and distracted them from the primary task of simply naming a colour. The difference in reaction time between smoking-related and neutral words was tiny, a few milliseconds (ms), but was not observed with current smokers or people who had never smoked. To me, this appeared to be an analogue of what happened with Bill. Regardless of the task in hand, simply saying 'red', 'blue' 'green' or 'yellow' was slower if the word was connected with alcohol, but unaffected by the neutral words.

Although a definitive role for selective attention in anxiety disorders had by then been proposed (Williams *et al.*, 1988), it was clear to me that attentional bias was equally important in relation to addictive disorders. The seminal work of Marlatt and Gordon (1985) had already highlighted the cue-specific nature of relapse in addiction, and how people could learn alternative coping strategies to forestall this. But what if an encounter with these so-called 'high-risk situations' reflected a cognitive bias rather than chance or circumstance? What if, after leaving the treatment centre or the rehabilitation unit, individuals were drawn to precisely the situations they were advised to avoid? Important questions, it seemed to me. But not just to me: cigarette smoking is estimated to cause 5 million deaths worldwide each year (Thome *et al.*, 2009). In the United Kingdom in 2009, 8,664 deaths were attributed to alcohol-use disorders (ONS, 2011). It is estimated in the *World Drug Report* (UNODC, 2009) that between 11 and 21 million people in 148 countries worldwide inject drugs, of whom between 0.8 and 6.6 million are infected with human immunodeficiency virus (HIV). Addiction is also associated with massive healthcare costs: Gustavsson *et al.* (2011) estimated that in 30 European countries (27 European Union member states plus Iceland, Norway and Switzerland) addictive disorders cost €65.7 billion in direct and indirect healthcare costs. For comparison, anxiety disorders were estimated to cost €74.4 billion, and mood disorders (unipolar and bipolar depression) €43.3. An entire volume would be needed to describe the full extent of human misery and costs attributable to the spectrum of substance misuse and addiction.

Here, the focus is on the cognitive and motivational processes that enable diverse behaviours such as smoking a cigarette, sipping an alcoholic beverage or injecting heroin to persist in parallel with awareness of the harmful consequences that ensue and a sincere desire to desist. In order to learn more about the role of cognitive bias in addiction, I conducted an experimental study using a modified Stroop test (Ryan, 2002a) with the invaluable help of the clients and colleagues in the clinic. It seemed to me that if attentional bias could operate at an early stage of cue reactivity it could thereby influence the frequency and intensity of urges and clinical outcome as indexed by relapse rates. I began to explore the theoretical and clinical implications of this mental process, which seems to occur unconsciously, involuntarily and, by all accounts, relentlessly. This, I thought, helped to explain the disparity between the commitment to recovery shown by many addicted individuals and the high frequency with which they failed. It still seemed sensible to teach coping strategies in anticipation of encountering the people, places and things that might trigger appetitive impulses. But sometimes this seemed to be too little, too late.

By then, I realized that my interest in the role of cognition in addiction was shared by many talented researchers and clinicians. This helped me recognize that selective attention can only be understood, or at least partially grasped, when seen as a property of a highly sophisticated system of cognitive or executive control. Inspired by their efforts and continuing my clinical practice in parallel, I began to develop the ideas that form the basis of this book. These were elaborated through a series of presentations and workshops at events such as the European Association of Behavioural and Cognitive Therapies and the World Congress of Behavioural and Cognitive Therapies in exotic locations such as Acapulco, Vancouver, Paris and Dubrovnik. This entailed a reappraisal of cognitive therapy for addiction that accentuated the core theme of this text: addiction is quintessentially a disorder of conflicted motivation that is reflected in impaired cognitive control, defined as the ability to flexibly guide behaviour in the pursuit of desired outcomes or goals.

However, in the clinical arena within which many of the readers of this book operate, this cognitive–motivational process can often be obscured by the diversity of the presenting problems associated with addictive behaviour. Accordingly, it is necessary to place this focus on cognitive control in a broader therapeutic framework known as *CHANGE*, an acronym of Change Habits and the Negative Generation of Emotion. An acronym is always a compromise but *CHANGE* serves to remind those tasked with overcoming addiction, whether therapist or treatment seeker, that this entails reversing compulsive habits and managing emotions. The journey of the book thus began in the clinic, then detoured through a process of research and innovation only to return once again to the clinical arena. Along the way, academic and clinical colleagues have generously shared their knowledge and skills. I am deeply indebted to them. In particular, I would like to thank W. Miles Cox (who kindly commented on a draft of this book) Michael Eysenck, Matt Field, Hugh Garavan, John Green, Marcus Munafò, Mick Power, Anne Richards, David Soto, Philip Tata and Reinout Wiers. I remain, however, responsible for any shortcomings in the text! I am equally indebted to those who came my way in the clinic with insightful and authentic accounts of their own addictions.

1

The Tenacity of Addiction

Introduction and Overview

Why does addiction exert such a tenacious grip on those who fall under its spell? In this book I propose that the answer to this question lies largely within the cognitive domain: the persistence of addiction is viewed as a failure or aberration of cognitive control motivated by the enduring and unconditional value assigned to substances or behaviours that activate neural reward systems. I shall outline how addictive behaviour endures because it recruits core cognitive processes such as attention, memory and decision making in pursuit of the goal of gratification, the associated alleviation of negative emotions, or both. This recruitment process is often covert, if not subversive, and operates implicitly or automatically in the context of impaired inhibitory control. The habituated drug user is effectively disarmed when exposed to a wide range of cues that generate powerful involuntary responses. The best, and often the only, option is to mount a rear-guard action from the command and control centre of the brain. This sets the scene for a reappraisal of cognitive therapy applied to addiction. Beginning with an overview of the plan and scope of the book, this introductory chapter outlines a cognitive perspective on addiction. It goes on to address shortcomings in historical and current therapeutic approaches to addictive behaviour and includes a brief review of the equivocal and occasionally puzzling findings generated in clinical trials. It concludes with an overview of *CHANGE*, the re-formulated account of psychological intervention based on cognitive, motivational and behavioural principles in a cognitive neuroscience framework that forms the basis of this text.

Terminology

I have avoided the use of the term *addict* unless quoting from other sources. I do not think the manifestation of a particular behaviour should be used to denote an individual, in the same way that I would avoid use of terms such as *a depressive* or *an obsessive* in other circumstances. Of course, many of those who develop addictive disorders choose to refer to themselves as 'addicts'. That is entirely appropriate for them, but I believe choosing to designate oneself as an addict is different from being so labelled by another. However, beginning with the title, I readily adopt the term *addiction*. Here, I apply a functional definition emphasizing the apparent involitional nature of addictive behaviour, its persistence in the face of repeated harm to self and others, and a tendency for drug seeking and taking to recur following cessation. In truth, addictive behaviour and its concomitant cognitive, behavioural and neurobiological facets occur on a continuum of varying, but often escalating, frequency and quantity or dosage. This is why attributing a static label such as *addict* is likely to miss the point, even if occasionally seeming to hit the nail on the head. There will be some interchange between the terms addiction, substance use and substance misuse according to the context. Generally, however, my use of the term addiction implies that the individual or group referred to meet standard diagnostic criteria for addictive disorders or dependence syndromes. Similarly, and again given pride of place on the front cover, I have opted for the term *cognitive therapy* rather than *cognitive behavioural therapy*. This decision is pragmatic rather than doctrinal but does authenticate the emphasis on cognition throughout the book. Both terms feature in the text, and anything deemed purely cognitive can easily be assimilated into the broader church of CBT.

Scope

Addiction has long been a source of fascination for theorists from a wide variety of scientific backgrounds. West (2001) listed a total of 98 theoretical models of addiction, which he classified broadly as either biological, psychological or social in orientation and content. Here, I do not attempt to review this diverse body of work. Nonetheless, West's taxonomy, referencing a 'biopsychosocial' framework, serves as a reminder that addiction is a complex, multifactorial, phenomenon. The main focus here is on understanding the neurocognitive and behavioural mechanisms of addiction and translating this knowledge into more effective therapeutic intervention. Most of the theoretical and empirical findings cited are based on either clinical trials or experimental paradigms involving drug administration, drug ingestion and drug withdrawal in humans and other species. For the most part, the substances at the root of the problems addressed in this text will therefore include opiates, cocaine, amphetamines, alcohol, nicotine and cannabis. At the time of writing, preparations for the fifth revision of the *Diagnostic and Statistical Manual of Mental Disorders* (DSM-V) are well underway. The term *dependence*, also central to the ICD-10 (WHO, 1992), is apparently being dropped. This is apparently due mainly to the possibility of conceptual confusion stemming from its dual meaning referring to either uncontrolled drug use, or normal neuroadaptation when, for example, narcotic analgesics are prescribed to alleviate chronic pain (O'Brien, 2011). The forthcoming taxonomy, due to be published in 2013, will therefore refer to 'Addiction and Related Disorders'. Subcategories will refer to 'alcohol use disorder', 'heroin use disorder' and so on.

Gambling and other compulsive appetitive behaviours

In the forthcoming diagnostic manual on addictive disorders, the chapter on addiction will also include compulsive gambling, currently classified as an impulse control disorder along with trichotillomania and kleptomania in DSM-IV (American Psychiatric Association, 1994). Consistent with this, Castellani and Rugle (1995) demonstrated that problem gambling is associated with tolerance, withdrawal, urges and cravings, high rates of relapse and high levels of co-morbidity for mental health problems. More fundamentally, from a cognitive neuroscience point of view, it is what goes on in the brain that matters, whether this is triggered by heroin, cocaine, alcohol or indeed gambling. By way of illustration, an intriguing series of case studies provides a more clinical dimension to the motivational power of dopamine, a key neurotransmitter in reward processing, in relation to gambling. Dodd *et al.* (2005) reported how they encountered 11 patients over a two-year period at a movement disorders clinic with idiopathic Parkinson's disease who developed pathological gambling. All of these patients were given dopamine agonist therapy such as pramipexole dihydrochloride. Seven of these patients developed pathological or compulsive gambling within 1–3 months of achieving the maintenance dose or with dose escalation. One 68-year-old man, with no history of gambling, acquired $200,000 of gambling debt. On cessation of dopamine agonist therapy his urge to gamble subsided and eventually ceased, an outcome also observed in the seven other patients that were available for follow-up. More generally, other behaviours with a propensity to become compulsive include online activities such as Internet addiction and gaming. My view is that a behaviour such as gambling that activates reward neurocircuitry with wins, and probably downregulates the same system with losses, is liable to become compulsive in susceptible individuals. Consequently, aspects of compulsive gambling and other behaviours where motivation to desist is compromised fall within the scope of this book.

The plan of the book

The book begins with a brief critical appraisal of existing approaches, in particular cognitive and behavioural approaches such as cognitive behavioural therapy (CBT) and cognitive therapy itself (Chapter 2). This review is highly selective insofar as it focuses on shortcomings and unanswered questions, such as the finding that markedly diverse therapeutic approaches, including CBT, deliver broadly equivalent clinical outcomes. In successive chapters (3 and 4), I address first the core learning processes that contribute to the development of addiction and their neurocognitive bases, as well as delineating the predispositional role of exposure to adversity. Next, a conceptual framework that accommodates implicit cognitive and behavioural processes along with more familiar targets such as consciously available beliefs is outlined. The conclusion is that the most plausible way to regulate the former is by augmenting the latter: strategies that enhance executive control, metacognition or awareness are more likely to deliver better outcomes. By emphasizing a component process such as executive or 'top-down' control, the therapist and client are provided with a conceptual compass with which to navigate through the voyage of recovery. Chapter 5 addresses the question of individual susceptibility to addiction: if, indeed, drugs and gambling wins are such powerful rewards, why, ultimately, do not all but a small minority develop compulsive or addictive syndromes? This marks the transition from the more theoretical and research based chapters to content that is more directly relevant to the clinical or applied arena, although remaining grounded in a cognitive neuroscience paradigm.

Most of the remainder of the book (Chapters 6, 7, 8 and 9) explicates key therapeutic phases from a cognitive control standpoint. The sequence that unfolds follows the 'Four M' structure (see Figure 1.1), which is the enactment of the *CHANGE* approach:

Motivation and engagement
Managing urges and craving
Mood management
Maintaining change.

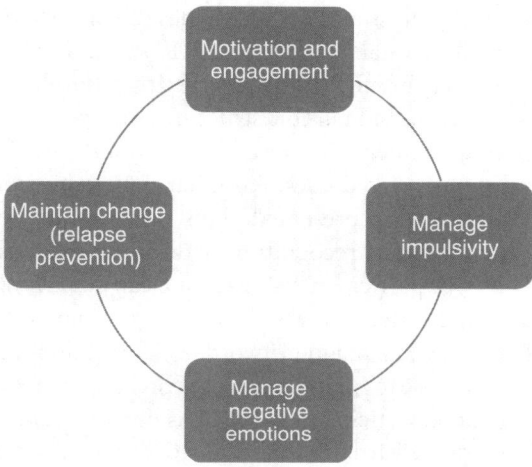

Figure 1.1 The Four M Model. Clockwise, these are the four key stages.

Chapter 10 aims to summarize, integrate and look forward in the context of a vibrant research arena with major implications for the concept and conduct of cognitive therapy.

Discovering Cognition

Existing accounts of cognitive therapy for addiction have not accommodated findings that cognitive processes, in particular those deemed automatic or implicit, are influential in maintaining addiction, or indeed as a potential means of leveraging change. In cognitive parlance, these models do not legislate for 'parallel processing' across controlled or automatic modes, with the latter being largely overlooked. Simply put, existing accounts fail to address what is the hallmark of addiction: compulsive drug seeking behaviour that appears to occur with little insight and often in the face of an explicit desire for restraint. Moreover, existing cognitive therapy approaches do not accommodate findings that cognitive efficiency is often impaired in those presenting with addictive disorders, whether stemming from pre-existing or acquired deficiencies. The client has developed a strong tendency for preferential cognitive processing and facilitated behavioural approach in the face of impaired cognitive control. Failure to acknowledge this leaves the therapist and client in the dark about an important source of variance that is influential at all stages of the therapeutic journey.

The findings of Childress and her colleagues (2008), who used advanced functional magnetic resonance imaging (fMRI) techniques to explore the neural signature of very briefly presented appetitive stimuli, are noteworthy. They found early activation of limbic structures such as the amygdala when the 22 participating abstinent cocaine addicts were shown subliminal, backward masked drug associated cues. A similar pattern was observed when covert sexual stimuli were presented. This design effectively eliminated the possibility of conscious recognition with backward masked exposure for a mere 33 ms, yet participants showed a clear pattern of activation in limbic structures implicated in reward processing. When tested with visible versions of these cues 'off-magnet' two days later, initial higher levels of brain activity in response to invisible cues was predictive of positive affective evaluation among the participants. As well as demonstrating the exquisite sensitivity of neural reward mechanisms to drug-related stimuli, these findings show that for habituated drug users the appetite for their drug of choice compares to powerful sexual drives: evidence perhaps that, for some, drugs are as good as, if not better than, sex. Further, Leventhal *et al.* (2008) found selective subliminal processing of smoking-related cues by nicotine-deprived smokers, again indicating non-conscious evaluative appraisal. It appears that, when exposed to significant cues, the brain makes up its mind very rapidly about what it wants. Extant theories (see, e.g., Marlatt, 1985; Beck, 1993) have difficulty in accounting for these cognitive events and processes, largely because information is processed at one level. Dual processing accounts, which form the basis of this text, have no such difficulty.

Implicit Cognition and Addiction

The definitive feature of implicit cognition is that 'traces of past experience affect some performance, even though the influential earlier experience is not remembered in the usual sense – that is, it is unavailable to self-report or introspection' (Greenwald and Banji, 1995, p. 4). These theorists illustrate the operation of implicit cognition with a generic example from experimental psychology. Participants are thus more likely to complete a word fragment or word stem using a word from a list to which they were previously casually exposed. Note that participants may not show explicit recall of the words but the effect of prior exposure nonetheless influences performance. The individual thus appears primed or predisposed to automatically generate a response that appears to evade introspection.

This is, of course, precisely what is happening in the brains of the cocaine-addicted people referred to above: the drug-associated cues have acquired considerable emotional and motivational potency that assured them of preferential processing even the absence of conscious awareness.

In the addiction clinic, prior exposure to a vast array of appetitive stimuli, both focal and contextual, is the norm. Learning theory correctly charts the acquisition of conditioned behaviour, but is less able to accommodate cognitive processes, especially if these are implicit rather than manifest. Wiers *et al.* (2006) sought to clarify the scope of implicit cognition approaches in the addictive behaviour field by proposing three broad categories: attentional bias research, memory bias research and the study of implicit associations. Wiers *et al.* (2006) concluded that, at least in the populations of problem drinkers addressed in their article, there was an implicit bias towards the detection of alcohol-related stimuli. Following engagement of attention, subsequent information processing was shaped by implicit memory associations. Understandably, given their covert nature, these processes remain largely unseen and unheard by addicted people and their therapists. Moreover, their influence and expression is often masked in the sanitized environment of the treatment centre or clinic, thus creating a somewhat illusory sense of progress. For example, an individual who has just completed a detoxification procedure might *explicitly* predict their future progress, but implicit factors might improve predictive utility and thus influence the level and intensity of treatment subsequently received. Indeed, preliminary findings from Cox *et al.* (2002) indicated that alcohol-dependent patients who showed escalating levels of attentional bias to alcohol cues through the treatment episode were more likely to relapse. This raises the question of the feasibility and utility of modifying or reversing cognitive biases that will be addressed in Chapter 7. This finding was replicated by Garland *et al.* (2012), who found that attentional bias and cue-induced high-frequency heart-rate variability (HFHRV), assessed post treatment, significantly predicted the occurrence and latency to relapse at six-month follow-up in a sample of 53 people in residential care. This was independent of treatment condition (a 10-session mindfulness-based intervention and a comparable therapeutic support group) and after controlling for severity of alcohol dependence.

Implicit cognition might well be subtle but is also pervasive and can be detrimental for both therapeutic engagement and clinical outcomes. Accordingly, cognitive therapy needs to accommodate a broader concept of cognition in addiction, delineating a role for implicit processes in parallel with the more familiar focus on conscious deliberation and re-appraisal. This re-conceptualization is the basis for developing the innovative approaches to formulating and intervening with addictive and impulsive appetitive behaviours that will be addressed in this text. The theoretical framework and clinical strategies are thus derived from CBT but framed within a cognitive neuroscience paradigm. I shall describe how this emergent paradigm can augment existing therapeutics and also generate innovative techniques that directly target the core cognitive and behavioural mechanisms of addiction.

Cognitive control is compromised in addiction

In the context of overcoming addiction, cognitive control is concerned with maintaining recovery goals and monitoring progress in goal pursuit. In particular, managing addictive impulses that have become redundant, unwanted or risky is vital. Cognitive control, especially inhibition, thus forms a key component of the broader executive functioning necessary for self-regulation. Other components of this function, associated with the prefrontal cortex, include *shifting* strategies in response to changing task requirements and *updating* by monitoring of goal pursuit. These cognitive operations – shifting, inhibiting and updating – have emerged as relatively independent factors in experimental investigation of executive functioning Miyake *et al.*, (2000). Impaired control over drug use by habituated users is of course a definitive feature of substance dependence and thus a rather obvious target for therapeutic intervention. Cognitive neuroscience findings provide confirmatory evidence for this. Chambers *et al.* (2009) reviewed evidence pointing to cocaine users, for example, showing impairments on several laboratory measures of impulse control such as having to withhold a well practised response or manifested in making riskier decisions. These deficiencies have been noted both under conditions of acute intoxication and also among abstinent restrained drug and alcohol users. Kaufman *et al.* (2003), for instance, using fMRI during a go/no go task, found significant cingulate, pre-supplementary motor and insular hyperactivity in a sample of 13 active cocaine users when compared with 14 cocaine naive controls. Forman and colleagues (2004), also using fMRI found abnormally decreased activity of this cingulo-frontoparietal–cerebellar neural network with a cohort of opiateaddicted individuals. These findings suggest that some drugs with addiction liability compromise command and control centres in the brain. This happens during intoxication but also carries over to abstinent periods. The most important faculty required for recovery, cognitive control or willpower, is thus rendered less effective when it is most needed.

Neuropsychological Findings

Conversely, clinical neuropsychological findings indicate that damage to cortical structures can dramatically disrupt appetitive behaviour. Yucel et al. (2007) used a combination of fMRI and proton magnetic resonance spectroscopy to investigate cognitive control in a cohort of 24 opiate-dependent individuals on either methadone or buprenorphine with drug-naive controls. They found that, while anterior cingulate cortex (ACC) activation was equivalent across the two groups, the opiate users failed to demonstrate the normal association between ACC physiological activity and behaviour measures (i.e. response errors) shown by the control group. There were abnormalities detected in neurochemical markers such as N-acetyl aspartate and glutamate. In addition, opiate users required greater involvement of the frontoparietal and cerebellar behavioural regulation network to achieve normal levels of cognitive control. Yucel et al. (2007, p. S99) speculated that 'The pattern of results across these studies implies that chronic drug use leads to the recruitment of a compensatory network of brain regions in order to successfully detect and resolve conflicts in response tendencies. However, even though normative behavioural performance may be achieved in structured laboratory experiments, the same neural systems may be more vulnerable to fail in the real world, where emotional and motivational influences (e.g. stress, craving, withdrawal, etc.) also tax these cognitive and neural resources'. Interestingly, both the clinic cohort and matched controls showed robust neurocognitive functioning as indicated by obtaining IQ scores of 112, above the normal range. The influence of opiate substitution therapy (average methadone, about 43 mg; average buprenorphine, 10 mg), or indeed premorbid cognitive performance deficits, cannot of course be ruled out as a source of differences between the clinic attendees and the control group. However, in the studies reviewed here, while participants from both experimental and control groups made errors such as pressing a button when they did not intend to, it was those with the addictive history who were somewhat underwhelmed at the neurobiological level, as evidenced by hypoactivity in the cingulate.

With regard to other substances, heavy marijuana use was associated with lower performance on tests of memory, executive functioning and manual dexterity in a sample of 22 regular users who had remained abstinent for 28 days prior to testing (Bolla et al., 2002). Eldreth et al. (2004) compared performance on a modified version of the Stroop task and brain activity between 11 heavy marijuana users who had been abstinent for 25 days and 11 matched comparators. The marijuana users showed no comparative deficits in performance on the Stroop task. However, the marijuana users showed *hypoactivity* in the ACC and the left lateral prefrontal cortex and *hyperactivity* in the hippocampus bilaterally, a pattern not observed in the comparator group. This suggests that the marijuana-using group was relying on a compensatory mechanism in the face of suboptimal error monitoring.

Turning to neurocognitive deficits associated with cocaine use, Bolla *et al.* (2004) used a variant of the Stroop test and positron emission tomography to explore cognitive conflict in 23-day-abstinent cocaine users. While engaged on the Stroop task, cocaine abusers showed less activation than non-drug-using comparison subjects in the left ACC and the right lateral prefrontal cortex but greater activation in the right ACC. This pattern was associated with response competition generated by the Stroop task. Resting scans showed no differences in neural circuitry such as the ACC, which subserves executive functioning. The abstinent cocaine users with the most intense of history of drug use showed the highest level of abnormality when cognitively challenged. Importantly, the two groups performed at equivalent levels on the cognitive tasks, being differentiated only at the neuronal level.

How should these findings be interpreted in the context of responding to addictive behaviour in the clinical arena? First, it is neither possible nor necessarily helpful to speculate on the issue of causality. In this regard, Garavan and Stout (2005) hypothesized that observed functional deficits such as those briefly reviewed above could be the product of pre-existing cognitive 'trait' variables such as poor impulse control that could be potentiated by acquired patterns of substance misuse, thus leading to more transient 'state' variables such as compromised cognitive control associated with recent intoxication. The fact that these deficits appear to endure for at least a month after cessation of drug use suggests that those involved in delivering therapeutic intervention should, at the very least, be aware of the fact that the client may be compromised in terms of cognitive control or at least have to exert more mental effort in dealing with situations where rapid decision or response inhibition is required.

As evidenced by the robust performance on neuropsychological tests, there did not appear to be global differences in cognitive functioning across the various groups of substance using and control participants. Instead, there appeared to be a specific deficit revealed by precise cognitive tests and neurobiological assays among the cohorts of drug users recruited. From the standpoint of embarking on a journey of rehabilitation that will inevitably involve complex new learning, it appears to me that a deficit in detecting errors or perhaps the necessity to exert more cognitive effort to compensate for this will inevitably prove challenging, if not exhausting. Moreover, these subtle alterations in cognitive processing remain largely unrecognized outside the cognitive neuroscience laboratory. At the very least, awareness of this should enable the addiction therapist to generate more accurate empathy as their clients encounter the inevitable challenges on the route to recovery.

Garavan and Stout (2005) concluded on the basis of their review that drug misusers evidenced a low level of awareness of errors on a range of laboratory tasks. This was associated with hypoactivity in the ACC, a structure vital to performance monitoring . The ACC is the early warning system for errors and is activated during action slips (Garavan *et al.*, 2003), and contributes to the 'D'oh!' feeling epitomized by Homer Simpson when he makes yet another error. In a sense, these findings validate phenomenological aspects of drug use. When clients state that they are struggling to cope with the challenges of restraint as they work towards recovery, the informed therapist can thus provide a more empathic response. As will be seen, recognizing deficits in cognitive control is the first step in developing the emerging 'neurocognitive' therapy addressed as outlined in Chapter 6 and elsewhere in this volume. This focus on cognition is thus intended to create a therapeutic space that bridges the gap between the neurobiological mechanisms of addiction and the need to devise plausible therapeutic strategies. The rationale is that CBT can be more accurately formulated and precisely targeted by understanding the enduring neurocognitive signature of addiction.

Addictive Behaviour is Primary, Not Compensatory

Second, existing or historical accounts emphasize or assume that addiction is *compensatory*: compulsive drug use and gambling are seen as a means of dulling or avoiding emotional pain, rather than seeking pleasure or reward. This follows a long tradition in psychology, largely unfettered by empirical support. In the psychodynamic tradition, Kohut (1971, p. 46), for example, viewed drug use as 'a replacement for a defect in the psychological structure'. The major failing of intuitive accounts of addiction such as this was circular reasoning. They echo historical accounts proposing that 'moral deficiency' was the cause of addiction on the decidedly shaky premise that individuals were lacking moral fibre simply because they were addicted. In turn, the addiction was paraded as evidence of the underlying moral frailty.

More recently, cognitive therapy accounts have similarly proposed addiction as a *reaction* to an event or an emotional state rather than a primary motive. Addiction stemmed from attempts to cope with or suppress maladaptive core beliefs such as 'I am helpless' or 'I am unlovable' (Beck *et al.*, 1993, p. 52). Cognitive therapists reading this text will doubtless have elicited these beliefs in the course of their work in addiction clinics and elsewhere. Clearly, negative emotions such as depression and anxiety can lead to drug taking, and dysphoria can be also be consequential to intoxication. However, vulnerability to emotional disorders *and* addictive disorders could also emerge and present in parallel because of their prevalence: lifetime prevalence rates for anxiety disorders in the USA, for example, have been estimated at 29% and mood disorders at 21% of the population (Kessler *et al.*, 2005) and an estimated 120 million of the adult population regularly consume alcohol (Anthony *et al.*, 1994).

It seems plausible that some individuals with coexisting emotional and addictive problems could have acquired these through different mechanisms or learning processes. In this regard, Hiroi and Agatsuma (2005) reviewed evidence indicating genetically distinct pathways leading to expressions of *either* drug dependence *or* comorbidity. Presumably, these could coexist. For instance, an individual could acquire an anxious disposition through a combination of genetic predisposition and exposure to adversity in childhood. The same individual could develop a dependence on cocaine or alcohol because of a different combination of genetic predisposition and an environmental factor such as easily available cocaine and hence greater exposure. Significantly, when cigarette smokers speak of their addiction, the listener rarely responds with speculation that this reflects some compensatory behaviour linked to disrupted attachment to parents, or being the victim of cruelty as a child. The addicted smoker is implicitly viewed in a manner more akin to that proposed in this text: regardless of his or her pre-existing vulnerabilities, it seems clear that the problem is inability to give up smoking. Similarly, a lifelong heroin user, recently detoxified, said to me in the course of a brief screening assessment: 'Basically I'm fine; I'm just an addict'. He did in fact appear to enjoy a sense of well-being. Many of course do not, and this can lead the formulation astray as the therapist and client strive to connect up the addictive behaviour with the negative emotional legacy. Generating a valid conceptualization of addiction is crucial if cognitive and cognitive behavioural approaches are to deliver enhanced outcomes. In the absence of conceptual clarity, confusion can thus emerge. Consider this statement from a client who resumed using cocaine and drinking alcohol after eight months abstinence:

> What is it about me, just when I get things right for a change, I start using again and end up relapsing. I seem to push the 'self-destruct button'. It must be that, deep down, I just want to be a failure (Ryan, 2006, p. 291).

Cognitive therapists (at least this one!) would most likely need to engage their own inhibitory systems to avoid tackling this maladaptive core belief. The *CHANGE* model does not ignore the possibility that such core beliefs are therapeutically significant, but questions whether they should be the primary focus. Here, a more parsimonious account of addictive behaviour is offered. The attention of the therapist and client when reviewing this episode focused on the more proximal antecedents of behaviour rather than searching for underlying vulnerabilities.

Drugs: no excuse needed!

Here, addiction is viewed as initially *appetitive* or *hedonic*, at least in the acquisition phase, when neural reward systems are first transformed by repeated drug ingestion. The hedonism or pleasure may well diminish with habituation but the approach behaviour remains as compelling as ever. It therefore contrasts sharply with common mental health problems such as anxiety and depression manifested (and maintained) by avoidance behaviour, or effortful suppression of unwanted thoughts or images. Existing cognitive therapy accounts of addiction (e.g., Beck *et al.*, 1993) view stress or interpersonal conflict as contexts for eliciting beliefs such as 'A drink will relax me', which in turn elicit automatic thoughts such as 'Drink!' or 'Smoke!'. These thoughts evoke craving and urges to use drugs. Without doubt, this is a potential pathway to a lapse or relapse, and a competent therapist would not hesitate in addressing this potentially maladaptive sequence of thought and action. Here, I propose that, while virtually any event or situation can become a precursor to drug use, there is a more direct cognitive–motivational process activated when drug cues are detected. Moreover, negative affect is by no means the only pathway, and *positive* affect or factors such as testing personal control also appear to precipitate relapse. Granted, these lapses did not prove as sustained as those associated with negative affect (Hodgins *et al.*, 1995). Nonetheless, a different picture emerged when a prospective design was employed to investigate the affective antecedents of relapse among a group of 133 smokers. Shiffman and Waters (2004) found that more enduring, day-to-day changes in stress and negative affect appeared to have little influence on lapse risk, but that more sudden increases in negativity, perhaps triggered by an argument and lasting for shorter periods of hours or minutes, were more likely to promote smoking lapses. They concluded that smokers aiming to give up are best advised to learn to cope with the challenges posed by the transient 'slings and arrows' of everyday life. Changes in affect, of whatever valence, are dynamically linked to addictive behaviour but are neither necessary nor sufficient to account for its genesis and enduring legacy. On occasion affective changes serve as triggers for compulsive drug taking or gambling, but often no excuse is needed. Addictive pursuits are intrinsically rewarding.

Changing Habits is the Priority

Therefore, in the current text I am according more immediacy and primacy to drug cues as powerful and *direct* motivators of behaviour in their own right. There is thus no need for an 'activating event' such as stress or interpersonal conflict for drug-seeking behaviour to be mobilized. Situations or scenarios associated with drug use will understandably evoke previously acquired, situation-specific, responses such as reaching for a drink or one's favourite drug, or immersing oneself in gambling. This is because, in reality, the potential activating event and the drug cue will often share the scene and the timeframe. As implied above, failure to grasp the appetitive essence of addiction has led to problems in how cognitive therapists conceptualize and formulate treatment plans. Cognitive and behavioural therapies have proved very effective in helping anxious and depressed people overcome avoidance. Arguably, instigating behavioural change is the quickest way to change cognitive processes. However, the behavioural signature of addictive disorders is *approach*. Orchestrating approach or exposure to addictive cues does not reliably or consistently lead to the therapeutic desensitization observed with, say, anxious patients (Conklin and Tiffany, 2002; see p. 159). Further, if cue exposure and response prevention does not work with an anxious person, the result is an unpleasant but usually transient increase in stress on the part of the patient and perhaps a slightly embarrassed therapist. In contrast, for an addicted individual exposed to drug-associated cues in a naturalistic setting, the consequences can be altogether more negative and enduring, as a lapse or relapse can ensue. The relapsing drug user risks losing parenting privileges, freedom, career, relationships, health or even life itself.

Diagnostic Criteria

Diagnostic criteria also appear circular, or at least remaining at a descriptive rather than explanatory level. Thus, the ICD-10 (WHO, 1992) criteria for substance dependence include the following: 'A cluster of behavioural, cognitive, and physiological phenomena that develop after repeated substance use and that typically include a strong desire to take the drug, difficulties in controlling its use, persisting in its use despite harmful consequences'. Again, the development of dependence, roughly equivalent to addiction in this context, emerges from repetitious substance use. The antecedents or the underlying mechanisms are ignored. This flawed reasoning is also echoed in disease entity or 'loss of control' accounts of addiction espoused by Alcoholics Anonymous (AA). Here, the sign or manifestation of the condition – inability to regulate appetitive behaviour – is reframed as the causative factor. Thus, individuals who cannot control their use of drugs or their propensity to gamble are deemed to be afflicted by a syndrome defined by inability to control the behaviour in question.

Towards Integration

Despite the logical shortcomings in the above, individuals can and do respond to well intentioned moral argument, the voice of the cognitive therapist or caring physician or the support of a self-help group. Indeed, there are commonalities between the more traditional views referred to above and the cognitive perspective espoused here: Somewhat ironically, the cognitive neuroscience findings highlighted in the foregoing suggest that self-regulation is indeed impaired in the context of addiction, resonant with the 'loss of control' concept that forms the basis of Twelve-Step approaches. There is one crucial difference: cognitive neuroscience illuminates hitherto unrecognized or unknown mechanisms or processes. Neuroimaging and experimental psychology findings, as above, have shown that appetitive stimuli are differentiated from neutral cues outside conscious awareness.

It appears therefore that the drivers of addictive behaviour are unreportable by the patient and can thus remain hidden from the clinician. Given the covert nature of the mechanisms of addiction, merely observing addictive behaviour, or seeking introspective reports, has not led to a convincing account of the *mechanisms* of addictive behaviour. For example, experimental cognitive psychology findings indicate that it is difficult to impede the rapid and preconscious *engagement* of attention but there is more therapeutic potential in focusing on the enhancement of *disengagement* of attention, because the latter is more amenable to cognitive control (see Chapter 6). Cognitive neuroscience thus promises to reveal more about the processes that govern addiction than is available through either introspection on the part of the addicted or the observations of the clinician. The aim of this text is to translate these revelations into viable therapeutic formulations and procedures.

Equivocal Findings from Research Trials

Third, cognitive therapy for addiction has not yielded the same robust therapeutic gains typically observed with, for example, anxious and depressed patients: cognitive therapy works, but does not consistently deliver added value when compared with other approaches such as Twelve-Step interventions. CBT has proved wanting, or at best inconsistent, when deployed against addiction, at least when compared with its impressive track record in tackling emotional disorders such as depression and anxiety. Even when our efforts are augmented by CBT, the apparently straightforward task of abiding by our promise not to do something often proves overwhelmingly difficult. Meta-analytic and controlled clinical trial findings attest to the stubborn nature of addiction. Intriguingly, markedly diverse therapeutic approaches including CBT motivational enhancement and Twelve-Step models have been found to deliver equivalent outcomes. As discussed in Chapter 2, this poses a particular challenge to CBT, which prides itself on the integrity and specificity of its core component processes.

Time for CHANGE

To recap, theorists and therapists first need to acknowledge that the cognitive processes that govern addiction are often autonomous. Addictive behaviour can therefore be initiated and proceed in the absence of awareness. The rivalry between these implicit cognitive and behavioural responses and explicit efforts to regulate impulsivity epitomizes the cognitive–motivational conflict that fosters addictive behaviour. Therapeutic intervention in response to addiction is thus more aptly viewed as a form of *conflict resolution* that directly or indirectly facilitates cognitive control. Interventions that foster cognitive control are more likely to deliver robust and enduring gains. Second, existing cognitive therapy accounts relegate addiction to a compensatory or consequential role symptomatic of underlying personal or emotional vulnerability. Here, I aim to reaffirm the primacy of addiction, regardless of the emotional or personal context from which it stems. Third, clinical outcomes observed after cognitive and behavioural interventions are often equivocal and sometimes negligible. Moreover, there is no empirically based consensus on the key mechanisms of change, as diverse therapies generate equivalent results. The *CHANGE* framework aims to address the above issues by acknowledging a role for implicit or automatic cognitive processes and emphasizing the primacy of addictive behaviour as a target for therapeutic intervention. However, emotional and neurocognitive factors are intrinsically linked to the initiation, maintenance and cessation of addictive behaviour. Accordingly, affect regulation and cognitive control skills are assigned a key role in enabling individuals to overcome addiction.

Evolution, Not Revolution

The aim of this book is not, however, to advocate abandoning tried and tested methods of therapeutic intervention with addictive behaviour and supplanting these with novel strategies, not least because for the most part the latter await the verdict of clinical trials. Rather, by delineating a core component process – cognitive or executive control – the aim is to accentuate common features in the mechanisms of change. As will be seen, viewing established therapeutic approaches such as cognitive therapy, motivational interviewing and Twelve-Step programmes through a cognitive processing prism reveals perhaps surprising commonality in the midst of diversity. Novel techniques that have only recently emerged from the experimenters' laboratories, such as cognitive bias modification or strategies for inhibiting automatic approach tendencies, will also be assigned a role in the evolving neurocognitive framework that forms the basis of this book. In this regard, the book resonates with contemporary efforts to anchor cognitive therapy in a more neurobiological framework. Disner et al. (2011), for example, described a neurobiological architecture based on Beck's (1967) cognitive model of depression. They proposed that the negative cognitive biases that characterize depression are facilitated by greater activity in subcortical emotion processing regions such as the thalamus and amygdala in tandem with attenuated top–down cognitive control mediated by areas such as the prefrontal cortex. The relevant point here is that extant models of cognitive therapy are fundamentally about how information is processed, especially that which is emotionally or motivationally significant.

In addition to exploiting emergent trends in applied cognitive science, I also intend to delineate a role for the ancient tradition of mindfulness. The conceptual thread running through such apparently diverse approaches is cognitive control: Remedial strategies capable of fostering disengagement, detachment or indeed greater awareness or insight offer the potential to derail the self-perpetuating spirals of desire and impulsivity that characterize addiction. However, merely identifying a component process such as cognitive control, or suggesting an addicted person simply adopts mindful awareness, is not necessarily therapeutic! The strength of the cognitive therapy approach is based on the twin pillars of conceptualization and formulation, both firmly embedded in a therapeutic alliance. The book is thus in keeping with the pragmatic empiricism that defines cognitive and behavioural therapies insofar as it eagerly embraces any technique or strategy that demonstrably enhances self-regulation, reduces distress and ultimately improves well-being.

Something Old, Something New

The reader will encounter much that is familiar and based on the inspirational work of other clinicians and researchers as well as much as yet unseen. From a clinical standpoint, a definitive feature of this book is the sequential manner in which therapeutic intervention is conceptualized, formulated and orchestrated. Motivational enhancement strategies thus precede interventions aimed at enhancing impulse control that in turn anticipate efforts at improving emotion regulation. Importantly, motivational enhancement strategies are seen as an integral part of the therapeutic intervention rather than just a preparatory phase. Motivation thus remains crucial, at all stages of the therapeutic process. This is because addiction represents a distortion of motivation that is at least partially maintained by implicit cognitive processes. This relentless processing remains dedicated to following the pre-treatment agenda of drug seeking and drug taking long after the individuals seeking treatment have explicitly declared their intention to change. The most important message is that greater understanding of the cognitive–motivational aspects of addiction will serve as a platform for a robust therapeutic alliance and the delivery of therapy that has a valid focus on appropriate intensity.

More detailed exploration of the therapeutic engagement, motivation and formulation marks the transition to the second part of the text, beginning with Chapter 5. Thus begins an elaboration of this model CHANGE (*Change Habits and Negative Generation of Emotion*). As outlined above, CHANGE is differentiated from existing approaches in four key areas.

- Addiction is viewed as a failure of cognitive control.
- CHANGE addresses both controlled and automatic cognitive processes as part of a formulated intervention.
- It recognizes the imperative of directly targeting addiction, notably with its emphasis on cognitive control and the promotion of therapeutic strategies to promote this.
- It explicates how to recognize and manage the psychological mechanisms in addiction, such as lack of insight, that can undermine the therapeutic alliance and sap the resolve of both patient and therapist.

CHANGE also aims to provide a route map for therapeutic intervention that should guide both therapist and client through a predictable sequence of stages referred to as the Four Ms. By acknowledging evidence of subtle but pervasive cognitive deficits in areas such as inhibition and error monitoring (see Chapter 3), the therapist is provided with clear justification for devoting time in session and assigning tasks between sessions that focus on problem-solving strategies and skills.

Overall, I aim to respect key tenets of cognitive and behavioural approaches. Fundamentally, CHANGE is thus collaborative, active, time limited and structured. It utilizes, for example, the complementarity between 'within session' change processes and 'between session' change processes. It thus finds common ground with recent accounts of cognitive therapy such as that by Bennett-Levy *et al.* (2004, p. 6), who defined the overall strategy of cognitive therapy as twofold:

to assist the patient to identify and reality-test unhelpful cognitions which underlie repeated negative patterns of emotion and behaviour; and
to develop and test new, more adaptive cognitions that can give rise to a more positive experience of the self, others, and the world.

Here, I can endorse this emphasis on remediation and coping. However, in the present context it is necessary to elaborate on 'cognitions' to include cognitive *processes*, in particular those that occur in advance of, or outside, conscious awareness. Parallel with this, it is important to acknowledge that, because addiction is not necessarily motivated or maintained by negative experience of 'self, others, and the world', encouraging the client to adopt a more positive cognitive appraisal of these domains is unlikely to provide an entirely adequate therapeutic response. That said, engendering a more positive cognitive appraisal is likely to *contribute* to a better treatment outcome. The positively biased person is – one assumes – more likely to encounter situations where novel, or hitherto ignored, rewards are more available. This is one reason why affect regulation is a key component of the *CHANGE* model, as will be seen in Chapter 3. The other reason is that negative affect is commonly observed following detoxification, and can also transform minor setbacks such as smoking one cigarette into a relapse via self-blame.

Subsequent chapters address the different stages of engagement, intervention, evaluation and maintenance of change. I shall include numerous examples of therapeutic intervention in clinical settings but the intention is not to write a treatment manual. Such texts already exist, for example that by Mitcheson *et al.* (2010), which I would recommend to readers less familiar with either CBT or working in the addiction field. A comprehensive web-based resource, www.skillsconsortium.org.uk. is also well worth visiting. Returning to the task at hand, the aim here is to delineate a role for cognition and motivation at various stages of therapeutic intervention. In so doing, I hope that the reader who is an aspiring or practising clinician will acquire a deeper insight into the psychology of addiction. In turn, this can lead to more accurate conceptualizations, more comprehensive formulation and hopefully in due course better outcomes that last.

2

Existing Cognitive Behavioural Accounts of Addiction and Substance Misuse

Cognitive behavioural approaches to addictive behaviours are grounded in cognitive and social learning approaches. Predictably, definitive features include an emphasis on functional analysis of addictive behaviour. This provides a framework for more sharply focused therapeutic intervention use. The so-called 'ABC' convention specifies the *antecedents*, *behaviour* and *consequences* of a given sequence of addictive behaviour. For example, a client recently described how he resumed drinking after having remained abstinent from alcohol for 10 weeks. The *antecedents* were an argument with his partner that led to him become angry and the thought 'She doesn't know how hard it's been'. The *behaviour* was buying 10 cans of lager and drinking them. The *consequences* were intoxication, apparently unaccompanied by any feeling of pleasure, feeling ill and experiencing high levels of guilt and remorse. A further definitive feature is the emphasis on teaching coping skills in an effort to forestall the default response of drug seeking and drug taking. The functional analysis thus enables the individual to recognize the situations or emotional states in which he or she is most vulnerable to substance use. The influential 'Relapse Prevention Skills Training' model (Marlatt and Gordon, 1985) and allied accounts (e.g. Annis and Davis, 1988) thus aim to tackle addiction by equipping the addicted person with a range of cognitive and behavioural coping skills to deploy when in these so-called 'high-risk situations'. The experienced clinician tends to focus on situations previously associated with lapsing, viewed as a short-term reversal of restraint, or relapsing, characterized as a return to pre-treatment levels of the problem behaviour. Marlatt and Gordon categorized the determinants of high-risk situations as *intrapersonal*, such

---

Cognitive Therapy for Addiction: Motivation and Change, First Edition. Frank Ryan.
© 2013 Frank Ryan. Published 2013 by John Wiley & Sons, Ltd.

as positive or negative emotions or urges, and *interpersonal*, such as conflict or social pressure. A re-conceptualization of the Marlatt and Gordon (1985) model (Witkiewitz and Marlatt, 2004) characterized relapse as a dynamic or multi-factorial process that is inherently difficult to predict, and hence prevent.

Beck *et al.* (1993) proposed a cognitive developmental model of addiction derived from extant accounts of emotional disorders such as depression and anxiety. Accordingly, susceptible individuals' core beliefs about substances and their effects are formed in response to critical life experiences. Thus, alcohol could be used initially to combat aversive emotional states linked to negative core beliefs about self, world or others (see Figure 2.1). In the event of a critical incident, essentially a type of high-risk situation, these beliefs are reactivated and generate automatic thoughts that trigger urges that enable acquisitive behaviour. For example, a core belief such as 'I am not a likeable person' could become associated with the belief 'I am

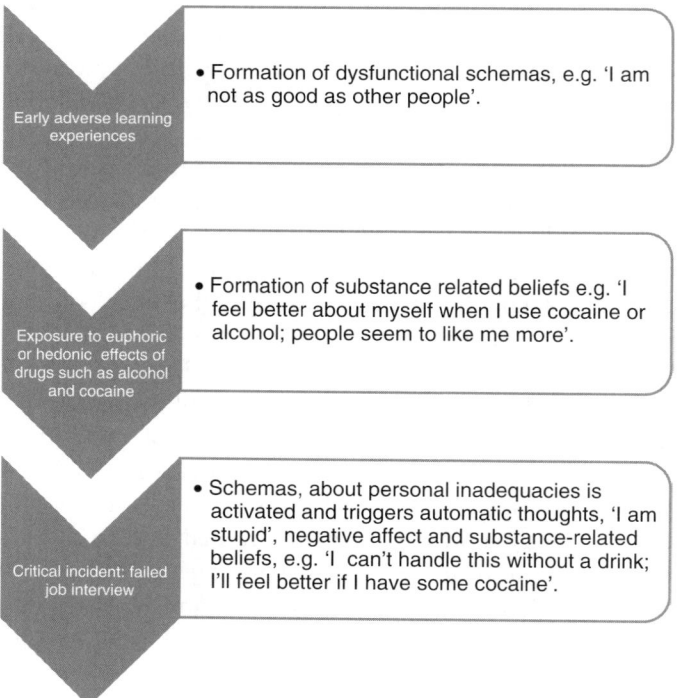

Figure 2.1 A cognitive developmental model of addiction.

more likeable when I drink alcohol'. In a given critical incident, automatic thoughts such as 'I need a drink' or 'I can't socialize without a drink' can influence behaviour.

The Evidential Basis of CBT for Addiction

CBT has brought key mechanisms of addiction into much sharper focus. This has allowed for the development of more precise therapeutic interventions that target aspects of the dynamic interaction between person, situation and appetitive impulse. The present text is a consolidation or evolution of CBT theory and practice. One of the strengths of CBT approach is its capacity to accommodate innovations. The formulation-based approach is crucial in this regard, as it enables the deployment of novel techniques to target psychological processes. The development of mindfulness-based cognitive therapy (MBCT), for example, illustrates this ethos. Mindfulness-based meditation comes from a very different tradition to that of CBT but has demonstrably brought added value to certain clinical populations such as those with chronic depression and high propensity to relapse (Segal *et al.*, 2002). As yet, mindfulness protocols have rarely been subjected to the rigours of controlled clinical trials with addicted populations. An exception to this is a single-site randomized controlled trial of mindfulness training for people trying to give up smoking. Brewer *et al.* (2011) found a greater point prevalence abstinence rate at the end of 17-week follow-up (31% versus 6%, $p = 0.012$) among a group of smokers were taught mindfulness compared with those who received a standard package of care.

Meta-analytic Findings

First, consider the findings of clinical trials reflected in meta-analytic studies. Dutra *et al.* (2008), for example, found cognitive behavioural therapy alone and relapse prevention produced low to moderate effect sizes (Cohen's $d = 0.28$ and 0.32) respectively. This contrasts unfavourably with median effect sizes of $d = 0.8$ and 0.9 observed with panic disorder and generalized disorder respectively, although an effect size of 0.3 was noted with depression (Westen and Morrison, 2001), based on data from 34 studies. This rather mixed message receives support from an earlier review. Irwin *et al.* (1999) found in their meta-analysis of 26 comparative treatment studies involving 9504 participants that the overall treatment effect of group-based relapse-prevention interventions for substance misuse was indeed small ($r = 0.14$), but statistically reliable. This modest figure reflects the relatively greater response on the part of individuals recruited to studies investigating alcohol dependence but disguises the negligible effect size noted with, for example, cocaine or nicotine addiction. However, the effect of relapse prevention on improving overall psychosocial adjustment was significantly larger ($r = 0.48$).

Behavioural Approaches

Specific behavioural techniques such as contingency management, based on operant conditioning, appear to deliver greater effect sizes than observed with broader CBT approaches. Variants of this approach include Behavioural Couples Therapy (O'Farrell and Fals-Stewart, 2006) and Social Behaviour Network Therapy (Copello *et al.*, 2006). They share an emphasis on reinforcing abstinence or adherence to the treatment goal by using either social or monetary reinforcements or combination of both. Clearly, these exemplify effective behaviour modification. From a cognitive control perspective, behavioural approaches that alter contingencies also directly influence the contents of working memory. The systematic and repetitious nature of reinforcement approaches is in effect a form of rehearsal or goal maintenance. From the model depicted in Figure 2.2, it is clear that whatever occupies the 'high ground' of working memory or executive control can exert influence over the surrounding cognitive terrain. Hypothetically, the maintenance and rehearsal of a clear behavioural goal should influence top-down processes such as the allocation of attentional resources. Moreover, by occupying a system that has limited capacity, these recovery orientated goals can reduce the likelihood of the working memory system defaulting to appetitive goals. These variants are limited to some extent, because they require the active participation of a non-substance-misusing partner or the cooperation of others in the addicted person's social network. A recent review of treatments using contingency management alone (Prendergast *et al.*, 2006) indicated moderate–high effect sizes ($d = 0.42$). Contingency management appeared more effective in treating opiate use ($d = 0.65$) and cocaine use ($d = 0.66$) compared with tobacco ($d = 0.31$) or polydrug misuse ($d = 0.42$).

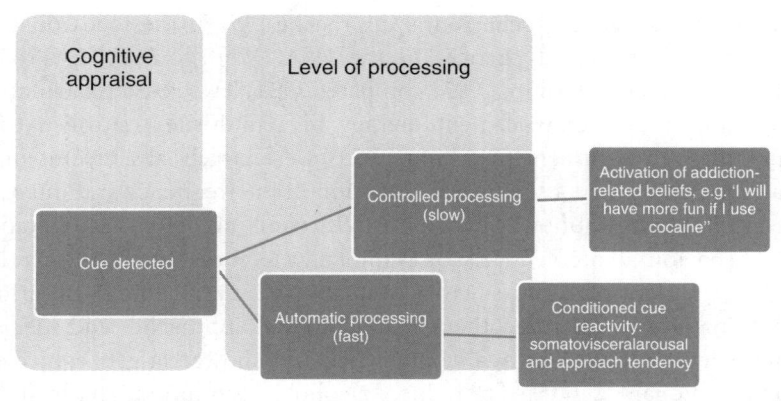

Figure 2.2 Two routes to addictive behaviour: a fast route triggered by preferential detection of potential drug cues; a slow route reliant on reflective or conscious deliberation.

Calibrating and comparing effect sizes calculated using different statistical analyses has its limitations. The data quoted here nonetheless illustrate that treatment effect sizes tend to be smaller and more varied with addictive disorders than with emotional disorders such as anxiety and depression. These meta-analytic findings appear to be telling us two things about responding therapeutically to addiction and coexisting mental health problems. On a positive note, we can advise our clients with concomitant panic disorder or generalized anxiety disorder that treatment can be very effective, and people with depression will also benefit to a significant degree. This will contribute to overcoming addictive impulses insofar as negative affect can be a powerful motivator. Second, and perhaps less positively, we would have to inform our clients that their addictive behaviour might prove more resistant to treatment, and will therefore require more intervention, probably over a longer timeframe. An important exception to this is that contingency management can change addictive behaviour, at least in the short term. Overall, however, this pattern of results suggests key mechanisms of change are being overlooked in conventional cognitive therapy applications.

Diverse Treatments Mostly Deliver Equivalent Outcomes

Findings from clinical outcome studies indicate that different treatment approaches tend to produce similar outcomes. This presents a particular challenge to cognitive behavioural approaches, given the focus on particular mechanisms of change. In the USA, *Project MATCH* (Project MATCH Research Group, 1997) compared CBT, Twelve-Step facilitation and motivational enhancement therapy in a multisite controlled trial. Hypothesized treatment matching effects were largely absent, but most participants showed a significant reduction in the frequency and intensity of alcohol consumption. The *COMBINE* (combined pharmacotherapies and behavioural interventions for alcohol dependence) study (Anton *et al.*, 2006), another large multi-site trial, evaluated the relative efficacy of various combinations of pharmacotherapy, behavioural approaches and medical management conditions Again, all participants showed largely equivalent therapeutic gain as indexed by reduced alcohol consumption. This included those receiving the brief but focused medical management condition. Similarly, in the UK, the *UKATT* (2005) alcohol treatment trial compared motivational enhancement therapy and Social Behavioural Network Therapy and found both equally effective: both groups, totalling 742, showed substantial, but equivalent, decreases of 44 per cent in alcohol consumption when followed up after 12 months.

What Are the Mechanisms of Change?

So far, so good: CBT at least seems to work as well as other approaches. But further results from controlled clinical trials evaluating CBT raise fundamental questions about efficacy. In a controlled study of cocaine dependence (Crits-Christoph *et al.*, 1999), both cognitive therapy and brief psychodynamic therapy led to significantly *poorer* outcomes indexed by rates of abstinence compared with traditional Twelve-Step counselling delivered to a combination of individual and group-based interventions. This was despite the fact that the Twelve-Step clients attended significantly fewer sessions. A further challenge to the emphasis on coping skills that is central to CBT emerges from a study by Litt *et al.* (2003). These researchers assigned 128 alcohol-dependent men and women to 26 weeks of group therapy consisting of either CBT aimed at developing coping skills or interactional therapy intended to examine interpersonal relationships. Both treatments yielded good reduced drinking outcomes throughout the 18-month follow-up period. Moreover, increased coping skills was a significant predictor of outcome but neither treatment was superior in this regard.

Partly in response to the findings of equivalent outcome with diverse interventions, Orford (2008) challenged addiction treatment researchers to focus on empirically supported common change processes. But what could these processes be? What is the common currency across such diverse terrain as Twelve-Step facilitation, motivational enhancement, CBT, behaviour and social network therapy, pharmacotherapy and structured advice sessions from a medical practitioner? Litt *et al.* (2003) considered *non-specific treatment effects*, suggesting, for example, that suitably motivated treatment seekers were in a position to capitalize on the opportunities for learning afforded by any structured treatment. Orford (2008a, p. 707) considered broader contextual factors to be plausible candidates:

> Such a model emphasises factors such as client commitment, therapist allegiance and the client–therapist alliance, and views personal change as being embedded within a complex, multi-component treatment system, itself nested within a broader life system that contains an array of inter-related factors promoting or constraining positive change.

This does not account for the fact that relatively straightforward behavioural techniques such as contingency management appear to deliver robust gains, although these fade with the contingency. More importantly, invoking a role for non-specific factors brings us no closer to understanding, let alone modifying, the mechanisms that account for the tenacity of addiction.

The Missing Variable?

The proposal that overcoming addiction entails an essentially cognitive conflict suggests that the extent to which therapeutic interventions can enhance cognitive control will index their therapeutic potency. This remains hypothetical, but is at least consistent with the finding that contingency management, CBT, Twelve-Step approaches, substance-focused counselling and motivational interviewing have been shown to be equally effective (or in many cases rather less than effective) in addressing addictive disorders. This points to the existence of a common factor or component process, which contrives to sustain self-control across a range of situations, in both the long term and short term. This is my candidate for 'the missing variable' that has eluded and baffled many clinical investigators. In fairness, this could be because cognitive control is a multifaceted variable. I propose that the extent to which diverse treatments foster and sustain an increased level of cognitive control will have a direct bearing on the efficacy. There is a hint of circularity in this proposition – good outcomes in addiction are *de facto* evidence of robust cognitive control – until it is established what are the components processes of cognitive control and how can these can be more deliberately accentuated in a therapeutic framework. As will hopefully become apparent in this text, the components of cognitive control are indeed becoming more clearly specified, and being translated into promising therapeutic strategies. Without the development of dual-representation theories, positing qualitatively different types of information processing, none of this would have been possible.

A Dual-Processing Framework

Strack and Deutsch (2004) have outlined a theoretical framework termed the Reflective Impulsive Model (RIM) that describes a two-systems model to account for aspects of human behaviour. In a subsequent article (Deutsch and Strack, 2006), they explored the implications of their model for addictive behaviour. The basic assumption of the model is that behaviour results from the operation of two distinct cognitive processing systems. These are a *reflective system* that is deliberate, intentional and decisive, and parallel but sometimes in opposition to this, an *impulsive system*. The latter is typically fast, effortless and implicit or intuitive. The RIM is one of several theoretical frameworks that shares a dual-processing architecture derived from earlier work by, for example, Shiffrin and Schneider (1977). The defining feature of these models is the recognition that information can be processed by two qualitatively distinct modes, *controlled* and *automatic*, corresponding to the reflective and impulsive systems. Once automatic processes are established, they acquire autonomy from controlled processes. In normal operation they are essentially capacity free, in marked contrast to the 'bottleneck' that constrains controlled processing.

Automatic processes are always 'switched on' and can interrupt or draw attention away from deliberate or controlled processes. One outcome of this is that the reflective system, where information is processed explicitly or rule based, is more prone to distraction or diversion. An apt example would be an individual trying to abstain from alcohol travelling to work. Here, controlled processing would be required to complete the journey and keep in mind the priorities and tasks that need to be addressed on arrival. There is now abundant evidence that individuals in this scenario would find their attention captured by stimuli associated with alcohol such as adverts, bars or retail outlets where alcohol is for sale. The essential point is that this attentional capture takes place regardless of the individual's decision to ignore such cues. Further, as will be seen in Chapter 7, once these cues have captured attention addicted individuals have difficulty in disengaging from this.

Bechara *et al*. (2006) described a neural architecture that provides a plausible basis for two cognitive systems, operating in parallel but sometimes in conflict as in the case of addiction. These theorists refer to an 'impulsive amygdala-dependent' system that signals pain or pleasure associated with *immediate* or short term outcomes that contrasts with a 'reflective prefrontal-dependent' neural system responsible for signalling *future* pain or pleasure (Bechara *et al*., 2006, p. 216). Both of these theoretical accounts, speaking to cognitive and neural systems respectively, posit a competitive process that precedes behavioural expression. In many scenarios, impulsive or short-term imperatives are easily reconciled with long-term objectives. A well-motivated but nonetheless hungry worker, for example, will diligently complete a tedious task before lunch. In this scenario, the individual appears able to choose an outcome that accommodates a range of motives and needs.

Bechara and colleagues propose that in the context of addiction there is a lack of equilibrium between the impulsive and reflective neural systems. Specifically, drawing on incentive models of addiction (e.g. Berridge and Robinson, 1995), they speculated that the sensitized impulsive system becomes more influential and more difficult for the reflective system to override. Moreover, the capacity to inhibit pre-potent responses is also compromised in individuals who have developed substance dependence (Noel *et al*., 2003), analogous to that observed in patients with ventromedial prefrontal lesions. Overall, dual-representation theories present major challenges to extant therapeutic approaches but also offer opportunities for the development of innovative cognitive and behavioural remedies. Table 2.1 shows how models where information is processed at different levels can accommodate different therapeutic procedures in response to both addictive behaviour and behaviour linked with negative emotional states, in keeping with the *CHANGE* framework. In reality, both automatic and controlled processes act in concert, as component processes can at least be partially differentiated as in the table. Implementation intentions,

Table 2.1 Dual processes mapped onto therapeutic interventions.

Focus of therapeutic intervention	Automatic process	Controlled process	Combined automatic and controlled processing
Addictive motivational processes and behaviour	Cognitive bias modification Behavioural approach modification Expectancy challenge Contingency management	CBT (e.g. relapse prevention skills training) Problem-solving skills training; cognitive skills training (e.g. working memory enhancement)	Mindfulness Implementation intentions (see p. 125)
Emotionally motivated behaviour	Exposure to cues associated with negative affect; cognitive bias modification	Cognitive behaviour therapy: identifying and modifying distorted thinking	Mindfulness

for instance (see p. 125) aim to recruit both automatic and controlled processes, by instigating rehearsal and activation of coping skills in response to cues. As will be seen (Chapter 4, pp. 58–59), what is encoded in working memory as a conscious goal can nonetheless influence attentional processing and behavioural activation automatically, and hence require little or no effort once the goal remains encoded.

In summary, the proposed reformulation of cognitive therapy applications for addictive behaviours is justified for three reasons. First, existing accounts of cognitive therapy for addiction have not accommodated findings that cognitive processes, in particular those deemed automatic or implicit, are influential in maintaining addiction. In cognitive parlance, these models do not legislate for 'parallel processing' across controlled or automatic modes, with the latter being largely overlooked. This leaves the therapist and client oblivious to an important source of variance that is influential at all stages of the therapeutic journey. Second, extant accounts fail to acknowledge that addiction is motivated by the compulsive and futile pursuit of rewards, or the promise of rewards associated with deranged appetites. This appetitive aspect, enacted by acquisitive behaviour, is entirely consistent with the robust outcomes observed when addicted individuals are offered alternative rewards to drugs on a contingent basis. Stimulating reward circuitry thus seems to be a cognitive or behavioural antidote to addiction. Conversely, it is also consistent with the underwhelming results often obtained when cognitive therapy is applied to addiction. Third, cognitive therapy for addiction discounts the neurocognitive basis of addiction: the facilitated, anticipatory processing of predictive cues in the face of impaired inhibitory mechanisms and compromised cognitive control. The failure to accommodate these aspects of addiction in the clinic contributes to the failure of CBT to deliver the same robust therapeutic gains typically observed with, for example, anxious and depressed patients. Yes, the therapy works, but does not consistently deliver added value when compared with other approaches such as Twelve-Step interventions. This suggests that key mechanisms of motivation and change are being overlooked in conventional cognitive therapy applications. The characterization of addiction as a disorder of appetitive motivation combined with deficiencies in cognitive control is the defining feature of this text.

3

Core Motivational Processes in Addiction

Is Addiction About Avoiding Pain or Seeking Reward?

Diverse psychological therapies, spanning the spectrum of psychodynamic to cognitive behavioural, have tended to account for addiction as a manifestation of either psychic disturbance or maladaptive coping strategy, as pointed out in Chapter 1. This has a direct effect on how motivation is understood in the context of addiction: if the goal of addiction is to alleviate emotional negativity or to compensate for perceived personal shortcomings, mitigation in this regard should lead to a good outcome. But what if the addiction has a more autonomous nature, more shaped by seeking pleasure or reward than avoiding pain or distress? Certainly, alleviating distress or surmounting personal difficulties might lead to therapeutic gain. But if addiction is intrinsically about the pursuit of reward the gains might not endure. In terms of conceptualizing, formulating and implementing cognitive and behavioural therapy strategies it is imperative that both therapist and client understand the essence of addiction. Cognitive and behavioural techniques that have evolved to address anxiety and depression, syndromes that are characterized by avoidance, need to be configured differently to address a syndrome that is driven less by emotional negativity and more by compulsive reward seeking.

Early behavioural accounts of addiction pre-empted the view espoused above that addictive behaviour was driven by negative reinforcement epitomized by a desire to avoid withdrawal discomfort. Thus, in attempting to account for the endurance and relapse proclivity in addiction, theorists such as Wikler (1948) focused on the apparently plausible notion that, having adapted or learned to tolerate the presence of a drug, individuals experience distress when the drug is not available at the synaptic

---

Cognitive Therapy for Addiction: Motivation and Change, First Edition. Frank Ryan.
© 2013 Frank Ryan. Published 2013 by John Wiley & Sons, Ltd.

level. The resulting dysregulation mobilizes the individual to redress the balance by engaging in drug seeking and taking. More sophisticated versions of withdrawal accounts of addiction have invoked a role for 'opponent processes' that interact dynamically with the hedonic or pleasurable outcomes of drug administration (Solomon, 1980; Koob and Le Moal, 1997). Accordingly, repeated use of drugs leads to enduring aberrations or deficits in neural reward mechanisms, both within systems (e.g., the mesocorticolimbic dopamine system) and between systems (e.g., the hypothalamic–pituitary–adrenal (HPA) axis and neural systems for regulating stress, both mediated by corticotropin-releasing factor (CRF), become maladapted or dysregulated by repeated exposure to drugs of abuse. On cessation of drug use, the resulting anhedonic state increases the likelihood of resumption or relapse. Koob and Le Moal (2005, p. 1443) refer to this as the 'dark side of addiction', characterized by 'chronic irritability, emotional pain, malaise, dysphoria, alexithymia, and loss of motivation for natural rewards'. This, the antithesis of reward or 'antireward', provides a powerful context for negative reinforcement that motivates compulsive drug-seeking behaviour and addiction. This anhedonic state might be experienced as 'authentic' depression or anxiety by the affected person, and indeed present itself to the psychotherapist as such. In the course of a recent clinical encounter I introduced this idea to a man who had been detoxified from alcohol and was complaining of feeling depressed. He replied that the concept of a 'dark side' of addiction implied that there was a 'bright side'. Ironically perhaps, from a neurocognitive perspective there is, or at least was, a 'bright side', although perhaps forgotten by the client.

How Formulation Can Go Astray

More generally, the negative affect carried over from acute intoxication represents a potential pitfall in terms of formulation from a cognitive therapy perspective. The clinician might, for instance, search for prior learning experiences in the client's narrative such as invalidation from attachment figures or traumatic exposure. This quest could be in vain, as the negative affect could reflect the enduring allostatic state rather than the expression of adversity in earlier life or other candidate vulnerability factors. Because current mood is depressed or anxious – regardless of the cause – autobiographical memory is biased accordingly. This leads to a distorted picture emerging on initial assessment. A valid and reliable assessment of a person's emotional or affective state is thus likely to be confounded by current or recent intensive substance use. In my own clinical experience, and despite awareness of the possibility of this interaction, I still experience the occasional (pleasant!) surprise of a client showing dramatic improvement in affect once substance misuse ceases. Conversely, I have met with few, if any, positive results when addressing concurrent mental health problems such as OCD and depression with clients on opiate substitution or significant drug or alcohol involvement.

Incentive Theories of Addiction

Withdrawal-based accounts struggle to account for the resumption of addiction, sometimes many years after quitting. For example, Gerald, a 70-year-old man, was recently referred to me. The reason for the referral was that Gerald was using crack cocaine on a daily basis. He was spending about £70 each day. Gerald was an amiable man who had worked successfully in the advertising industry, where he had first encountered cocaine when in his 30s. He had made several attempts to give up; the most successful had ended 18 months earlier after 13 years of abstinence. Leading up to resuming cocaine use he recalled thinking 'I'm bored'. His drug taking quickly became habitual once again and his reflection was 'I'm still amazed that I carry on doing something when I don't even like it'. There is now abundant evidence suggesting that it is the capacity for drugs to activate dopaminergic transmission that invests them with such enduring potency (see for example Volkow *et al.*, 2002). Some drugs, such as cocaine, amphetamine, methamphetamine and ecstasy, appear to increase dopamine levels more directly by either facilitating dopamine release or inhibiting reuptake. Other drugs, such as alcohol, nicotine, opiates and marijuana, stimulate GABAergic or glutamatergic neurons that culminate in increased levels of dopamine mainly by disrupting reuptake.

Further, the unnatural surge in dopamine levels elicited by drug ingestion can drain normal rewards of their dopaminergic potency. Schultz (2002) pointed out that drugs *directly* target neural reward-processing centres, in contrast to natural rewards such as food or water. This results in elevation of dopamine levels in areas such as the nucleus accumbens that is significantly greater than that elicited by conventional rewards. Crucially, this dopamine release consolidates associative learning. It appears, therefore, that exposure to the reinforcing effects of drugs can activate elementary learning mechanisms from the outset. Contingent dopamine release reinforces the preceding instrumental behaviour and invests associated cues with motivational properties through classical conditioning mechanisms. In turn, these elementary learning mechanisms recruit cognitive control processes such as selective attention. In habituated drug takers, this chemical cascade appears to create a motivational state subjectively experienced, according to Everitt and Robbins (2005), as 'must do!'. In Gerald's case this proved to be enduring. As will be seen below, drug ingestion does not generally comply with Maslow's (1943) dictum 'a satisfied need is not a motivator of behaviour'. Conversely, rather than providing satiation, exposure to drug effects triggers a cycle of craving, intoxication, withdrawal and further binging.

The cognitive and motivational dynamics of addiction have been elegantly captured in the *impaired Response Inhibition and Salience Attribution* (iRISA) framework (Goldstein and Volkow, 2002). In this model, substance and substance-related cues acquire increased salience while non-drug reinforcers become less prominent during cycles of regimented drug taking, bingeing or withdrawal. Parallel with this, the ability to inhibit drug seeking and taking and other maladaptive behaviours is impaired. Inhibitory processes are predicated on dorsal prefrontal cortex (PFC) subregions such as the dorsolateral PFC (DLPFC), the inferior frontal gyrus and the dorsal anterior cingulate cortex (dACC). Incentive salience and consequential drug wanting, attention bias and drug seeking are subserved by regions such as the medial orbitofrontal cortex (mOFC), the ventromedial PFC and rostroventral ACC (see Goldstein and Volkow, 2011) (Figure 3.1). In the normal, non-addicted, non-intoxicated state, here represented by the light-gray ovals (Figure 3.1(a)), cognitive control is maintained by dorsal PFC regions. This suppresses the 'hot', more ventral PFC functions, here represented by the dark gray ovals, that drive not just impulses for drug seeking but emotions for fear, anger or sexual desire. During cue reactivity (Figure 3.1(b)), when craving or withdrawal may be elicited, drug-related cognitive processes, behaviours and emotions challenge cognitive control, inducing approach–avoidance conflict. Intoxication and bingeing occur when cognitive control is impaired (Figure 3.1(c)).

Learning Mechanisms in Addiction

Both classical (stimulus–stimulus) and operant (stimulus–response) learning mechanisms have been invoked to account for the acquisition of

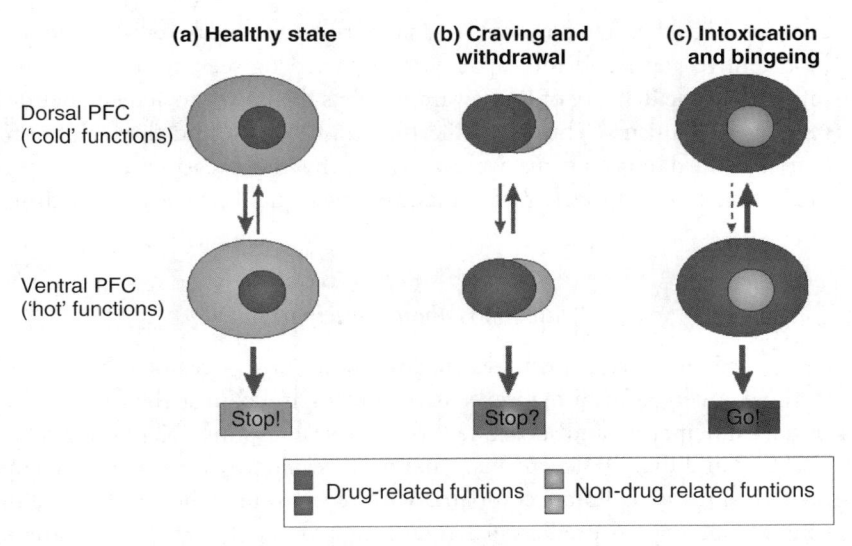

Figure 3.1 A model of PFC involvement in iRISA in addiction.

addictive behaviour. The former controls behaviour by means of antecedent cues and the latter by the 'value' or utility attached to the outcome. Drawing on animal laboratory work, Yin and Knowlton (2006, p. 167) described how classical and operant processes operating in tandem can lead to addictive behaviour:

1. *Stimulus–outcome (S-O) association.* Laboratory or environmental cues elicit preparatory responses (as in the classic Pavlovian salivation response) in anticipation of a biologically relevant outcome or unconditional response. Essentially, what is conditioned or learned is which cues predict which outcomes. This type of learning is relatively insensitive to subsequent manipulation of the action–outcome relationship see (A-O contingency, below) or 'reward devaluation', particularly when the outcome is delivery of a drug that activates neural reward circuitry. In other words the behaviour – drug seeking and use – perseveres even when the outcome is adverse or at least not leading to the delivery of the anticipated or expected reward. This might shed light on the disappointing results often found with exposure paradigms (see Conklin and Tiffany, 2002) that entail exposure to the reward signal but withholding of the expected reward or source of gratification. Despite the hoped-for deconditioning process, the

cue – perhaps the sight and smell of a favourite alcoholic beverage – retains its incentive value and the capacity to trigger drug seeking. It is the cue rather than the delivery of the reward that has the power to activate neural reward mechanisms. Thus, O'Doherty *et al.* (2002) found that midbrain neural reward mechanisms were activated by the presentation of cues predicting a pleasant taste rather than the subsequent delivery of the drop of glucose.

Addiction is about anticipation

Recent evidence from primates suggests that cortical regions analogous to those involved in human executive control are exquisitely sensitive to reward anticipation and subsequent behavioural response. Kennerley *et al.* (2011) found that OFC neurons dynamically evaluate the value of current reward-motivated choices compared with recent ones, whereas ACC neurons encode reward-prediction errors using a broader common valuation currency. It thus seems that reward processing is compartmentalized to a degree, even within prefrontal zones. This reward prediction or anticipation can occur very rapidly. Environmental or interoceptive cues can activate neural reward mechanisms indexed by, for example, extracellular dopamine levels in less than one second. Phillips *et al.* (2003) used electrochemical methods to measure dopamine levels every 100 ms in cocaine-habituated and cocaine-naive rats. Cues associated with cocaine elicited more rapid dopamine signalling compared with that triggered by the drug itself, but only in animals who had been previously trained to seek and ingest cocaine. Thus, what distinguished the habituated animals from the naive animals was *a conditioned response* that led to pre-emptive reward signalling, rather than the actual reward associated with the delivery of the drug molecules to neural receptors.

Consistent with this, recent findings with cigarette smokers suggest that the speed with which drugs arrive at their neural destination and the subsequent degree of concentration might not be as influential as hitherto thought. Rose *et al.* (2010), for example, evaluated the related hypotheses that addictive cigarette smoking was in part driven by rapid accumulation of nicotine and peaks or spikes of nicotine concentration in the brain. They recruited 13 dependent and 10 non-dependent cigarette smokers and measured the kinetics of nicotine accumulation in the brain. Using a PET scanner they found that nicotine levels rose progressively in both groups (in fact, more slowly among the dependent smokers, apparently due to delayed 'washout' as nicotine levels tended to remain chronically high due to regular use). The key finding was that there were no 'spikes' in nicotine availability in the brain following smoke inhalation. Wise and Kiyatkin (2011) proposed that peripheral activation of nicotinic receptors that are highly concentrated in the lungs acts as a conditional stimulus, and it is this information that is relayed quickly to the brain, well in advance of the nicotine itself. They further proposed that other drugs such as heroin and cocaine also activate peripheral receptors that signal receipt of a drug to the experienced user. Here, I interpret these findings as justification for prioritizing cognitive control as a focus for therapeutic intervention. The habituated drug user is effectively disarmed when exposed to a wide range of cues generating powerful involuntary responses. The best, and often the only, option is to mount a rearguard action from the command and control centre of the brain.

2. *Action–outcome (A-O) association.* An organism learns the relationship between the procedures or actions necessary to obtain drug ingestion and outcome. If deemed pleasurable or hedonic this operant behaviour will be reinforced, and perpetuated through the generation of further reinforcement. In humans, information bearing on the value or utility of the outcome would initially be available to introspection. Thus, the individual would be in a position to declare that 'I smoked that cigarette because I chose to and I wanted to experience the combination of stimulating but also relaxing effects'. While this type of learning can be rapidly acquired, it is also sensitive to subsequent manipulation of the A-O contingency or reward devaluation. If an individual fails to experience the anticipated reaction the association is weakened. For example, if the recreational smoker experienced a coughing fit or nausea, the combined lack of the predicted reward and the aversive experience would devalue the outcome and reduce the likelihood of the behaviour recurring. Other negative impacts such as cost or the belief that smoking is now perceived as 'uncool' can also alter the balance that comes with the more flexible learning phase. For the majority of people who use drugs or gamble recreationally a balanced appraisal of utility and outcomes forestalls the development of more intensive or compulsive behaviour at this stage.

3. *Stimulus–response (S-R) association.* In contexts where biologically salient rewards are available, an association between the environmental stimuli (e.g., cues in the laboratory) and the operant such as the lever press

is gradually formed. Once acquired, this association becomes relatively insensitive to subsequent changes to outcome value. Thus, the behaviour becomes habitual and enduring. Robbins and Everitt (2002, p. 632) concluded that addiction might be understood as 'the aberrant engagement of Pavlovian and instrumental learning processes'. According to these theorists, appetitive drug seeking is initially mediated by such structures as the amygdala, hippocampus, cingulate and medial pre-frontal cortex. However, they speculated that the crucial transition from the relatively more flexible A-O learning to more rigid S-R, that is, from more voluntary to more compulsive drug use, could reflect a transition at the neural level from prefrontal cortical to striatal control.

It is important to recognize that the above core learning processes occur in parallel and can be interactive. Pavlovian–instrumental transfer, for instance, occurs when appetitive Pavlovian stimuli greatly increase the vigour with which participants execute instrumentally trained responses for expected outcomes but for others also. Talmi et al. (2008) demonstrated this in a laboratory study with human participants. The participants first learned to earn monetary rewards by effortfully squeezing a handgrip (instrumental or action–outcome conditioning). Subsequently, the participants learned to associate visual cues with similar monetary rewards or the absence of any reward (stimulus–outcome or classical conditioning procedure). In the third phase of the experiment participants were shown either reward-predictive (C+) or reward-non-predictive cues (C−) prior to being given the opportunity to squeeze the grip to earn rewards (Pavlovian-instrumental transfer). As predicted, participants exerted significantly more effort, measured by the number of grip squeezes registered in the time window, when primed by the reward-predictive stimulus. Talmi et al. captured fMRI data during this procedure and found that Pavlovian to instrumental transfer was associated with increased activity in the nucleus accumbens and amygdala, structures that mediate between appetitive stimuli and behavioural response. This illustrates a potential mechanism through which habituated drug users might be galvanized into drug seeking routines that are more vigorous and sustained when exposed to reward-predictive stimuli. It also offers a potential target for therapeutic change, although simple desensitizing or extinction procedures have not delivered consistent gain in this regard. Restoring the balance between these neural systems, whereby more self-control is likely, remains a key objective in combating addictive behaviour.

Distorted Motivation and Aberrant Learning: the Emergence of Compulsion

A contrasting theoretical approach emphasizes the appetitive or reward-seeking nature of drug use. According to this model (Robinson and Berridge, 1993, 2003), components of neural reward circuits become sensitized (i.e., more responsive, the opposite of tolerance) to drug effects with repeated use. Crucially, the incentive value of the drug is attributed to stimuli that predict drug availability. Such stimuli prove to be fascinating to habituated drug users or, as succinctly put by Berridge *et al.* (2009), serve as 'motivational magnets'. This investment of cues with powerful motivational properties gives addictive drug use its characteristic compulsive quality. Robinson and Berridge refer to this as *incentive salience*, which triggers excessive 'wanting'. They distinguish this from the purely hedonic, pleasurable motive intuitively invoked to account for chronic drug use. Further, Berridge *et al.* (2009) differentiate 'wanting' from 'liking' both physiologically and neurobiologically. Wanting is associated with dopaminergic activation, whereas opioid, endocannabinoid and GABA–benzodiazepine neurotransmitter systems are implicated in generating pleasurable ('liking') reactions by activating 'hedonic hotspots' in limbic structures such as the ventral pallidum. The neural substrates for 'wanting' are thus more widely distributed and more easily activated than the substrates for 'liking'. For example, suppression of endogenous dopamine neurotransmission reduces 'wanting' but not 'liking'. Conversely, 'wanting' without 'liking' can be induced in laboratory animals by pharmacological or genetic manipulations that maintain high levels of dopamine in areas such as the nucleus accumbens.

'Wanting and Liking' in the Clinic

Crucially, the liking or more commonly the 'no longer liking' expressed by those who wish to change patterns of addictive behaviour is open to introspection and can be discussed in therapy. This accords self-reported like or dislike more credibility than it deserves, while the 'wanting' or compulsion remains latent until unleashed by salient triggers. Robinson and Berridge also proposed that repetitious use of psychoactive substances sculpts neural reward circuitry in a more enduring fashion, rendering the mesolimbic dopaminergic system hypersensitive to stimuli associated with drug availability in the longer term. This means that subsequent exposure to stimuli associated with drug availability activates higher-order cognitive processes via attentional capture. Consistent with this, Grant *et al.* (1996), in an early neuroimaging study of cocaine-addicted participants, found evidence of more global cognitive processing in areas such as the dorsolateral and medial orbitofrontal cortex following exposure to drug-related stimuli. These discriminative stimuli appear to function as secondary reinforcers through association with dopaminergic activation of reward neurocircuitry. Therefore, they acquire a competitive advantage in gaining the attention of those who have become 'sensitized' by prior learning. Accordingly, addicted people find their attention grabbed by cues that can trigger craving and urges to resume addictive pursuits. Field and Cox (2008, p. 1) thus proposed that 'through classical conditioning, substance-related stimuli elicit the expectancy of substance availability, and this expectancy causes both attentional bias for substance-related stimuli and subjective craving.'

As referred to above, Everitt and Robbins (2005) proposed that initially drug seeking is under the control of instrumental response−outcome contingencies in which drug seeking behaviour appears more voluntary and goal directed. With repetition, the behaviour becomes more stimulus driven and more automatic. This increased rigidity of response could be related to lower levels of striatal dopaminergic transmission, presumably through neuroadaptation to the dopamine 'highs' following drug intake. Parallel with this, executive control could also be compromised in people prone to addiction. In this regard, Garavan *et al.* (2008) found that, ironically, cognitive control was *enhanced* on a laboratory task along with increased orbitofrontal activity when cocaine was administered to regular users. Hypoactivity, relative to drug-naive controls, disappeared in the same prefrontal regions. This transient enhancement merely emphasizes that in the absence of the drug there was a deficiency of sorts, reminiscent of an alcohol-dependent woman who confided to me 'I was born two gin and tonics short of normal'. This leads to a variation of the 'self-medication' hypothesis implied in this instance: psychoactive substances are used to control impulsivity rather than to alleviate dysphoric states such as anxiety and depression. Thus children and adults with attentional deficit disorder show reduced response impulsivity when given stimulant drugs such as methylphenidate (see Aron *et al.*, 2003). Findings that impulsivity can be downregulated by psychoactive drugs suggest that this impulsive tendency precedes rather than follows addiction. From a remedial perspective, the challenge remains one of augmenting cognitive control.

The Role of Secondary Reinforcers

Robbins and Everitt also emphasized the secondary reinforcement value (i.e., analogous to money representing the rewards it can deliver to us) that drug cues can acquire. These triggers, the familiar people, places and things that predict drug availability, serve as discriminative stimuli capable of eliciting compulsive habitual behaviour. This contributes to the endurance of addiction: drugs with abuse potential are often hidden or difficult to find but compulsive drug seeking continues despite this. The conditioned reinforcers preserve the behaviour that, sooner or later, yields the primary reward. By way of illustration, consider Stephen, a client with a 25-year history of injecting heroin use who was recently referred to me. In the course of the initial consultation it emerged that his motivation in attending was that it would facilitate his quest from a psychiatrist colleague for a prescription of diamorphine, an opiate that he could inject. He told me that, during an interruption to his normal supply of heroin, he continued to search for an elusive vein into which he would inject water. Because of the poor state of his veins (he also had a chronically infected abscess in his leg) this was often a painful and markedly hazardous procedure, but he continued nonetheless. In this case, the drug-seeking behaviour has become dissociated from actual drug delivery and appears to endure not only in the absence of the primary reward of the drug but in the face of pain, discomfort and the prospect of acquiring life-threatening illnesses. Whatever the learning and motivational processes are that govern this they are clearly aberrant.

Beyond Pleasure and Pain: a Psychoanalytic Perspective

According to a contemporary commentator, Freud's phrase 'beyond the pleasure principle' indicates that he recognized that 'instinctive urges work within us in relative independence of pleasure and pain'. Further, they are conditioned 'by their success and failure, and by their conflicts' McDougall (1925, p. 43). It would appear that the 'motivated unconscious' depicted by Freud was at least amenable to an interpretation based more on the outcome attained by the urge-driven behaviour then the subjective experience of pleasure or pain. A more recent attempt to reconcile psychodynamic models with cognitive neuroscience (Solms and Nersessian, 1999) similarly proposed that motivational value is calibrated in degrees of *pleasure* and *unpleasure*, according to which 'more pleasure' equates to 'more likely to satisfy my inner needs,' and 'more unpleasure' accords with 'less likely to satisfy them, or more likely to frustrate them.' Again, note that the subjective experience of pleasure, or not as the case may be, is secondary to the outcome. This accords with the dissociation between subjective pleasure or liking and more compulsive, driven behaviour that denotes wanting. Somewhat surprisingly, this is consistent with the model of addictive behaviour proposed here, and the neurobiological model described by Robinson and Berridge (2003), although the unconscious mechanisms here are primarily cognitive but with motivational valence. The consistency emerges from the dissociation between pleasure or liking and the compulsive wanting that develops into addictive behaviour. To paraphrase Freud, it is a case of 'where liking was there shall wanting be' in the case of addiction.

Conclusion

While emphasizing different pathways (the development of pathological wanting; the increasing stereotypical habit acquisition), both incentive and aberrant-learning accounts depict addictive behaviour as becoming less amenable to cognitive control. In the process, valuable insights emerge for the clinician and the treatment seeker alike. Robinson and Berridge, for example, draw crucial distinctions between subjective pleasure and compulsive wanting. Robbins and Everitt provide a cogent account of how compulsive habits develop and persist. Both theories provide an explanatory and predictive framework for relapse, even in the long term. While negative-reinforcement models offer a less parsimonious and more questionable account of relapse in the longer term, alleviation of withdrawal discomfort and negative affect are clearly influential both in increasing the incentive value of addictive pursuits in the first instance and as a precursor to resumed use after abstinence is attained. These provide the rationale for the *CHANGE* approach, aimed at sequentially addressing incentive-driven compulsion and emotional dysregulation.

4

A Cognitive Approach to Understanding the Compulsive Nature of Addiction

In this chapter I shall outline theoretical perspectives on cognitive control mechanisms with particular emphasis on the role of attention in regulating behaviour. Overcoming addiction requires enhanced control over two cognitive mechanisms: first, enhanced detection and preferential processing of motivationally relevant information; second, the need to inhibit the associated responses. This is challenging because the former is automatic and thus less effortful, but inhibition is deliberate and thus taxes cognitive capacity. Moreover, crucial components of the neurocircuitry supporting cognitive control, in particular response inhibition, can be compromised by repeated exposure to drugs of abuse, or by the effects of acute intoxication. Baler and Volkow (2006), for example, highlighted the intimate relationships between the circuits disrupted by drugs of abuse and the neural systems that underlie self-control.

But what is the relevance or indeed utility of this theoretical framework *apropos* clinical intervention? Failure to acknowledge the influence of automatic cognition and the facility with which it can trigger impulsive behaviour such as addiction has misled both addicted individuals and clinicians in two important areas. First, the role of voluntary control has been misunderstood and/or exaggerated. It now appears that, given the necessary stimulation, appetitive approach behaviours that are fast and automatic have a head start over slower inhibitory responses. (See Figure 4.1.)

Second, the inevitable expression of largely involuntary addictive behaviour has been mistakenly attributed to a range of factors such as lack of motivation, lack of commitment or indeed inadequate treatments or incompetent therapists. Blame, that very common thinking error, can

---

Cognitive Therapy for Addiction: Motivation and Change, First Edition. Frank Ryan.
© 2013 Frank Ryan. Published 2013 by John Wiley & Sons, Ltd.

Top-down processes: goal maintenance and monitoring relying on effective inhibitory mechanisms

Bottom-up processes: motivationally salient stimuli grab attention and trigger cue reactivity including action tendencies

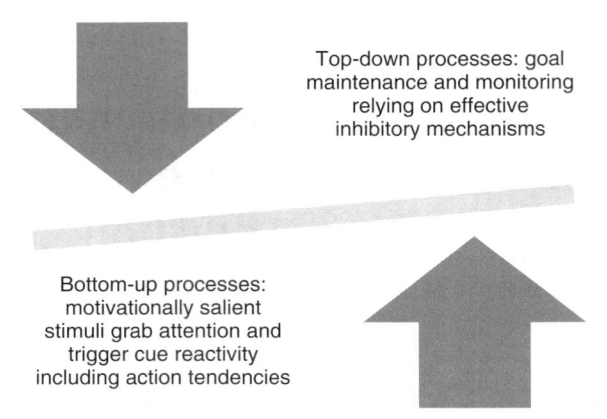

Figure 4.1 The dynamics of cognitive control. Top-down processes subserved by prefrontal circuits DLPFC, dACC, inferior frontal gyrus and ventrolateral prefrontal cortex. Bottom-up processes are driven by a network of limbic structures indexed, for example, by early amygdala activation due to preferential processing. Once activated, relatively automated appetitive action tendencies – habits – are enabled and sustained by striatal-based learning mechanisms. In reality, this is a much more interactive process, as addictive behaviour results from a combination of impaired top-down control and enhanced bottom-up processing. In therapeutic contexts, intervention can be directed at bolstering the former by, for example, fostering goal maintenance or modifying the latter by cognitive bias modification or reversing behavioural approach tendencies.

enter the treatment room as clients and therapists alike seek to account for failure. As will be seen in Chapter 6, this attributional bias has the potential to undermine the cornerstone of cognitive therapy, the therapeutic alliance, and sap the motivation of both client and therapist.

Theories of Attention

Several theorists have distinguished between a goal-directed, purposive aspect of attention and a more stimulus-driven, reflexive component (e.g., Corbetta and Shulman, 2002; Posner and Petersen, 1990). The former is volitional and guided by declarative knowledge such as expectations and schematically encoded information. According to Posner and Petersen, these functions are supported by anterior cortical circuitry, especially prefrontal areas. In contrast, the latter, more reactive system is responsive to biological or behaviourally relevant stimuli, especially those not currently attended to. These functions are associated with more posterior neural networks in the temporoparietal and ventral frontal cortex. Conventionally, these two systems are referred to as 'top down' and 'bottom up', corresponding to controlled and automatic modes of information processing respectively. The two systems are assumed to operate in a complementary manner. For example, I am using top-down attentional strategies to write this paragraph, but if the doorbell rings this will capture attention whether or not I was expecting it, or indeed whether or not it was a welcome interruption: the doorbell captures my attention whether it is goal relevant or not. Another example is when stimuli that are task or goal relevant (e.g., finding a mail box in an unfamiliar neighbourhood, or finding a friend in a crowded room) become more salient or 'pop out' from the background. These examples illustrate how the effective and efficient pursuit of goals is facilitated by the seamless operation of top-down and bottom-up processes. When preferred goals become less preferred, this facilitation nonetheless continues, especially when the former goals have acquired the high incentive value ascribed to addiction-relevant stimuli.

Top-Down Influences Can Be Automatic

This apparently automatic top-down modulation is usually, like much implicit processing, helpful. As pointed out above, without this capacity, it would take much longer to detect a familiar face in the crowd, or a mailbox in a congested street. All well and good, as long as one is single minded, or fortunate, enough to live a simple and uncluttered life. A more typical scenario perhaps is to be at one's desk struggling with competing priorities, including a deferred lunch, when a colleague with whom you share a room arrives with his or her own freshly microwaved, aromatic lunch. Here, more cognitive control is needed to adjudicate over the maintenance of whatever is judged to be the most important goal. But that goal maintenance can be compromised by both bottom-up and top-down processes. First, the colleague's meal can capture attention and assign the goal of 'finding lunch' prominence in working memory (WM). Second, if lunch becomes the goal, associated cues will acquire greater propensity to distract from other goals. A key theme in this book is that, in the context of addiction, implicit processes such as the allocation and maintenance of attention are slow to adapt to the new rule, 'no-go', and loyally continue to implement the 'go' rule that compels the individual to seek and find cues that point to appetitive rewards. This rivalry between implicit processes and deliberate efforts to resist appetitive impulses is the key dynamic in addiction and the authentic representation of ambivalence. It thus represents a legitimate target for therapeutic intervention.

Automatic Processes Can Be Practically Limitless

The ability to search for relevant environmental clues, or cues, automatically is efficient and relatively resistant to overload. Thus, Koch and Tsuchiya (2006) concluded that on average in the visual faculty alone we have to deal with about one megabyte of raw data each second, based on an estimated one million nerve fibres leaving each human eye. It is perhaps not surprising therefore that experimental findings show that detection rate or efficiency is relatively unaffected by the amount of distracters or potential targets (i.e., whether there are 10 or 100 faces). Selective attention has evolved to deal with this vast quantity of information. Evans and Treisman (2005), for example, used a rapid serial visual presentation (RSVP) paradigm to present 288 'target' images of vehicles or animals interspersed by 2,456 distracter images in visual scenes. As implied by the term RSVP, the visual scenes were presented very rapidly, in blocks of six. Each presentation took 450 milliseconds (ms), allowing just 75 ms for each scene to be processed. These investigators found up to 80% correct detection rates for target stimuli (animals or vehicles), although more contextual or semantic processing was less apparent. Thus, participants were able to indicate fairly accurately whether they saw a vehicle or an animal in a given scene, but were less adept at stating whether it was a truck or a rabbit, or if it was on the left or the right of the picture. These results pointed to rapid but crude feature analysis operating in advance of more attention-demanding identification. This remarkable ability to operate in parallel, with little or no demands on attention or need for conscious awareness, is of course advantageous in most scenarios.

Motivationally Relevant Cues are Prioritized

In addiction, however, cues acquire an artificially high salience both because of their motivational significance and the associated high frequency with which they have been processed. The highly evolved faculty to detect goal-relevant or survival-related stimuli is thus recruited to detect drug-related stimuli. Further, it appears that this preferential processing is somewhat immune from neglect or repression. The refractory period known as the 'attentional blink' (Raymond et al., 1992) occurs when two masked targets (T1 and T2) are presented within very brief periods of each other (usually less than 400 ms) and embedded in a stream of distracters. T2 is usually poorly identified when it is presented within a short time interval of T1. Participants appear not to notice the second of the two targets. Previously (Ryan, 2002b), I speculated that the attentional blink might exert its inhibitory influence in the context of addiction because the multiplicity of cues would overload its apparent limited capacity. I speculated that this might contribute to inconsistent responses to appetitive cues across various domains of cue reactivity such as craving, somatovisceral arousal and addictive behaviour as outlined by Carter and Tiffany (1999). Subsequent findings indicated that this may not be the case. Waters et al. (2007) found that attentional blink was reduced for smoking words, compared with neutral words, among a sample of 55 heavy smokers. The participants had to identify two target words (T1 and T2), which were either smoking related or neutral and embedded in 14 distracters. All 16 stimuli were presented rapidly, appearing on the screen for just 130 ms. The attentional blink appeared to operate as normal with neutral stimuli, inhibiting identification or recognition of T2 when it immediately followed T1. Performance was significantly less impaired when it came to identifying smoking-related stimuli.

A more recent study with problem gamblers (Brevers et al., 2011) generated similar findings in a controlled study. Here, the attentional blink 'survived' at 200 ms, but not at 400 ms, in the group of 35 problem gamblers that they recruited. With a longer time interval there is presumably less competition for attentional resources and the subtle attentional blink is not apparent. However, it does appear that, under conditions of more restricted attentional resources, smoking- or gambling-related words are more likely to be consciously identified than neutral words by individuals who are addicted smokers or compulsive gamblers. It is reasonable to hypothesize that this facilitation of substance- or gambling-related cues could also operate with other types of addiction. This implies that motivationally relevant cues appear to be resistant to key inhibitory processes such as the attentional blink that operate entirely outside conscious control. It seems that when evaluative processes assign a positive valence to addiction-related stimuli they ensure it is a long-term investment.

Biased Competition

The attentional blink phenomenon highlights the inherently competitive nature of cognitive processing. In any given environment or situation there is invariably more information than an individual can either want, or need, to process. Desimone and Duncan (1995) proposed that visual stimuli are not processed independently at the neuronal level but interact with each other in a mutually suppressive way. Thus, presentation of two or more stimuli can lead to *less* neuronal activation in parts of the visual cortex because different neuronal representations can be mutually suppressive. In effect, stimuli competing for neural representation partially 'cancel themselves out' as soon as they are available in the receptive or perceptual field. Information is thus processed in a competitive manner, beginning at the single-cell level. Clearly, this 'bottom-up' selective process can be shaped by evolutionary imperatives or motivational priorities. Finding somewhere to eat in unfamiliar surroundings or identifying a friend's or a loved one's face in a large crowd is no doubt facilitated by biasing of filtering out the hundreds or possibly thousands of distracters.

Beck and Kastner (2009) placed the biased-competition model in a broader neurocognitive framework, particularly in terms of 'top-down' influences. They refer to an 'attentional template', in which a sought-after or valued object is held in working memory in order to promote target selection and filter out distracters. This, of course, implicates executive control and areas such as the prefrontal cortex. Here, I propose that habituated drug users and gamblers will have acquired an attentional template, in effect a mindset, which infiltrates the intrinsic competitive nature of cognitive processing. A cognitive therapist will perhaps recognize the schema-like properties in this concept, although here I envisage a less generic cognitive structure. For example, a cognitive schema that constructs a worldview congruent with threat or failure can accommodate a wide range of stimuli, situations and scenarios, but the template proposed here is far more specific and focal, in keeping with the attentional template outlined by Beck and Kastner (2009). It also accords with recent reappraisals suggesting that the capacity of working memory is considerably less than 'the magical number seven plus or minus two' proposed by Miller (1956). Jonides *et al.* (2008) reviewed the literature and concluded that capacity, the number of items directly accessible or the focus of attention, could be limited to four plus or minus one, with perhaps only *one* piece of information being the focus of attention on a moment to moment basis.

Clearly, if only one piece of information were defined as simply an item or a number we would be unable to achieve a simple mental arithmetic task such as adding five and six. Jonides and colleagues therefore proposed that attention indeed focuses on just one piece of information but this is defined not as a single item or stimulus but a 'functional context' that could be defined by time, stimulus characteristics or momentary task relevance. When applied to that very particular type of goal driven behaviour that defines addiction this emphasizes in effect how single minded we can be in pursuing goals in a highly motivated manner. The complex issue of working-memory capacity will not be resolved in these chapters, but the trend does appear to be one that emphasizes how restrictive working-memory capacity is at any given moment. This scarce resource, vital to effective self-regulation, is the prize available to whatever stimulus representation is 'first past the post', and it is indeed a case of the winner takes all.

Attention and Volition

Traditional models of addiction assume that mental preoccupation with one's favourite drug or compulsion would activate craving and urgency that in turn serves as a final common pathway to drug seeking and drug taking. Cognitive models of attention ascribed a more multifaceted role to attention. Norman and Shallice (1986), for example, attempted to explicate the role that attention plays in the *control of action*. They first of all point out that the term 'automatic' has at least four different meanings:

- the way certain tasks can be carried out in the absence of awareness, for example walking down a familiar pathway;
- the manner in which an action may be initiated without deliberate attention or awareness, for example sipping from a glass of water or picking peanuts from a bowl;
- situations where attention is automatically drawn to something, for example the sudden appearance of a face at a window;
- the more technical use of the term in contemporary cognitive psychology where actions or tasks are deemed automatic if they do not appear to interfere with other tasks, that is are not constrained by limited capacity.

Norman and Shallice were particularly concerned with volitional and involitional regulation of action. Their starting point was that action or complex task performance appears to rely on the interaction of automatic processes 'supervised' or regulated by deliberate attentional control mechanisms that could either suppress unwanted actions or enhance desired ones. Norman and Shallice assign a precise role to attention. They contrast the relatively slow (at least 100 ms) pace of processing steps for deliberate control of attention with the requirement for skilled action sequences to be initiated with accuracy to the nearest 20 ms. Instead, therefore, of attention being involved in the 'micromanagement' or moment-by-moment regulation of behaviour, Norman and Shallice (2000) proposed that attentional resources are relevant primarily at the *initiation* and determination of a given action schema. They assume, plausibly, that competition between numerous potential action schemas is where the real battle for scarce cognitive resources is joined. They invoke the theoretical mechanism termed 'contention scheduling' to adjudicate in this conflict. They propose (p. 379) that this process 'resolves competition for selection, preventing competitive use of common related structures, and negotiating co-operative, shared use of common structures or operations when that is possible'. Consequently, once the given action schema has reached the necessary activation level it is once again a case of winner takes all.

Appetitive Cues Usually Win

Drawing on another sporting metaphor, 'a level playing field' does not exist in the context of addiction: appetitive cues have acquired a competitive advantage when it comes to attracting the attentional resources necessary to activate behavioural schemata. This is indeed a transient advantage, but in the highly competitive context of information processing milliseconds do matter. This is likely to be largely stimulus-driven or 'bottom-up' processing. By definition, addictive behaviour is well practised and thereby encoded in behavioural or action schemata. Well practised behaviour can routinely be invoked in the absence of valid motivation. Reason (1984) referred to these as 'action slips'. For example, one of his research participants described how, on his way to the back porch to get his car out, he put on his gardening outfit as if to work in his garden. Recently, and well before my normal bedtime, I went to the bedroom to retrieve a book but instead removed my watch and began getting ready for bed! These 'capture errors', while sometimes amusing, illustrate the fact that purposeful, apparently goal directed behaviour can be purely stimulus driven and involitional: in the examples mentioned above, neither gardening nor an early night was the conscious goal but these were pursued nonetheless. Note, however, that neither of the default behaviours involving the garden or the bedroom can be usually viewed as compulsive or incentivized. Accordingly, once the error is detected the correct behaviour course can be resumed, perhaps with a wry smile. This sharply contrasts with what is known about the evocative power of stimuli associated with addictive behaviour. Once these have captured attention even momentarily, they are likely to have triggered more powerful action tendencies regardless of whether this was task congruent or not. This resonates with a key theme of this text. A universal feature of cognition such as distractibility or loss of task focus or conflict monitoring assumes an altogether different meaning in the context of addictive behaviour. The magnetic effect of addictive cues can prove harder to override and other goals can fade into insignificance.

Purposeful Behaviour Can Occur in the Absence of Consciousness

Dijksterhuis and Aarts (2010) reviewed evidence from neuroscience, cognitive psychology and social cognition in order to understand the relation between goals, attention and consciousness. One of their conclusions was that goal-directed volitional behaviour can be initiated by events or stimuli occurring outside awareness. An example of this would be presenting a subliminal stimulus or incidental ambient exposure to words such as 'success'. This challenges the intuitively appealing notion that voluntary action relies on conscious decision making. Earlier experimental evidence indicating that consciousness was not necessary to trigger volitional behaviour was provided by the seminal studies of Libet *et al.* (1983). They designed an experimental paradigm that required participants to make a free choice about when to simply move their index fingers. The participants were asked to report when they made the decision to move one of their fingers and predictably this proceeded the action. Crucially however, electrophysiological measures revealed action potentials about one second prior to conscious awareness of making a decision. As Dijksterhuis and Aarts (2010) point out, the findings are not necessarily easy to interpret, because the participants were not deciding *whether* to move their finger but *when* to move their finger. Dijksterhuis and Aarts (2010, p. 469) nonetheless concluded in their review that there is abundant evidence that 'people become consciously aware of an act only after they unconsciously decide to engage in it. In addition, at least some volitional behaviour does not require any conscious awareness at all: Goals and motivation can be unconsciously primed'. Purposeful, goal-directed behaviour nonetheless requires attention; otherwise, it would be unfocused and rarely successful. Dijksterhuis and Aarts (2010) proposed that attention and consciousness, while intuitively linked, can be differentiated. They applied a 2 × 2 taxonomy whereby stimuli are either attended to or not and whether they are reportable or not. Thus, attention can be engaged as in pursuing goal-directed behaviour in the absence of conscious awareness and, conversely, we can be conscious of stimuli without paying much, if any, attention to them.

Attentional Bias and Craving

Incentive-focused models of addiction (Robinson and Berridge, 1993; Ryan, 2002b; Franken, 2003; Kavanagh *et al.*, 2005) assume that substance-related stimuli acquire a motivational salience that gives them a head start in the competition to gain attention. Thus, a substance cue 'grabs attention, becomes attractive and "wanted," and thus guides behavior to the incentive' (Robinson and Berridge, 1993, p. 261). I attempted to place this in a more cognitive context by proposing that 'cue reactivity and the experience of craving are meaningfully related to perceptual and cognitive processes that occur before, during, and after cue exposure' (Ryan, 2002b, p. 68); the prediction is that there should be a strong, possibly reciprocal, relationship between escalating craving and increasing attentional bias. Preliminary findings (Ryan, 2002a) provided somewhat indirect support for this, with multiple-regression analysis revealing that indices of alcohol dependence, such as scores on the Severity of Alcohol Dependence Questionnaire (Stockwell *et al.*, 1979) and self-reported alcohol consumption predicted the degree of interference on a Modified Stroop test. This task requires the participant to name the colour of the ink used to print words that are either neutral (in this case not related to alcohol) or significant, such as 'Wine', 'Binge' or 'Vodka'. Interference was measured by comparing the reaction time to colour name alcohol-related words as opposed to neutral words. It is thought that this superficially simple task reflects the facility with which an individual can inhibit the prepotent tendency to read the word or conversely the extent to which the word meaning distracts the individual by capturing attention. In functional terms it appears to index automaticity.

Field and his colleagues recently conducted a meta-analysis of 68 datasets investigating the relationship between attentional bias, measured by a range of techniques such as eye movement tracking and the visual probe, and measures of subjective craving (Field *et al.*, 2009). They found a modest relationship of $r = 0.19$, further reduced to $r = 0.13$ following a statistical correction for publication bias, between attentional bias and expressions of craving. This suggests 4% and 2% of shared variance, respectively. Mining subsets of the data produced a more nuanced set of findings. First, in the subset of 12 studies in which craving was experimentally manipulated a more robust correlation of $r = 0.23$ was apparent among participants with higher induced craving, compared with $r = 0.08$ among those whose subjective craving was not thus manipulated. Second, when Field *et al.* analysed subsets of data that used *direct* measures of attentional bias, such as eye-movement tracking, they found a more robust correlation, $r = 0.36$. Third, regardless of how attentional bias was measured, there was a higher correlation between cues associated with caffeine, cannabis, cocaine and heroin compared with cues associated with alcohol and tobacco. Finally, further stratification of the data indicated that there was no apparent difference in the relationship between attentional bias and craving amongst those who were engaged in treatment and those who were not actively seeking treatment.

It appears therefore that attentional bias is significantly related to phenomenological aspects of addiction such as craving, but the dynamics of this relationship are not yet fully understood. One way to achieve greater understanding of this relationship would be to manipulate cognitive bias in clinical settings, in a manner similar to innovations with therapeutics of anxiety disorders. Findings showing that attentional bias may form part of a cognitive vulnerability factor that meaningfully relates to key components of addiction, such as craving, are scientifically important. They set the scene for more rigorous evaluation using controlled trials in clinical settings with appropriate follow-up. Some of this evidence will be examined in Chapter 7. The key question is whether cognitive bias modification, or more specifically the reversal of attentional bias, has clinical utility, whether as a stand-alone procedure or as a 'bolted-on' extra to existing treatments. The available evidence is reviewed in the next section.

Implicit cognition and behaviour

A definitive aspect of implicit functioning is that it occurs in advance of or outside conscious awareness or is otherwise unavailable to introspection. Findings that abstaining smokers, for example, show evidence of unconsciously processing smoking-related cues (Leventhal et al., 2008) provide further evidence that drug-relevant information can be processed outside awareness, or in advance of conscious control. These researchers presented subliminal (17 ms) pictures of smoking-related, affective and neutral stimuli to nicotine-deprived smokers, non-deprived smokers and nonsmokers. Their method allowed them to assess what cues were unconsciously 'preferred'. Smokers deprived of nicotine for at least 12 hours prior to testing showed a bias to where the 'unseen' picture of smoking paraphernalia appeared on a screen. This was not apparent in nondeprived smokers or nonsmokers. This shows the essentially motivational nature of the cognitive processing in the context of addiction. When the motivational value of the stimulus is presumably increased through deprivation, it becomes more salient. Consistent with this, Ingjaldsson et al. (2003) divided detoxified alcohol-dependent individuals according to whether they were low or high on measures of craving and presented them with subliminal (20 ms) masked slides of alcohol stimuli. Psychophysiological measures of cardiovascular reactions showed that in the high-craving group the heart rate reduced immediately after exposure to subliminal alcohol cues, suggesting an orientation or alerting response. This effect was not found within the low-craving or the control group. Moreover, when presented with 'supraliminal', that is visible, alcohol cues, the groups did not show cardiovascular differences.

Cognitive Cycle of Preoccupation

Previously (Ryan, 2002b), I proposed that the detection of drug cues is automatically facilitated regardless of the conscious goal of the restrained drug user (e.g. 'I want to avoid triggers for using drugs'). Due to the relentless nature of this hypervigilance, drug cues tend to engage attention even if they are unpredictable and occur over a lengthy period. Once detected, the ensuing evaluative appraisal assigns the cue a positive valence by default. This primary appraisal can elicit components of cue reactivity such as physiological arousal, behaviour and cognitions (e.g. expectancies) in advance of, or parallel with, the recruitment of focal attention. These components of cue reactivity are subjected to more elaborate appraisal mediated by attentional and inferential biases. This account accentuated the role of attentional processes and primary appraisal mechanisms. I concluded (p. 74) that 'Cognitive biases can thus subvert the most fervently held desire for abstinence or restraint by generating a model of the environment where cues for the proscribed substance are virtually ubiquitous'. Assigning an influential role to cognitive biases was neither adequate conceptually nor did it provide a viable basis for therapeutic intervention. With regard to the latter, addressing or modifying cognitive biases presents considerable challenges from a therapeutic standpoint. Certainly, conventional cognitive therapy techniques were not applicable. Moreover, while influential in maintaining cycles of addictive behaviour, automatic cognitive biases such as the preferential allocation of attention to drug-associated cues was by no means the only information processing that occurred. Controlled processes are also available and could be exploited to regulate less consciously regulated processes.

Accordingly, I attempted to place this partial account into a broader cognitive context (Ryan, 2006 and Figure 4.2), focusing on the role of working memory as an 'executive-attention' mechanism that maintains stimulus

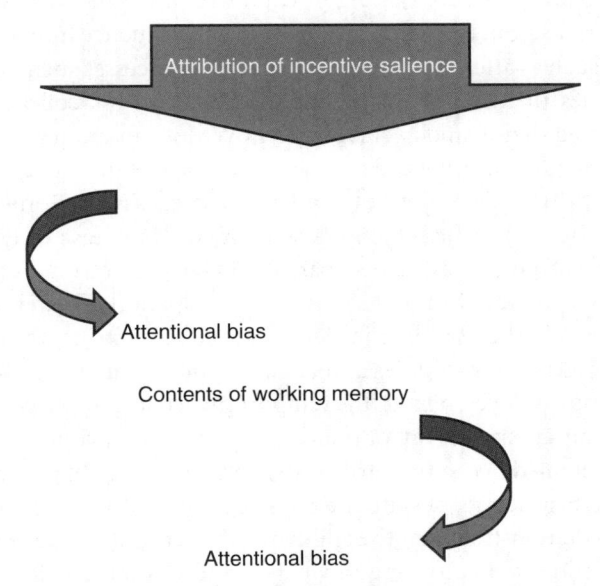

Figure 4.2 Cognitive cycle of preoccupation.

representations, action plans and goals (see, e.g., Kane and Engle, 2003). Attentional bias towards cues associated with drug-derived gratification is assumed to facilitate access to WM, which in turn increases the likelihood of subsequent cues being detected. This processing takes place automatically, regardless of the conscious desire of the individual to avoid evocative cues. If the gratification goal is supplanted, attentional allocation will obediently align itself with the new objective. This focus on working memory provided, I hoped, a more congenial context that provided both therapist and client with more therapeutic traction: the contents of WM could be both reported by the client and influenced by the therapist. This promised an arena for collaborative engagement where intervention focused on regulation of attentional allocation by influencing the contents of WM. For example, specifying restraint as a goal, or an alternative goal incompatible with satiation, was presumed to reduce the liklihood of appetitive cues capturing attention. Occupying the 'high ground' of WM enabled more top-down regulation of bottom-up attentional processes. Importantly, the focus on goal specification and goal maintenance helps bridge the gap between cognitive processing and motivational psychology. The concept of *current concern* (Cox and Klinger, 1988; Klinger and Cox, 2011), for example, applies when an individual is actively pursuing a goal. Goal pursuit is associated with pervasive biasing of cognitive processes such as attention recall and reflection. Note that goal pursuit can influence implicit cognitive processes such as attention as well as deliberate processes such as reflection.

In a series of ingenious experiments, Soto and his colleagues (2007) demonstrated that if an object is stored in WM it can influence attentional deployment *automatically* and at a very early stage of perceptual processing (Soto *et al.*, 2010). Typically, Soto and his colleagues used geometric figures as stimuli, but here I shall paraphrase their work for ease of explanation. For instance, an individual participant could be instructed to retain certain stimuli, say an image of an apple, in WM in anticipation of a later recognition test. This would then become irrelevant as the participant was required to classify objects as, say, squares and circles. Crucially however, if the square or circle was displayed next to the temporarily irrelevant image of an apple there was an apparently involuntary delay with the primary recognition task. The retained but temporarily task irrelevant image of the apple would thus prove distracting, despite the conscious goal of the participant. This appears to demonstrate that the ability to select stimuli in the environment could be influenced according to whether the stimuli match the contents of WM or not. In therapeutic intervention contexts, this suggests that one way to influence attentional processing is by manipulating the contents of WM. Specification of a new goal, for example 'when I arrive at the birthday party I will search for as many nonalcoholic beverages as I can find', could recruit the apparent perceptual biasing effect of WM to engender attention bias for these alcohol-free drinks. Theoretically, thus could counterbalance attentional bias predicated on addiction or compulsive use of alcohol.

The suggestion is that occupying the 'high ground' of WM with a non-addictive stimulus provides the individual with a head start in attentional engagement of 'neutral' rather than addictive cues. Importantly, because the biasing is involuntary, it is less likely to deplete coping resources that might be subsequently needed. For example Susan, a 35-year-old woman recently seen in my clinic, was sucessfully detoxified from alcohol only to find that she was highly anxious in social situations. In an effort to address this, she agreed to use coping skills such as engaging in more eye contact and discounting thoughts such as 'They think I'm stupid; they'll think I'm an alcoholic'. The need to use further coping strategies such as drink-refusal skills meant that Susan risked developing 'coping fatigue'. The relatively simple task of identifying nonalcoholic drinks, involving the retention of a goal in WM, proved easy and allowed more cognitive capacity for Susan to use practice competencies such as social interaction and engagement. On this occasion she remained alcohol free and stayed at the party for over an hour, the minimum period agreed in advance.

As described in the paragraphs above, Soto and his colleagues designed experiments showing that one way to influence attentional processing is by manipulating the contents of WM. However, the relationship between task complexity, cognitive load and distractibility is complex. Lavie (2005) concluded that a high perceptual load, for example having to count letters in a word rather than specify whether it was a noun or a verb, that engages full attention can reduce the lure of the distracter. According to Lavie's account, known as load theory, this is because there is no spare capacity available to register any additional perceptual inputs. This can sometimes have disastrous consequences: for instance, if a driver is using a mobile phone – and thus fully engaged – when driving, he or she may show a form of 'attentional blindness' to a red traffic signal or a pedestrian. However, if the consequences of distraction are likely to be unhelpful or negative, for example if a person is at home reading a book but finds their attention turns to online betting, the benefits of full engagement of attention are apparent by default.

Applied to clinical contexts, load theory implies that inhibiting processing of certain stimuli can have a therapeutic benefit. With regard to anxiety disorders, for example, Lavie (2005) speculated that the gating of attention can happen at very early stages, even when emotional stimuli, usually regarded as automatically demanding of attention, are presented as task irrelevant, that is, distracters. Thus, Pessoa *et al*. (2005) found that under conditions of high perceptual load the amygdala did not differentiate between emotive faces (angry, happy or sad) and neutral faces. It seemed that the amygdala responded differentially to faces with emotional content only when sufficient attentional resources were available to process those faces: when attentional resources were required for another task, differential responses to emotional expression were eliminated. There are no comparable investigations of which I am aware probing the relationship between perceptual load and processing of addictive cues, but these findings raise the possibility that strategic manipulation of cognitive factors such as perceptual load can reduce distraction because there is no spare cognitive capacity.

Recalling the fMRI findings of Childress *et al*. (2008), showing early neural activation by cocaine-related stimuli, the prediction is that if the participants had been provided with more cognitive challenge the subliminal cues would not have triggered neural activation. The nature of the challenge is crucial, however, because while high perceptual load can *reduce* distraction, high WM load (as in Soto *et al*., 2007) *increases* distracter interference. This suggests that cognitive control is needed for actively maintaining the distinction between targets and distracters. When cognitive control is poor, perhaps because WM capacity is low or highly loaded, engaging in a task with high perceptual load is likely to reduce distraction. Conversely, if the task is low on perceptual load distraction is more likely to ensue (see Figure 4.3). In terms of resisting distraction, the top left quadrant represents

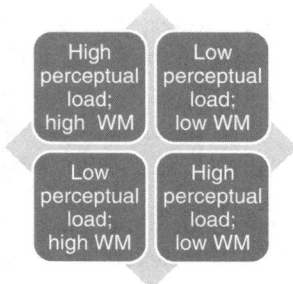

Figure 4.3 Getting the balance right between capacity and overload.

the most robust position with a combination of high perceptual load and a high degree of cognitive flexibility. The top right quadrant represents a more fragile scenario with a high tendency towards distraction through bottom-up processing and compromised cognitive control perhaps due to low WM capacity. The two lower quadrants represent intermediate positions with perceptual load potentially compensating for deficits in cognitive control (left quadrant) and robust cognitive control overriding distractions that might occur due to low perceptual loading (right quadrant).

In real-life settings, a situation where this type of cognitive vulnerability could arise might typically be due to the routine demands of a job that requires continual shifting and updating of the contents of WM. Clearly, this would also entail increased perceptual load but not necessarily focused on a single task. Many jobs require monitoring and updating, for example. According to the model depicted in Figure 4.3, the combination of high WM load and low perceptual load would increase the risk of an individual becoming more distracted by ambient cues. If that person is aiming to restrain him - or herself from drinking or using drugs, the prediction is that the cues that would capture attention may well be substance or addiction related.

5

Vulnerability Factors In Addiction

Individual Differences in Addiction Liability

The majority of people who occasionally experience the effects of drugs such as alcohol, cocaine and heroin do not become addicted (Anthony *et al.*, 1994; Wagner and Anthony, 2002). This indicates that some adaptation, or more accurately maladaptation, takes place in the subset of those who become addicted. Presumably, some individuals could be predisposed to be more sensitive to drug-associated pleasure or reward or have deficits in self-control when faced with such potential rewards. Negative reinforcement could also be influential in those prone to negative emotional states that can be ameliorated by exposure to the neurochemical impact of drugs. In this chapter I shall explore affective and cognitive factors that contribute to individual vulnerability to addiction. Addiction emerges from a complex interplay of genetic and environmental factors (see Figure 5.1). The theme is that addictive disorders and the common behavioural and mental health problems than often coincide can plausibly be viewed as sharing a common heritage, for example genetic loading and/or exposure to adversity, especially in early life. This could represent one pathway to addiction but is not of course the only pathway. Profiling it in this text is intended to correct what is often an implicit assumption that addiction is, in effect, a *reaction* to emotional turmoil. Because of their motivational significance, affective factors such as depression and anxiety are more likely to mobilize emotionally vulnerable individuals to seek professional help. These factors are more available or salient to both treatment seeker and caregivers than the rather more covert phenomenology of impulsivity.

Personality Traits

More stable dispositions that influence behaviour across time and context, known as traits, are regarded as the components of a given person's

Cognitive Therapy for Addiction: Motivation and Change, First Edition. Frank Ryan.
© 2013 Frank Ryan. Published 2013 by John Wiley & Sons, Ltd.

64 Cognitive Therapy for Addiction

Vulnerability derived from genetic and epigenetic factors

Expressed as poor impulse control | and emotional negativity or instability

⬇

Exposure to adversity and/or availability of psychoactive substances, possibly as part of a repetitous cycle

Development of deliberate drug-acquisitive behaviour (action–outcome learning). | Formation of strengthening stimulus–stimulus links (associative or classical conditioning).

⬇

Induction of increasingly automatic cognitive and behavioural processes underpinned by stimulus–response or 'habit learning'

Impaired cognitive control reflected especially in suboptimal goal maintenance and compromised cognitive control. Indexed by attentional bias.

⬇

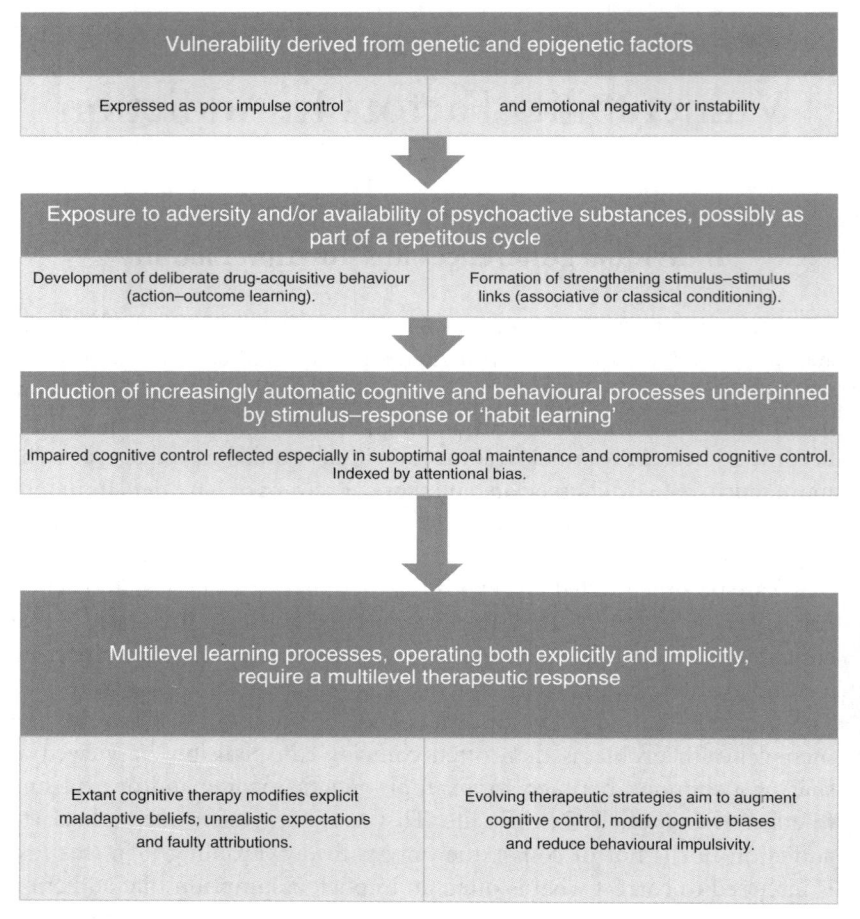

Multilevel learning processes, operating both explicitly and implicitly, require a multilevel therapeutic response

Extant cognitive therapy modifies explicit maladaptive beliefs, unrealistic expectations and faulty attributions. | Evolving therapeutic strategies aim to augment cognitive control, modify cognitive biases and reduce behavioural impulsivity.

Figure 5.1 Vulnerability factors for addiction and emotional disorder.

personality or character. The oft-quoted maxim by Oscar Wilde (1892), 'I can resist everything but temptation', implies (albeit paradoxically!) a disposition to gratification that is pertinent here. Is it valid or helpful to refer to an 'addictive personality', defined as a tendency to be unable to resist temptation as stated humorously by Lord Darlington, Oscar Wilde's character in *Lady Windermere's Fan*? In a word, no! The reasoning underlying the notion of an addictive personality is circular, as evidence of diverse patterns of addictive behaviour is used to justify the disposition inferred from the behaviour. Moreover, at the neuronal level apparently diverse compulsive behaviours are eliciting similar outcomes, such as alterations in dopaminergic, glutamatergic or GABAergic transmission. In common with many intuitive theories, exceptions are ignored. For example, I recently saw a 32-year-old man with high levels of opiate dependence who had overcome his dependence on alcohol two years earlier. Remaining in the realm of the anecdote, I have also seen many individuals who had selectively overcome, or indeed relapsed with, addiction 'A', leaving addiction 'B' unaffected. Nonetheless, there are individual differences in addiction liability, which justifies this brief diversion into personality theory.

The 'Big Five' Personality Factors

There is emerging consensus on the factorial structure of human personality as being the 'Big Five', or the Five-Factor Model (FFM): Neuroticism (N), Extraversion (E), Openness (O), Agreeableness (A) and Conscientiousness (C) (see Matthews *et al.*, 2009, for a recent review). Combinations of these diverse dispositions no doubt could render an individual susceptible to developing an addictive disorder. For example, individuals ranked high on E and possibly low on C could be deemed susceptible because extroverts are more sensitive to the reward signals and, feeling less conscientious (low C), would display less perseverance in the face of temptation. Equally, however, individuals more disposed to anxiety (high N) could also be deemed vulnerable, because of sensitivity to punitive stimuli such as those that could be associated with withdrawal discomfort in the context of addiction. It appears plausible therefore that certain combinations of personality characteristics could well predispose individuals to more intensive pursuits of drug- or gambling-derived rewards. While there is no consensus on what constitutes an 'addictive personality' as a generic entity, at the individual or ideographic level personality factors such as impulsivity or emotional instability are surely relevant to formulation and therapeutic intervention.

Gray's theory (e.g. 1991) proposed two major neurobehavioural systems, the behavioural activation system (BAS) and the behavioural inhibition system (BIS), which react to reward and threat signals respectively. More impulsive individuals tend to be stable extraverts, more sensitive to reward signals mediated by the BAS, based on forebrain structures such as the striatum. Due to the increased sensitivity reactivity of this system, highly impulsive people are more motivated by rewards than less impulsive people. This contrasts with the classic Eysenckian construct of extraversion, which assumed that extroverts (in effect impulsives) were characteristically underaroused neuronally and hence craved stimulation, novelty or the attention of others. On the other hand, highly anxious individuals, tending towards neurotic introversion, are more sensitive to threat signals. This generates testable predictions, for example that extraverts will learn optimally in rewarding conditions and introverts' learning is better where punishment prevails (Pickering et al., 1995).

Clearly, the notion of a predisposition to reward sensitivity has implications for addiction susceptibility. Franken (2003), for example, found that a cohort of attendees at a drug treatment centre scored higher on standard measures of dimensions of the BAS compared with both attendees at an Alcohol Treatment Centre and controls recruited from the normal population. In the next section I shall briefly address enduring dysfunctional patterns in areas such as emotionality and impulsivity. These results suggest that disinhibition is a complex phenomenon that may be mediated either by BIS hypoactivity, BAS hyperactivity or even BIS hyperactivity. Further, impulsivity or disinhibition is influenced by the involvement of variables such as gender, personality, motivation, task and subject's Anx state (p. 239). Lynam (2011) estimated that impulsivity or inhibitory failure feature in as many as 18 designated psychiatric disorders (DSM-IV; American Psychiatric Association, 1994). Inhibitory failure remains nonetheless a definitive component of addictive disorders and serves as an essential target for therapeutic intervention.

Personality Disorders

Personality disorders share high levels of coincidence with substance misuse disorders, at least among those who seeking treatment (Weaver et al., 2002). Here, a meaningful discussion of the merits or demerits of assigning diagnostic labels to people with enduring emotional behavioural and interpersonal difficulties is not possible. Following on from the discussion above about traits, a dimensional approach appears to offer more parsimony. Livesley et al. (1998) conducted a principal-component analysis that yielded four components they labelled the 'the four As'. In order to achieve the mnemonic effect the terms are rather obscure, so I have clarified each term accordingly: Asthenic (emotional dysregulation), Anti-social (dissocial behaviour), Avoidance (inhibitedness) and Anankastic (compulsivity) (see Matthews et al., 2009, Chapter 11).

Whiteside and Lynam (2001) proposed that the FFM issues for personality traits reflect five relatively distinct pathways to impulsive behaviour.

Negative urgency: the tendency to act rationally when experiencing negative emotions, for example 'When I am upset, I often act without thinking and sometimes reach for a drink'.
Lack of perseverance: the tendency to give up on a task more easily, in effect a lack of willpower. The manifestation of this personality trait could be endorsing the item 'I tend to give up easily', strongly discounting the statement 'Once I start something I'm determined to finish it'.
Lack of premeditation: the tendency to act without considering the consequences, especially those in the medium to long term, for example strongly disagreeing with a statement such as before deciding to do something I carefully weigh up the "pros and cons".
Sensation seeking: essentially the same as the FFM construct reflecting a preference for novelty seeking, risk-taking and openness to new experience.
Positive urgency: this disposition refers to the tendency to act rashly when experiencing positive affect, feeling excited in response to positive life events (see also Lynam, 2011).

Addiction therapists need to be aware of these enduring tendencies, as they can create a context for relapse if and when abstinence is achieved. Assessment can be achieved by evaluating the personal history for patterns of behavioural or emotional problems that appear somewhat independent from the effects of chronic drug or alcohol use. Instruments such as the NEO-Personality Inventory – Revised (NEO-PI-R, Costa and McCrae, 1992) or the much briefer Barratt Impulsiveness Scale (Patton *et al.*, 1995) can be used to clarify or quantify any indications of enduring dysfunctional traits or impulsivity, respectively. In the next section I shall look at possible pathways to addiction from this more developmental perspective.

Affective Vulnerability Factors

Looking at individual differences in addiction propensity from a lifespan or developmental perspective, Sinha (2009) concluded that repeated and uncontrollable negative life experiences interact with individual genetic susceptibility to alter neurotransmission in stress-related pathways such as corticotrophin-releasing factor (CRF), norepinephrine, glucocorticoids, gamma-aminobutyric acid (GABA), neuropeptide Y (NPY), brain-derived neurotrophic factor (BDNF), serotonin, glutamate and dopamine systems. Fumagalli *et al.* (2007) reviewed evidence from animal laboratory research pointing to the sensitizing impact of adversity in gestation or perinatally. Perinatal adversities impact, for example, on receptors in the GABAergic system, an important regulator of response to stress by virtue of its inhibitory role. Moreover, even though environmental stress such as maternal deprivation in the research using nonhuman species reviewed by Fumagalli *et al.* (2007) occurred over a brief window in the developmental span, it led to enduring behavioural deficits and measurable changes in neuronal mechanisms and processes. First, this was because if neurogenesis is disrupted at a critical stage the opportunity for restoration of recovery does not recur. Second, Fumagalli and colleagues noted that perinatal adversities were associated with epigenetic influence, the process whereby gene expression can be altered in the long term by environmental or other non-genetic factors. Consistent with this, genetic or heritable factors are now recognized as significant contributors to addiction susceptibility (see, e.g., Hiroi and Agatsuma, 2005). While heritability is an influential factor, this is not to say that there is any empirical consensus on which genes, or more specifically their functional variants or polymorphisms, can be accorded candidate status for increasing susceptibility to addiction. The inherited contribution to complex human patterns of behaviour such as impulsivity or sensation seeking, here deemed relevant to addiction, is likely to derive from the combined effects of hundreds, if not thousands, of different genetic loci. (See Munafo and Flint, 2011.)

Further, dopamine neurons that signal reward can also be excited by acute *aversive* events (see Ungless *et al.*, 2010.) At first glance, these findings appear to be at odds with evidence of dopamine release in response to rewards, or predicted rewards, together with dopamine suppression in response to withheld rewards or punishment (see Wise, 1988). Ungless *et al.* (2010) suggest that phasic and tonic excitation at (aversive) stimulus offset can become more chronic and contribute to the changes in dopamine release. Although much of this research is based on animal laboratory work, findings that activation of parts of the dopaminergic reward circuitry is associated with aversive stimuli are consistent with treatment-outcome studies highlighting the relationship between adverse mood and resumed substance use.

Regardless of the complex neurochemical substrate of negative affect, in humans appraisal processes play a crucial mediational role between a given situation and the subsequent emotional response. Thus, a socially anxious individual might find social interaction unpleasant because he or she has a belief 'they think I'm stupid'. Comparing this with an appraisal such as 'they think I'm amusing' accentuates the power of evaluative processes. From the foregoing, this negative automatic thought would generate negative affect via a complex neurochemical cascade. Conversely, teaching the socially apprehensive individual to recognize and reconstruct such thoughts should serve to reduce negative aspect and the associated liability to substance misuse.

Brain-Derived Neurotrophic Factors

Another neurochemical candidate for predisposing individuals to addictive disorders is neurotrophins such as BDNF. These are polypeptide proteins involved in regulating and modulating other neuronal functions. Crucially, they maintain neuronal plasticity and govern the survival, differentiation and maintenance of functions of specific groups of neurons (Thoenen, 1995) such as dopamine receptors. Neurotrophins such as BDNF appear to be integral to the maintenance of plasticity of the central nervous system, especially when challenged by stress or adverse environmental conditions. BDNF thus appears to be a plausible candidate for at least contributing to resilience in the face of adversity. Physical exercise following brain damage, or as a means of cognitive enhancement, has also been associated with increased BDNF-dependent synaptic plasticity and recovery. Because of its regulatory function, BDNF is also recruited to achieve neuroadaptation or homoeostasis when the brain is exposed to drugs. McGinty *et al.* (2010) concluded in their review that the empirical data suggested that BDNF, when localized in the prefrontal cortex rather than other areas, attenuates reinstatement to cocaine seeking. They speculated that it achieved this by normalizing cocaine-induced neuroadaptations that alter glutamate neurotransmission within the nucleus accumbens.

It thus appears that neurotrophic factors such as BDNF are on one hand inhibited by exposure to adversity, particularly perinatally and at early stages of neurogenesis, and on the other hand important in orchestrating neuronal activity in combating the chemical challenge of drugs. Consistent with this, Fumagalli *et al.* (2009) found in his own laboratory in Milan that in chronically stressed animals BDNF was not recruited when they were exposed to cocaine, in contrast to the non-stressed control animals.

Recalling that BDNF has an overarching 'maintenance' regulatory function with more differentiated groups of neurons, the stressed cohort did not appear to have access to sufficient BDNF to attenuate or counteract the cellular demands caused by exposure to cocaine challenge. The implication is that cellular resilience may be at risk, because chronic stress might contribute to an increase in the threshold for the activation of the trophic response, thus rendering the animals more vulnerable to cocaine. This means that stress-induced impairments of acute BDNF upregulation typically promoted by cocaine might be damaging for cortical neurons.

In clinical or functional terms, the implication is that exposure to stress, especially at critical stages of development, can contribute to subtle but pervasive deficits in neuronal systems that have become exposed by the inevitable challenges with which life presents us. Moreover, neuronal plasticity modulated by neurotrophic molecules such as BDNF is also key to mobilizing the brain's response to being suddenly flooded by molecules delivered by drug ingestion. These mimic endogenous chemicals, or disrupt their transmission, thus creating dramatic imbalance. This raises the possibility that prior exposure to stress increases susceptibility to the neurotoxic effects of drugs. This could account in part for the high level of emotional disorders such as anxiety and depression observed in those seeking treatment for addictive disorders. However, rather than suggest that addiction is a response to dysphoria, a form of 'self-medication', the proposal is that vulnerability to *both* addiction and emotional dysregulation could be influenced by adversity early in development. This provides further justification for addressing emotional-regulation skills (Managing Mood, the third M) in the treatment framework outlined here.

Neurocognitive Vulnerability

Turning to cognitive processing factors, another influential candidate variable is pre-existing deficiency in components of executive control such as inhibition or working memory capacity. Ersche *et al.* (2012) recently discovered abnormalities in frontostriatal systems in a cohort of 50 comprising both stimulant-dependent individuals and their biological siblings who did not have a history of drug dependence or misuse. These abnormalities concerned connectivity between motivational or 'go' circuits and regions involved in inhibition, such as the right inferior frontal cortex correlated with the Stop Signal Reaction Time task, an experimental measure of inhibitory control. (See also Chapter 7 and a review by MacKillop et al., 2011.) It appeared that *both* addicted and non-addicted siblings had deficits in impulse control linked to underlying abnormalities in relevant brain regions. This suggests that, while inherited deficits in impulse control confer a significant risk of addiction, the risk can be overcome by many. This reduction of risk could be associated with differing environmental exposure or the development of resilience possibly linked to factors such as behavioural flexibility. In this regard, the non-addicted siblings had relatively larger volume in the medial orbitofrontal cortex, involved in adapting to changing contexts, and the precuneus, a parietal structure nestling between the two cerebral hemispheres, implicated in consciousness, perception and episodic memory. It could be that the siblings fortunate to avoid drug dependence relied on the counterbalancing effect of cognitive control that, for whatever reason, remained unavailable to their addicted brothers and sisters. The implication is that neurocognitive risk factors for addiction, while heritable, are not deterministic. Further, there appears to be scope for overcoming these deficiencies in naturalistic, developmental contexts, albeit using mechanisms that are not fully defined. Cognitive neuroscience is nonetheless providing valuable clues as to the nature of the processes involved, specifically the component processes of executive control.

Findings from the Addiction Clinic

Moving from the laboratory to the clinical arena, research with clinic recruits confirms the reciprocal or dynamic links between dysphoria and drug-seeking behaviour. Witkiewitz and Villarroel (2009), for instance, found a strong association between negative affect and resumed alcohol use after a period of abstinence. These researchers applied an associative latent transition analysis to the Project MATCH (Project MATCH Research Group, 1997) outpatient data ($n = 952$) and aftercare data ($n = 774$). Changes in drinking following treatment were significantly associated with current affect, and prior changes in negative affect were related to prior changes in drinking. The results suggest that a therapeutic focus on the relationship between negative affect and alcohol use could decrease the probability of lapses. The findings also lend support to therapeutic programmes that teach affect regulation, but imply that forestalling resumed drinking is in itself a means of maintaining good mental health. It appears reasonable to assume a similar reciprocal relationship would exist between negative affect and other drugs with similar therapeutic implications.

Recalling the discussion in Chapter 2 on the relative motivational significance of avoidance of aversive states as opposed to the lure of hedonic reward, this debate is perhaps less vital in the addiction clinic. It is nonetheless important to differentiate between negative affect stemming from withdrawal discomfort and that emanating from more general sources, for example stress linked to work or depression linked to personal loss. In this regard, Perkins *et al.* (2010) found that smoking resumption in nicotine-deprived cigarette smokers robustly reduced dysphoria linked to abstinence but was associated with more modest reduction in experimentally induced negative affect (e.g. by viewing upsetting slides or preparing a revealing speech). This finding validates the framework proposed here that enables formulation-based treatment to target both the impulse-control issues linked to addiction and the negative affect frequently associated with addiction. The practical implication is that, in order to be effective, treatment programmes need to address both addictive and affective issues in tandem. However, the cognitive therapist needs to be astute in differentiating between genetic predispositions, the more enduring negative affect that might stem from adversity earlier on in development and maturation and the more short-lived dysphoria associated with relatively abrupt cessation of drug delivery. This accentuates the need for eliciting a detailed personal history from the individual seeking help with an addictive disorder but who also reports significant negative effect. From a cognitive-therapy perspective it is vital to specify the source of the emotional negativity. In Chapter 8 I shall specify three sources: pre-existing negative affect due to personality traits and/or exposure to adverse life events, negative emotions stemming from the after-effects of drug intoxication and negative emotions arising from setbacks or lapses.

From Research to Practice

In the foregoing, addiction has been depicted as a syndrome forged by the interaction of genetic, developmental, affective and social factors. In order to conceptualize cases and produce valid formulations, it is important that the cognitive therapist accounts for the interaction of these factors. Therapeutic intervention needs to acknowledge what can be changed but also what may not be so amenable to remediation. Evidence, for example, that early exposure to adversity can impair the brain's innate recovery mechanisms, or that impaired inhibitory control predates addiction, points to an enduring syndrome that will not change easily. By recognizing the challenge of addiction and delineating the core learning and motivational processes, the *CHANGE* model outlined here aims to bring a more pragmatic and evidence-based approach to the therapeutic arena. This sets the scene for the following chapters, which address the challenge of initiating and maintaining change.

6

Motivation and Engagement

Impaired Insight and the Therapeutic Relationship

The compulsive nature of addiction often remains latent or implicit in the clinic, despite becoming increasingly stimulus driven in naturalistic settings. This contrasts with how emotionally driven disorders such as anxiety and depression present in clinical settings. A depressed or anxious patient will frequently express strong emotions behaviourally as well as by self-reports and physiological arousal, whereas an addicted individual will often appear somewhat detached from the compulsive nature of the problem. Michael, for instance, a depressed 58-year-old man who came to see me recently, became distraught when reflecting back on the difficulties he had encountered due to his chronic anxiety, associated avoidance and alcohol dependence. His appraisals, 'I've achieved nothing; I've wasted my life', were entirely congruent with his sad mood and self-directed anger. The transparent manner with which Michael was able to report his thoughts made him a good candidate for traditional cognitive therapy, beginning with a reappraisal of his biased thinking. Similarly, Tim, a 47-year-old man with pervasive obsessive–compulsive tendencies involving mental rituals, told me that throughout the session he was struggling to focus on the interview as he felt compelled to count angles in the furniture in the room and engage in other neutralizing rituals. Again, this enabled a more accurate assessment of his problems by means of close observation and exploration of his compulsive thinking and obsessive behaviour 'in the moment'. In both these cases the presenting problem is transported directly into the clinical arena and is thus available for examination and ultimately modification.

Addictive disorders present differently however. Both of these men also had chronic substance misuse problems with regard to alcohol and cocaine respectively. Despite attributing much of their lives' difficulties to their inability to regulate their drug use, there was little, if any, cognitive,

---

Cognitive Therapy for Addiction: Motivation and Change, First Edition. Frank Ryan.
© 2013 Frank Ryan. Published 2013 by John Wiley & Sons, Ltd.

behavioural or motivational evidence of this in the consulting room: craving, urgency, preoccupation or suddenly leaving the clinic in order to procure drugs were notably absent. Further, close enquiry about recent drug use of often reveals little of the mindset or thought process of the client, although of course it reveals important information about environmental and contextual cues and triggers. Consider Suzy, a 35-year-old woman with a 15-year history of compulsive and excessive drinking together with recreational use of cocaine. She told me that, at six weeks of abstinence from both substances, she was doing 'really well' and had not experienced any urges or craving since being seen a week earlier. However, when next reviewed she told me that after she had consumed two or three drinks at a friend's birthday party she accepted cocaine from another friend. The coping strategies rehearsed in advance for this planned encounter were not deployed. Suzy was not able to account for her lapse, although she was self-critical, accusing herself of lacking motivation. This scenario is, no doubt, a familiar one to therapists and their clients in the addiction arena. Here, I intend to examine problems in the therapeutic relationship from a dual-processing perspective.

Ambivalence is a systemic problem with a systemic solution

From a dual-processing perspective the ambivalence or motivational conflict that characterizes addictive behaviour is a clash of systems rather than an uneven balance sheet. The reflective system can enable lengthy deliberation about the merits and demerits of cocaine, for example, and sometimes the outcome is indeed a decision to give up. The impulsive system, however, does not have the flexibility to entertain conflicting tendencies, and hence enables the intrinsically more simple pursuit of satiation. Put simply, the impulsive system is not influenced by the outcome of weighing up the pros and cons of continuing or stopping a given behaviour. In the face-to-face encounter in the therapy room the impulsive system remains in the background, letting the reflective system do what it does best: thinking and talking. This can invalidate or distort the motivational enhancement process, as the source of impulsivity is not fully acknowledged or recognized. In due course the impulsive system will assert itself, for example when executive control is compromised by tiredness, stress or unexpected cue exposure. I shall outline how assessment and engagement strategies can be modified and applied to accommodate distorted decision making and impaired cognitive control. This scenario (see Table 6.1) depicts an altogether more difficult, but I would argue more realistic, route to addiction resolution than that implied by motivational augmentation via empathy, feedback and facilitated decision making.

Impaired insight

Traditional accounts of addiction emphasized the role of 'denial', the negation of problems associated with addiction by the affected individual. In the words of another client, 'alcoholism is a disorder that tells you that do not have it'. Goldstein *et al.* (2009) considered lack of insight or self-awareness with regard to drug addiction as indications of altered or impaired functioning in corticolimbic regions associated with interoception, behavioural control, habit formation and evaluative learning as follows.

- The insula subserves interoceptive representation of somatic and emotional states, including craving. Interestingly, Naqvi *et al.* (2007) reported that a cohort of 19 smokers with brain damage involving the insula were 100 times more likely than a cohort of 50 smokers with brain damage not involving the insula to lose the urge to smoke and subsequently give up smoking.
- The anterior cingulate cortex, involved in behaviour regulation and error monitoring. It will be recalled that there is evidence that chronic misusers of cocaine, heroin, alcohol, cannabis and other drugs evidence underactivity in this key component of cognitive control (Garavan and Stout, 2005). Carter and van Veen (2007) have proposed that the role of the ACC is to detect conflict between concurrently active, competing representations and to engage the dorsolateral prefrontal cortex (DLPFC) to resolve this. This leads to top-down or executive control being leveraged to improve performance. Compromised ACC and DLPFC functioning, as observed in chronic drug users, therefore compromises cognitive control.
- The dorsal striatum is a key conduit for dopaminergic transmission triggered by drug use. Everitt *et al.* (2008) proposed, albeit based largely on evidence from nonhuman-animal studies, that the transition from controlled to compulsive drug seeking represents a switch at the neural level from prefrontal cortical to dorsal striatal control over addictive behaviours. Applied to humans, this implies that the more compulsive drug seeking becomes, the more remote it is from the cortical areas that might support insight and decision making. However, as pointed out by Stacy and Wiers (2010), habit theories may be more applicable to subsets of drugs such as nicotine due to the high frequency of cigarette smoking. This has obvious implications for psychotherapeutic approaches such as motivational interviewing (MI), or indeed cognitive therapy, that rely on elicitation of beliefs and motives in order to facilitate decision making.

Table 6.1 Outline of the CHANGE/Four-M Model.

	Stage/step	Intervention/core competency	Outcome	Outcome measure
Stage 1 (1–4 weeks) 2–4 hours	Motivate and engage	Motivational interviewing skills: active listening, expressing accurate empathy, giving feedback. Contingency management. Explain role of implicit processes; identify alternative goals; form implementation intentions.	Higher levels of engagement and retention. Agreement on and specification of therapeutic goals	Psychometric measures of motivation, commitment and stages of change (e.g. SOCRATES). Lower DNA and higher percentage retained rates.
Stage 2 (4–8 weeks) 4–8 hours	Manage craving and impulses	Identifying triggers via self-report and self-monitoring; coping skills for urges and craving; contingency management. Implementation intentions for high risk situations; goal rehearsal. Cognitive bias modification; training in working memory/executive control skills. Bolstering willpower; mindfulness practice.	Reduced frequency and intensity of drug/alcohol use or compulsive gambling.	Lower levels of craving or impulsivity (psychometric scales or self-reports). Increased self-efficacy.

Stage	Focus	Interventions	Goals	Measures
Stage 3 (8–12 weeks) 4–12 hours	Mood regulation (8–12 weeks)	Learning coping skills for unwanted emotional arousal; contingency management (CM designed to continue for 12 weeks). Training in working memory/executive control skills. Mindfulness practice.	Lower levels of emotional distress; reduced incentive for substance misuse.	Lower levels of self-reported mood disturbance and/or *PHQ* scale
Stage 4 (12 weeks+) 4 hours	Maintaining gains, relapse prevention (3–24 months)	Long-term goal setting and goal maintenance; fostering use of coping skills and social support. Mindfulness.	Longer latency to relapse; higher proportion of days drug free; lifestyle change or employment	Percentage time free from substance misuse. Longer time to relapse. List of goals achieved.

By definition, it is not possible to have insight regarding stimuli of which one is unaware. The Childress *et al.* (2008) study referred to in Chapter 1 is relevant here. The very early detection (33 ms) of drug-relevant cues, as evidenced by activation in areas such as the amygdala observed in abstinent cocaine users, means that *pre-emptive* conscious control is impossible. Mobilizing the necessary inhibitory or diversionary processes can take several hundred milliseconds. This enables speculation that stimuli that are not consciously detected can be, if anything, more influential than those that can be appraised consciously. There appears to be converging evidence from psychophysiology research, cognitive processing studies and neuroimaging findings with individuals addicted to alcohol, tobacco and cocaine that stimuli that evade conscious detection are nonetheless differentiated preconsciously. However, this lack of awareness of stimuli does not necessarily prevent these same stimuli from capturing attention and triggering purposeful (here, drug-seeking) behaviour.

The Sad Case of Julia

This lack of insight can have profoundly negative consequences. A year ago, I saw Julia, a 39-year-old woman, in my clinic. She told me that, over a period of several years, her three children had been placed in care because of her history of crack cocaine addiction. She described how she had left rehab and remained drug free for over a year before becoming pregnant. With less than three months of her term remaining she met a supplier of crack cocaine who lived nearby. Within a week she was using daily, despite being closely monitored by health- and social-care professionals: she knew the consequences. Julia did not recall experiencing any particular craving or urge initially but she continued to use until she was due to give birth. Prior to this, the crack dealer had pleaded with her to stop, probably as she was distressing his other customers. Inevitably, she was not given the opportunity to care for her newborn and apparently healthy baby, who was placed in care from birth. She returned home alone. What was striking about this sad episode was that Julia subscribed to the view any observer would: this was a personal tragedy for her, and the children she had witnessed being removed from her care one by one. Yet she had proved powerless to defer the gratification offered by her drug of choice pending the longer-term and infinitely more gratifying rewards of parenthood. Note also that Julia had by all accounts been drug free for over 18 months prior to her relapse. What cognitive or motivational processes could account for this? Julia was an articulate lady but introspection did not yield any particular insights. She appeared to sleepwalk into this avoidable catastrophe. Any input I could provide was too little, too late. In any event, I encouraged Julia to view her behaviour when confronted with the possibility of getting cocaine as being, albeit momentarily, governed by an impulsive system over which she had neither control nor insight when it really mattered. Sadly, any consideration of this did not enable her to undo the consequences of her relapse but recognition of the involuntary processes involved helped reduce her tendency towards self-blame and depression. This vignette starkly illustrates the challenge facing those aiming to recover from addiction. In the following paragraphs I shall attempt to develop some insight into the cognitive processes that might have had a bearing on Julia's behaviour.

Conflicted Motivation is the Key

Historically, motivational approaches were a reaction to the confrontational stance advocated by traditional approaches such as Twelve-Step in an effort to break down 'denial'. In the case of Julia, this would entail orchestrating a situation where she would admit that she was addicted and powerless in the face of temptation. By confronting ambivalence rather than putative denial, MI provided a more nuanced and engaging approach. MI is thus appropriately aimed at leveraging people into treatment programmes, or encouraging them to simply attend for the next session. The mechanisms and utility of MI approaches are, however, neither fully clear nor fully established as drivers of change. To be sure, a nascent decision to give up is sometimes translated into long-term change, but more often the resolution is not implemented or fails to endure (see Burke et al., 2003). Moreover, the mechanisms of this implementation process are unclear because it is difficult to establish a causal link between a therapeutic mechanism such as evoking commitment to change and clinical outcomes. Miller and Rose (2009) nonetheless considered a range of possible therapeutic mechanisms, such as therapist attributes including empathy, client behaviour such as 'change talk', or evocation of faith or hope. Linguistic analysis (Amrhein et al., 2003) of how people negotiate and decide to change suggested their utterances could be differentiated according to the following motivational components: desire, ability, reasons, readiness, need and commitment. The extant motivational model assumes that, given the right coaching, the essentially rational person who happens to be addicted will make a decision that is in his or her own best interests. In many cases, this would work: most people are open to persuasion in the face of a well-presented case for change or flexibility. But addiction can be an exception, as demonstrated by the sad case of Julia. Whether reflecting denial, negation or simply selfishness, her behaviour seems difficult to understand. Unless, that is, Julia was herself unable to fathom her own motives. As briefly reviewed above, neuroscientific findings do indicate a lack of interoceptive awareness in addiction. This suggests that one person's ascription of denial (the observer) is another's lack of insight (the addicted one).

Goal Setting and Maintenance

Because the MI dialogue takes place mainly in the reflective or declarative mode, it is assumed that the addicted individual will be able to authentically chart their motivational status. It is hoped, for instance, that by listing positive and negative attributes of drug-using behaviour individuals will re-evaluate their choices and resolve to change. Clearly, working with clients to explore the positives and negatives of their addictive lifestyle is likely to be useful, especially if done in the empathic and nonjudgemental manner that characterizes the spirit of MI. This evaluative process can of course facilitate decision making and goal setting, priorities at the engagement stage of therapy. When risks to health, relationships and livelihood are juxtaposed with the transient rewards of the addictive pursuit, the balance sheet often appears rather heavily weighted towards giving up. For example, a parent could acknowledge the pleasurable effects of cocaine while at the same time recognizing that this has a negative effect on her ability to care for her young child. The discrepancy between self-gratification and the valued role of being a good parent evoked by this process creates tension that the motivational therapist can exploit by steering the client towards making a decision apropos her drug use. This could entail simply agreeing to come back for another motivational encounter, an undertaking to avoid using in certain situations or perhaps making a commitment to give up. In cognitive-processing terms this goal definition and goal maintenance are key to cognitive control.

The Importance of Between-Session Change

It seems reasonable to conclude that MI can facilitate decision making and increase commitment to change *within the session*. Here, the reflective mode is fully engaged, the client dutifully swayed by the force of logic. Ultimately, this approach, termed 'cognitive algebra' (Stacy and Wiers, 2010), fails to account for the characteristic tendency of habitual behaviour to proceed by default at critical decision points or when significant cues are available, especially *between sessions*. These cues only need to capture attention momentarily in order to initiate action (see Norman and Shallice, 1986, and Chapter 4). MI thus assumes greater insight into the motivational drivers of addiction than is likely or even possible. This reduces the therapist's ability to empathize accurately with the clients that they are ardently trying to motivate. MI also assumes a more rational decision-making process than is likely to be the case, thereby assigning more credence to undertakings of restraint proffered by the client. In effect, this is an example of a 'planning fallacy' (Tversky and Kahneman, 1974; Kahneman, 2003) and sets the scene for failure. Consequently, the therapeutic alliance can be undermined in some of the ways explored below. MI nonetheless remains a valid and flexible approach that can accommodate the emerging findings and new perspectives outlined here. The emphasis on empathy, decision making and goal setting is fully justified at the beginning of a therapeutic journey aimed at overcoming impulsive behaviour.

Neurocognitive Perspectives on Motivation

In the *CHANGE* model engagement is, predictably, the first phase (see Table 6.1) and aims to help the client to form attainable goals. The related tasks of goal setting and goal maintenance are seen as core components of self-regulation or cognitive control. As discussed in Chapter 3, goals encoded in WM are crucial to organizing behaviour and can exert top-down influence on selective attention: goal setting is thus seen a means of exerting cognitive control. In the later sections of this chapter I shall address formulation, again drawing on a model that accommodates the operation of implicit cognitive and behavioural processes. This includes an exploration of how therapists conceptualize addiction and the possibility of implicit biases influencing formulation. A particular focus is on nurturing the therapeutic alliance in the context of a behaviour that occurs impulsively, with little warning and often little insight into its precursors. In turn, this sets the scene for Chapters 7 and 8 (managing impulses and mood) that describe addressing impaired cognitive control in the context of addiction and coexisting problems, somewhat arbitrarily signified by 'M' for managing impulses and 'M' for mood. To this end, some examples and strategies are provided.

Motivational Interviewing in Practice

FRAMES

As we saw at the beginning of this chapter, the conceptual basis of MI can be challenged as it assumes a rather more rational decision-making process in the face of impulsivity than is in fact the case. It nonetheless has enabled the development of a useful framework for engaging and preparing people for therapeutic intervention.

FRAMES is an acronym that captures the key ingredients for building motivation and commitment.

- F represents individualized feedback about the person's status, in particular with regard to motivation itself. A typical general opening response would be as follows: 'Thank you for taking the time and effort to complete the questionnaires and answer all those other questions about your drinking. Based on what you have told me, your most recent drinking is in fact in the range associated with health problems, and it also seems that you can struggle with keeping it under control. Would you like me to tell you more about some of the risks linked to this?'
- R represents the emphasis on the clients taking responsibility for their decision to commit to change while at the same time accentuating the fact that there is usually some discretion about the timing and focus on change embarked on, for example 'Its really good that you choose to come in today. At the very least we can look at the various options there are available for you; but if you are up for it you can maybe choose one'.
- A is about the provision of clear advice. If there is an obvious risk, for example high levels of intoxication, poly-substance use or hazardous injecting, it is important to urge the person to minimize or reduce this, employing a nonjudgemental tone, for example 'Even if you have been very careful about not sharing your injecting equipment there we can't rule out the risk that you have been exposed to an infection like

hepatitis B over the years, or that you might be accidently exposed in the future. I think it's a very good idea to get vaccinated. It just requires three quick injections over the next few weeks. Then you've ruled out one possible source of ill health. What do you think?'

M signifies a menu of change options. This follows on from encouraging the client to take responsibility by perhaps choosing where and when therapy can begin and what the priorities are, for example 'We're just coming up to the holiday season and it's still possible to arrange a detox before the New Year. Some people prefer to defer a detox until the New Year as they think it would be difficult to quit drinking at this time of year. What are your thoughts?'

E connotes empathy and should be warm, person centred and accurate.

S stands for self-efficacy. It is important to use every available opportunity to bolster the clients' belief that they can strive to obtain their treatment objectives to the best of their ability.

A *dual-processing approach to ambivalence.* As outlined at the beginning of this chapter, there are also fundamental limitations to the degree of insight individuals can have regarding the drivers of their addictive behaviour. Reflection can, no doubt, generate valuable insights but does not directly impact on implicit cognition and behavioural approach tendencies. Motivational enhancement approaches do have credibility in two key areas. First, the reflective empathic and patient style or spirit of MI is well matched to the resistive aspect of addiction. Recognizing that ambivalence is a normal aspect of everyday decision making is a good basis on which to empathize with a client choosing between two courses of action. This helps build a robust therapeutic alliance. A typical agenda for an MI session would be something like this.

Opening strategy: do not jump to conclusions! Ask permission or elicit consent before addressing what may obviously seem the presenting problem to you, that is, hazardous or addictive substance misuse, but might not be appraised similarly by the person sitting opposite you. If the issue is raised by the client, the therapist can usually assume that he or she has permission to explore this. If not, the therapist could ask: 'What brings you here today?' or, if the client appears very reluctant to raise the subject, 'Where does the [problem substance use or gambling] fit in here?'

Ask about lifestyle, stresses and problem behavior.
A typical day.

Current concerns.

The good things and the less good things about the current drug use (if the subject is raised by the client.

Elicit self-motivational statements or 'change talk': for example 'It sounds like your partner is worried about your drinking, but I was wondering how you feel about it?'; 'What would be good things about [reducing or eliminating drug and alcohol use] (a) intermediate or short term or (b) in, say, six months' time?'

Listen with accurate empathy: 'It sounds like you want to quit but when you tried treatment before you went back to using cocaine'. Note that the tone is reflective rather than proscriptive or dogmatic. Other phrases that signal reflection and/or empathy could be 'What I'm hearing is you are worried about your drug use but until your [legal/housing/work/relationship] issue is resolved you don't feel able to tackle it'.

For example, Eleanor, a 37-year-old information technology (IT) manager, was reportedly drinking between 15 and 20 units of alcohol each evening. But she did not regard this as the primary problem. She completed the sentence 'My main problems are...' as follows: 'Insomnia, stress at work because my boss resents me and I don't have a man in my life'. Follow-up questions revealed that for Eleanor alcohol was a *solution* rather than a problem. She believed it helped her to 'switch off' after a frustrating day at work, reduced her negative rumination regarding her unwanted single status and finally helped her to sleep. These perceived positive outcomes exerted a strong motivational influence. Instead of disputing or challenging the underlying beliefs and expectancies (often the default response of enthusiastic cognitive therapists!), the motivational approach emphasizes the avoidance of argument embodied in the phrase 'rolling with [the] resistance'. In this regard, MI shares a dialectical approach to behaviour modification (Linehan, 1993), cycling between acceptance and change.

Second, a focus on decision making and goal setting is a good way to start a therapeutic journey. These latter two components of the motivational approach stand out because they are consistent with the neurocognitive approach advocated here. Decision making and formation of goals are intrinsically cognitive endeavours. Regardless of, indeed in spite of, impaired cognition linked to the persistence of addiction, robust decision making and goal maintenance offer to enhance control over implicit cognition and behavioural impulses.

Systematic motivational counselling

Systematic motivational counselling (SMC; Cox and Klinger, 1988, 2011) is based on the premise that psychological disorders reflect maladaptive motivational patterns. People commit themselves to inappropriate or self-destructive goals such as the pursuit of alcohol or other substances. This commitment can often be at the expense of adaptive goal pursuits, particularly when substance misuse is the overvalued goal. Systemic motivational counselling focuses on helping the client disengage from inappropriate goals and initiate and maintain more adaptive goals. SMC is individualized in order to reflect the diverse goals each person adopts.

In my view, there is likely to be a relationship between personality traits such as impulsivity or emotional stability (or its absence, historically termed neuroticism) and goal selection. Thus, an emotionally stable person who had become dependent on alcohol might benefit from pursuing different recovery-focused goals to an impulsive or emotionally less stable individual. By way of illustration, the former might benefit from becoming involved in mutual-aid or self-help groups, where he or she could prove a calm presence. More impulsive or less stable individuals might need to be pointed to different goals such as physical exercise, sport or travel. Speculative, of course, but brief interventions that accommodate personality attributes appear to benefit schoolchildren and adolescents with regard to reducing alcohol and substance use alongside other clinical symptoms such as negative affect (Conrod *et al.*, 2010). The same could apply to adults.

SMC is not necessarily a stand-alone treatment and can easily be applied at any stage of a treatment or intervention, from assessment onwards. Thus, identifying goals and developing goal pursuit strategies can help the client early on in developing a treatment plan but subsequently can also help specify vocational, social or educational goals. Clearly, the SMC approach can complement cognitive and cognitive behavioural strategies that emphasize problem solving and overcoming impediments to goal pursuit such as anxious avoidance or safety-seeking behaviour. Once goals are identified and negotiated, they can be divided into subgoals that can be worked on between counselling sessions.

Effective goal setting. The characteristics of effective goal setting are prescribed by Willutzki and Koban (2011) as follows.

- Well-defined goals should be positively formulated. For example, clients who are aiming to overcome addiction often complain of boredom, leading to specifying a goal such as 'I don't want to be bored' or 'I don't want to have any more sleepless nights'. More positive, goal-directed strategies would include the next time I feel bored my goal will be to engage in exercise/meditation/reading/AA meeting/gardening (according to personal preference!).

- Goals should be personally relevant and resonate with personal values and aspirations. For example, a 34-year-old man with a chronic history of opiate and alcohol dependence who I saw a few years ago disclosed that he had always struggled with reading and writing but had also aspired to gaining further education. He was able to access a course for adults with literacy difficulties and was diagnosed with hitherto unrecognized dyslexia. This proved instrumental in helping him access a university degree course within two years.
- Goals should be specific and stepwise as well as being defined in behavioural terms, for example the therapist could ask 'what would the first step look like?' if the goal was rebuilding a relationship with a life partner, family member or employer.
- The goal should be within the person's competence: less 'I don't want to have to deal with stress'; more 'I want to learn to manage stress more effectively when I am in challenging situations'.
- Goals require sustained effort over time and the client needs to be prepared for this but also coached or mentored so that he or she pursues the chosen goal.

Recently, Joe, one of my clients who had been detoxified from alcohol, specified returning to work in the IT industry as a goal. Subgoals consisted of updating his resume and registering with specialist IT recruitment agencies. Prior to negotiating this goal and associated subgoals, Joe was readily able to specify what needed to be done, but did not implement this in the form of a goal pursuit strategy. Having updated his resume, his feedback to me was that he enjoyed doing it and he spent less time dwelling on the harm he had caused through his chronic alcohol misuse over the years and the prospect of committing to lifelong abstinence.

Formulating and Planning the Intervention

Building a therapeutic alliance: distinct features in addiction

The combination of partial insight on behalf of the client and misconception on the part of the therapist can prevent the formation of a robust therapeutic alliance and undermine the development of collaborative case conceptualization. In particular, there is a risk of overreliance on heuristics – cognitive shortcuts that can aid decision making, but can also lead to erroneous conclusions. Kuyken *et al.* (2009) outlined how therapists' decision making can be subverted by their own, often implicit, cognitive biases. This, in turn, was derived from the seminal work of Tversky and Kahneman (1974; Kahneman, 2003), who described how three broad categories of heuristics impact on the reasoning and decision making: *representativeness, availability* and *anchoring*. The *representativeness* heuristic applies when people are asked to judge the probability that an object or event 'A' belongs to a class or process 'B'. In the addiction clinic this leads to the conclusion that the presenting problem, addiction (A), in effect represents something else, such as underlying emotional vulnerability or a defective self-image (B). The error in this case would be implicitly assuming that because people with underlying emotional disorders or low self-esteem are prone to substance misuse problems, the individual in the consulting room is necessarily representative of the population. The *availability* heuristic can also contribute to a less valid case conceptualization. Here, the biased decision making on behalf of the therapist is influenced by the salience or availability of information provided by the person seeking therapy. In an addiction or substance-misuse treatment setting this could be, again, evidence of emotional dysregulation, insomnia or perhaps reports of marital discord or stress in the workplace. However, these concerns, clearly pressing and salient to the client, might all stem from excessive drug and alcohol use, plausible candidates indeed for affecting emotions, sleep, relationships and productivity. Impaired control in this regard should therefore be given prominence in any conceptualization.

Anchoring, or *'anchoring and adjustment'*, bias is a tendency to over- or underestimate probability based on limited data or an invalid reference point, and is a further source of error in case conceptualization. Anchoring thus appears to explain why judgments tend to be excessively influenced by an initial impression, value or perspective. For example, if one were asked: 'Is the population of the USA more or less than 200 million?', estimates would be biased or anchored to this value even though it is a significant underestimate (the true figure is closer to 310 million!). In case formulation and conceptualization, if one were to start with a reference point (the 'anchor') that is not entirely valid – perhaps due to being misled by representativeness and availability biases – any subsequent therapeutic intervention could drift off course. If the 'anchor' or reference point following initial assessment is, for example, emotional vulnerability or poor stress management skills rather than impaired impulse control, the therapeutic intervention is jeopardized. To a distressed client and busy therapist this apparently plausible reasoning offers a viable way forward with the therapeutic process.

Focusing on one facet of the presenting problem – whether this is a collateral problem such as anxiety or the addictive behaviour itself – creates a context for the activation of what is termed the *focusing illusion*. An illustrative example of this heuristic is 'If I got a rise I would be much happier'. True, a pay rise is always welcome, but it rarely delivers enduring happiness. This focal bias can lead to problems as the treatment plan unfolds. For example, both client and therapist can over-emphasize (or 'focalize') the benefits of abstinence or restraint from drug use or gambling. In this regard, the implicit belief could be along the lines 'If I am successful in maintaining abstinence I shall be much happier'. It is imperative of course that the client is invested in the goal of restraint (goal maintenance is emphasized throughout the text!), but this has to be nuanced accordingly.

Attributional Biases: the Blame Game

When faced with challenging and frustrating issues, people are minded to look for causal explanations. When emotions are aroused and motivation is conflicted, as of course happens in the context of addiction, this process can be distorted. In particular, when faced with repeated setbacks, both client and therapist can develop faulty attributional processes along the following lines:

Scenario 1. Client blames him- or herself: 'I'm lacking willpower and I'm useless anyway'. In this case, I would respond as follows: 'Addiction is really a disease of willpower: repeated drug taking reduces your capacity to control your behaviour because it changes the way your brain works. It does this in a clever way that allows one part of you to say quite sincerely "I want to quit" while another part of you still wants to carry on regardless. It's like the saying "old habits die hard". That is why it is important that you've chosen to commit to therapy. We all need a helping hand when it comes to tackling unwanted habits'.

Scenario 2. Therapist blames client: 'You are not committed, come back when you're motivated (stop wasting my time!)'. I hope that, having chosen to read this book, you are less likely to adopt such a biased and judgemental stance! However, in practice attributional bias can of course be more subtle than this rather strident example. A hard-pressed therapist, however well informed, can default to this type of self-serving attribution. The reflective practitioner would be well advised to recall that addiction is essentially a failure of self-regulation and an attribution that, in effect, blames the victim flies in the face of the evidence. It is also circular reasoning. Moreover, the insights and undertakings proffered by the client in the consulting room – 'I really intend to quit this time because my relationship is more important than anything else' – can be somewhat misleading, serving to raise what ultimately can prove to be false hopes of recovery. It might also be helpful to reflect on situations when one's own willpower was bypassed. My guess is that a more nuanced attribution will emerge from this introspection, assigning a portion of the causality to being stressed, tired or hungry!

Scenario 3. Therapist blames him- or herself: 'I'm no good at this. My clients never seem to improve'. Again, this attributional bias may operate more subtly than in the example above. It is nonetheless important to maintain self-efficacy in the face of inevitable setbacks. First, on a more general level, it is helpful to bear in mind that relapse is an all-too-common outcome, but often driven by factors extraneous to the therapeutic intervention. Thus, factors associated with a good outcome such as being in employment or in a stable relationship can compromise therapeutic gain when abstinent regardless of the competencies of the therapist in either scenario. Second, awareness of the neurocognitive mechanisms of addiction addressed in this text provides a plausible rationale for why treatment regularly fails. Here, the addiction is seen as a syndrome where substance or gambling cues acquire motivational power while other reinforcers lose their potency in the context of impaired inhibitory processes.

Case Formulation

Assuming that the requisite motivational work has been done, the *CHANGE* approach aims to develop a tailor-made formulation for each individual.

This is because there are at least two overlapping sets of issues: substance misuse and emotional dysregulation. This is a version of what I say to clients.

> We've covered a lot of difficult territory over the past few meetings. You've shared stories about your childhood and how tough things were for you. I've heard how you coped with that, although it sometimes felt like a real struggle. Things went well until your divorce two years ago. You found that you began to drink heavily and use cocaine again. This led to you to resign from your job or 'jump before you were pushed' as you put it. But the economic situation has made it difficult for everybody, including you, who might be looking for a job. Not being successful in your job-seeking has left you feeling very down and I concluded that you were depressed: You said that you were feeling sad, having negative thoughts and not wanting to get up in the morning even though you were awake for hours. You were also drinking about a bottle of vodka a day and using cocaine at weekends. I know you are feeling a bit hopeless at the moment but by coming into the Centre you have made the right decision. We will both work together on your treatment plan in the course of the next session or two. We need to focus on *two things*: first the alcohol and cocaine use, then the low mood. There are important reasons for tackling the issues in that order and I'll just summarize if I may. First, while I know you believe alcohol helps you switch off and get to sleep, it can also disrupt sleep and make you feel anxious or depressed. Cocaine is also a bit of a fair-weather friend, as you can feel on top of the world for a while after using but again the after-effects can lead to a worsening of mood. In fact, it is not clear to me how much of your current depressed and anxious mood is due to the after-effects of cocaine and alcohol or the reaction to the losses and setbacks in your life in the past couple of years. That's why we need to work together to tackle the alcohol and cocaine before we address the emotional issues like depression. What do you think?

According to Persons (1989, 2008), a case formulation should provide a framework for integrating the following components (italics in original; 2008):

a description of the client's *symptoms*, *disorders* and *problems*
specific hypotheses about the underlying *mechanisms* causing or contributing to the initiation and maintenance of the disorder in question
it further proposes the recent *precipitants* of the presenting problem, in effect the 'why seek help now?' question
the *origins* of the mechanisms, often in the therapy seeker's earlier life.

Tarrier and Calam (2002) suggested that, in addition, the following factors should be addressed:

conceptualizing the dysfunctional system, especially focusing on maintenance factors
the historical vulnerability and epidemiological factors
the influence of social and interpersonal behaviour.

This approach preserves the more conventional CT emphasis on explicit, reportable cognitions that are key mediators in drug seeking and taking or affective precursors to addictive behaviour. The dual-process model applied here adds additional mechanisms by invoking a role for implicit processes. Additional implicit processes can easily be accommodated into this framework and thus guide the delivery and evaluation of the intervention.

A case-formulation approach is used in this text with the aim of providing a flexible framework for delivering cognitive therapy. The flexibility is essential because the evidential base for psychological therapies such as CBT is largely derived from clinical trials, where for methodological reasons inclusion and exclusion criteria mean that participants have relatively 'pure' manifestations of psychological disorder. Thus, clinical trials for emotional disorders recruit participants with anxiety and depressive symptoms and tend to exclude substance-misusing and addicted people. Conversely, clinical investigators probing treatment for addictive spectrum disorders tend to exclude participants with co-morbid mental-health difficulties deemed unrelated to the addictive process. This presents the clinician who aspires to deliver empirically supported therapy (EST) with the problem of what treatment manual(s) to reach for, and in what order: the one focused on emotional disorder, addiction or personality disorder? The *CHANGE* model aims to provide unambiguous guidance for at least what to reach for first: the protocol that addresses addictive behaviour. However, this should not be a reflexive decision, but one based on a detailed formulation. For example, just because addiction is necessarily the primary target of therapeutic intervention does not mean that it is in fact the primary problem in a historical context. The formulation should aim to explicate the context that accounts for the initiation, acquisition and maintenance of the addictive behaviour. This creates the platform for reversing or inhibiting the process. In this regard, Persons (2008, p. 2) highlighted a number of situations where applying a protocol-based EST can be difficult. I have derived examples from my own clinical case load.

1. *The client has multiple disorders and problems.* Typically, clients referred for CBT in structured treatment settings present with several problems. By definition, those referred will meet criteria for disorders relating to hazardous use, misuse or dependence on drugs. Treatment seekers will also vary in terms of the current level of drug or alcohol involvement: some will still be using their drug(s) of choice, possibly not recognizing that this is the main problem; some will have decided to give up and others will have already done so. A more complete appraisal of the individual's current concerns and personal history will generally reveal more problems of psychiatric or psychological nature, often in the context of conflicted interpersonal relationships or criminal offending behaviour.

2. *The client has multiple providers.* Persons (2008) cites an example of a woman seeking treatment for panic disorder who is taking benzodiazepines prescribed by her own doctor. In substance-misuse-treatment settings, concurrent use of prescribed or nonprescribed substances is quite common. This can undermine the delivery of a protocol-based therapy such as CBT. For example, a client with chronic insomnia I was working with would occasionally seek benzodiazepines from his doctor, although it had been agreed that this was impeding his progress using cognitive behavioural strategies. A more systemic issue is the tradition of attending Twelve-Step groups in parallel with engagement in clinical interventions such as CBT. These can be complementary, as when both approaches are aiming for the same objective, such as abstinence. On occasion, however, more complicated scenarios can occur. For example, a client reported that she was criticized when she disclosed at an AA meeting that she was taking antidepressants prescribed by my psychiatrist colleague. Here, the treatment protocol was a robust combination of CBT and pharmacotherapy, but this was being potentially undermined by participation in a Twelve-Step program.

3. *Situations not referenced in empirically derived protocols, or scenarios for which there is no agreed protocol.* For clarity, I do not intend to address the substantive issue of evidence-based practice for addiction under this heading. This is addressed in Chapter 2 and is a recurring issue throughout the text. Rather, my aim is to illustrate the diverse range of presenting problems in a specialist addiction-treatment setting.

For example, Joanna, aged 43, recently came to my clinic shortly after she was detoxified from chronic alcohol excess. She said that her problem was that she was unable to meet a life partner, often beginning relationships but ending them abruptly. There was an isolationist trend revealed in her history, but she was not socially anxious and not lacking in self-confidence. She was thus able to cope very well with meeting people from an Internet dating site, but even when these met her criteria she elected to end the relationship. In a similar vein, many clients describe the main problems and goals as finding a partner or finding a job. CBT can be very effective in devising a strategic approach to addressing these problems, but a specially tailored programme is often required. For example, if a client's previous occupation was deemed a risk factor in the development of an alcohol problem, careful consideration is required here if she is thinking about resuming that role.

4. *The client does not adhere to the requirements of therapeutic protocol.* Adherence to therapeutic protocols can often be challenging to clients because they are being encouraged to approach or confront situations or emotions that they have long avoided. In addiction, the converse applies and therapeutic adherence often involves avoiding situations or emotions strongly linked to appetitive behaviour. Further, if a client with an addictive disorder exhibits the index behaviour they succeed in directly altering their functioning at a neurobiological neurocognitive level. Put simply, a lack of adherence can lead to intoxication and a failure to complete homework assignments or indeed attend the next appointment.

5. *Difficulty in embracing the therapeutic alliance and treatment failure.* Here, I propose that addiction presents unique barriers to therapeutic engagement. This stems directly from the involuntary nature of addictive syndromes and their essentially treatment-resistant nature. As I argue in this text, much of the cognitive processing that regulates addictive behaviour takes place in advance of conscious awareness. The client is thus prevented from gaining full insight. Moreover, because therapists' conceptual frameworks have not generally accommodated the role of nonconscious processes, their professional insight into the mechanisms of addiction has also been incomplete, if not distorted.

Persons (2008) explored the roots of how the therapeutic relationship is conceptualized. The two broad approaches are the *Necessary but Not Sufficient* (NBNS) and the *Relationship as Treatment* view. The NBNS approach emphasizes the importance of attributes such as warmth, trust, respect and collaboration. However, these are a platform or context within which the main work of therapy such as cognitive restructuring or behavioural change can be accomplished. All well and good, as long as the client can reciprocate the well-intentioned overtures of the therapist. In many cases, it is precisely the treatment seeker's difficulty in establishing and maintaining trusting relationships that creates the vulnerability that propels them into treatment. As Persons (2008) points out, this creates a Catch-22 situation where the basic building block of therapy, the therapeutic alliance, becomes an obstacle. This is where the Relationship as Treatment approach demonstrates its worth. Here, the patient's behaviour in the consulting room is correctly seen as a sample of behaviours and thought processes that occur outside the clinical setting. Accordingly, if an individual has learned to be guarded when talking about him- or herself, for example, this defensive strategy will also be deployed in the course of the consultation.

Table 6.2 Formulating for co-occurring addiction and emotional disorder according to the CHANGE model.

	Formulation Sheet	
Kevin	*Situational or developmental*	*Substance specific*
Origins (family and developmental)	Abusive aunt Parents remote, less caring	Father heavy drinker (possible genetic loading) Culture (Glasgow)
Origins (adult traumas and experiences)	Assault during robbery and near-death experience	
Mechanisms	Safety behaviours; avoidance; rumination; NATs: 'They'll pick on me because I'm tall'	Inhibiting effects of alcohol on anxiety. NATs/expectancies: 'Alcohol helps me sleep; alcohol helps me relax.'
Problem	General anxiety (chronic worry)	
Problem	Dysphoria	'Binge' drinking
Problem	Insomnia	
Precipitants	Threatened by neighbour (2003); threatened on bus (2005). Continuing pressure of running business.	GP withdrew Bz prescription (2007). 'Rebound' anxiety and insomnia.

NATs, negative automatic thoughts.

The 'relationship as treatment' view can be traced back to psychodynamic approaches and is reflected in the client-centred therapy developed by Carl Rogers. This links the approach to motivational enhancement approaches that are on one level "psychodynamic" insofar as the therapist engages in therapeutic manoeuvres designed to elicit specific outcomes in the session, with perhaps less direct emphasis on what happens between sessions. For example, the therapist tries to *increase* ambivalence, thereby creating dissonance and hopefully eliciting motivational statements or goals. Throughout, the therapist maintains a warm, nonjudgemental and empathic stance that is likely to be a novel experience for the treatment-seeking individual. MI deploys explicit strategies to foster a highly nuanced interpersonal space. This, in turn, facilitates decision making and goal setting that would aim to alleviate matters of substance misuse or addiction. However, as noted by Persons (2008), a limitation of the relationship as therapy approach is when the cues or context for the dysfunctional behaviour are not present in the therapeutic assessment session, for example marital conflict when the other party is unavailable or unwilling to engage in therapy. This is similar to the latent aspect of addictive impulses in therapeutic settings illustrated by the vignettes of Michael and Tim mentioned above. This can misrepresent essential aspects of addiction and confuse treatment planning. In effect, the individual with the addictive disorder would appear to have made more progress than was in fact the case. Accordingly, because emotional disorder and addictive behaviour are deemed to have separate but often interacting pathways, it is sometimes helpful to formulate in parallel, as in Table 6.2. In this case invalidation experiences in childhood fostered anxious arousal, distorted thinking, rumination and avoidance. Alcohol use was subsequently reinforced both positively (hedonic effect) and negatively (tension reduction). Drug seeking to forestall insomnia was another component in the case formulation.

Summary

The tendency for addictive behavior to be initiated and proceed outside of conscious awareness curtails insight and can frustrate therapeutic engagement. The motivational conflict that characterizes addiction is not adequately captured by standard motivational techniques, such as evaluating the relative benefits of change versus no change. Nonetheless, the spirit of motivational interviewing resonates well with the resistive aspect of addiction and helps clients identify recovery goals. Case formulation can also be challenged by attributional biases on the part of both client and therapist. Moreover, formulation leads to reflect the fact that the mechanisms by which addiction develops can be distinct from those that foster emotional disorders.

7

Managing Impulses

Introduction and Overview

This chapter begins with comments on structuring a session and an overview of techniques aimed at cultivating resilience among those seeking help for addictive disorders. The premise is that addiction is a default state that will almost inevitably manifest itself to some degree between sessions. The therapist therefore needs to attend closely to what is happening in the consulting room, but remain alert to the influence on the treatment-seeker of latent cognitive vulnerability factors such as attentional bias, implicit approach tendencies and faulty decision making operating in the coming weeks and days. The next section of the chapter will introduce and evaluate emerging cognitive neuroscience findings aimed at enhancing cognitive control under the following categories:

- cognitive bias and behavioural approach reversal
- neuropharmacological techniques
- cognitive enhancement
- neurorehabilitation (brain training techniques)
- cognitive control techniques.

Following on from this, I shall outline three therapeutic strategies that the addiction therapist can use 'out of the box': behavioural experiments, forming implementation intentions and contingency management. These tried and tested therapeutic tactics serve to increase cognitive control in diverse, and sometimes unintended, ways.

Structuring the Session

Following one or more sessions assigned to motivation and engagement, the format for the subsequent sessions adheres to a conventional cognitive therapy structure. The emphasis is on consolidating and maintaining a collaborative stance in the face of what is, at least in part, a treatment-resistant syndrome. While flexibility is important, the typical session would include the following phases.

- Update on developments since previous encounter, with particular emphasis on any expression of addictive behaviour, negative mood states and current concerns.
- Setting the agenda, possibly asking the client to specify the priorities if the list of concerns or problematic issues is extensive. Specifying the stage of *CHANGE* (one of the Four Ms) of treatment, for example managing impulses, managing mood, maintaining change
- Reviewing any between-session assignment homework
- Introducing and then elaborating on the primary topic of the session, for example coping with impulses
- Negotiating homework for the coming week, for example an implementation strategy or a behavioural experiment
- Summary and feedback
- Schedule next appointment, reinforcing the importance of attendance even if the therapeutic objectives met by the homework are not accomplished.

Building Resilience

The central theme of this text is that addiction emerges and endures because of progressive failures in self-regulation, specifically with regard to impulse control. The aim is to elucidate the mechanisms where possible and to apply any insights gained to improve outcomes. To recap, addictive behaviour acquires momentum due to powerful incentives offered by drugs and gambling. Through repetition and an apparent indemnity against loss of value, addictive behaviours acquire a degree of autonomy that often overwhelms the resolve of the individual to give up. Parallel with this, repeated ingestion of drugs appears to be associated with abnormalities in cognitive control. By analogy, it is surely unfortunate if, while driving, the accelerator jams or is at the very least overreacting to the driver's right foot. The situation would, however, be immeasurably worse should the brakes begin to fail at the same time. Assume, further, that this mechanical meltdown takes place in just a fraction of a second, before the driver can realize the immediate danger. This, then, is how I see the challenge faced by those attempting to overcome the compulsive habits that characterize addiction. This struggle can take its toll on the commitment of the individual and the resolve of the therapist. It is therefore imperative that the therapist uses every available opportunity to build resilience and emphasize the client's strengths. The message to the client needs to be nuanced along the lines 'while you need to be very much on your guard in those situations when you used cocaine that we just discussed, I know that there are also many occasions when you showed greater restraint and coped really well'.

Kuyken *et al.* (2009, p. 108) suggested that the following questions can used to identify beliefs and attributes linked to resilience. I have modified and paraphrased to match the present context.

- What rules or beliefs can help you be resilient in the face of craving and urges?
  Here, the client could be guided to reflect on occasions where they successfully coped with craving by using distraction, mindful awareness or the support of others.
- What rules or beliefs should you follow if you are suddenly offered your drug of choice?
  This overlaps somewhat with the previous item, but having a drink shoved in the hand or being ushered into a bathroom to use cocaine is a common occurrence. This is a scenario where implementation intentions are called for, as subsequently outlined in this Chapter. An example is '*If* I am offered cocaine *then* I will immediately say "Thanks for the offer, but no thanks! I've quit"'; or '*If* an alcoholic drink is placed in my hand, *then* I will put it down and say "No thanks, but I'd love a fruit juice"'.
- Ideally, what qualities would you like to show when you come face to face with an opportunity to buy [your drug of choice]?
  This is an opportunity for the client to focus their attention on positive characteristics such as thinking of others, using commonsense or staying calm in a difficult situation.
- What beliefs [about you/others/the world] help you display these qualities?
  Here, the therapist could use information gleaned from the assessment sessions to provide cues if needed. For example, if the client has coped with much adversity in life, eliciting beliefs about being able to cope over extended periods are helpful given the extended time taken to recover from addictive disorders. Core beliefs about others and the world can also be elicited and re-structured if necessary. For example, a 41-year-old

man who was unfairly disciplined at work was referred due to an increase in his alcohol consumption to hazardous levels. His primary emotion was anger, associated with beliefs that the world was unfair and people were untrustworthy. When he re-evaluated these beliefs he discovered that for the most part his experience of life had, on the contrary, reflected good fortune and most people in his life had in fact been trustworthy. This enabled him to be more understanding of others and more open in his dealings with his employers and others. His anger and stress levels reduced, as did his alcohol consumption.

- If you coped in the best way you can imagine, what would you be thinking [about yourself/others/the world]?
  Here, an appropriate response could be 'When I put my mind to it I can enjoy myself and relax socially and I actually get more positive feedback from others. Feeling apprehensive about being sober is not really justified'.

Eliciting strengths, associated positive beliefs and anticipatory coping strategies related to oneself and others is of course good practice with a range of psychological disorders. Further, from a cognitive control perspective this refocusing of attention and directly influencing the contents of WM (e.g. the formation of a prospective memory encoded as the implementation intention 'If I am offered cocaine, then I will politely but firmly say no'). The assumption here is that identifying cognitive control tasks that draw on WM capacity will, if deployed appropriately, disrupt the default goal of drug acquisition facilitated by preferential attentional allocation.

Impulse Control

Impulsivity is a multifaceted construct including processes such as behavioural inhibition, impaired decision making and lapses in attention (de Wit, 2009). Psychometric studies have revealed further attributes of the construct of impulse control. Whiteside *et al.* (2005) factor analysed widely used measures of impulsivity and extracted four orthogonal factors and the conventional extraversion dimension.

Factor 1. Lack of premeditation, for example usually by a negative loading on an item such as 'I'll usually think carefully before doing anything'.

Factor 2. Urgency, for example 'I often act without thinking'.
Factor 3. Lack of perseverance linked to personality factor Conscientiousness, for example 'I tend to give up easily'.
Factor 4. Sensation seeking, tendency to novel and risky experiences.
Factor 5. Extraversion, a tendency to be outgoing, warm and gregarious.

Emerging findings from cognitive neuroscience have provided significant new insights into the area of response inhibition or impulse control. A striking finding is that behaviour, especially highly motivated or well practised responses, can be initiated and to some degree proceed in the absence of conscious awareness. Note that these models (e.g. Dijksterhuis and Aarts, 2010; Strack and Deutsch, 2004) do not propose that behaviour proceeds in the absence of *attention*, but it can progress in the absence of *conscious awareness*. This is because the allocation of attention can be dissociated from conscious awareness, specifically at an early stage stimulus appraisal and encoding. Thus, when the cue has appetitive motivational significance its accelerated attentional processing can trigger approach behaviour before controlled cognition can be mobilized to inhibit the approach tendency, assuming restraint is the goal.

Craving and Urge Report

The notion that craving precedes, and therefore drives, addictive behaviour has strong intuitive appeal with both addicted people and often their friends, families and therapists. Thus, while craving should be anticipated and avoided whenever possible, it at least has some utility as a final warning of imminent irresolution. Empirical findings have shown that this is not necessarily the case. Carter and Tiffany (1999) highlighted the inconsistent relationship between the different components of cue reactivity: craving, physiological arousal and behaviour such as actual drug seeking and taking do not cohere closely. First, there is a weak or unreliable relationship between subjective reports of craving and other indices of cue reactivity. A review of 13 studies led Tiffany (1990) to conclude that the relationship between physiological measures and self-reported urges accounted for a modest 15–27% of the variance. Similarly, the relationship between reported strength of urges and actual consumption measures correlated 0.40, approximating to 16% of the variance. Second, craving reports following cue exposure proved to be only modestly predictive of subsequent alcohol use (see, e.g., Litt *et al.*, 2003). Third, and perhaps most intriguing, is the replicated finding that subsets of addicted people do not respond to drug-like cues: 30% of alcoholic participants in some cue-exposure studies failed to report increased urge to drink. Similarly, Powell *et al.* (1992) reported that 36% of their opiate-addicted cohort reported no increase in craving when shown slides of their favourite drug. To any clinician this is puzzling, as clients' self-reports attest to a more direct and consistent relationship between cues, motivation and behaviour. Clearly, this relationship holds in the majority of cases, but the question of the apparent inconsistency of the relationship between subjective experience of craving and urgency remains.

Cognitive Processing and Craving

Earlier, I proposed (Ryan, 2002b) that cognitive processes, in effect intervening variables, mediate the stimulus and response. In most cases the cognitive process is facilitative, in keeping with the fact that in many cases drug cues do elicit craving or desire and appetitive behaviour. This facilitative cognitive bias is, of course, central to the theoretical and applied framework described in this text: preferential processing of cues is seen as the driver of the preoccupation commonly reported by addicted individuals. However, inconsistent relationships between craving (the subjective experience of wanting or being urged to consume the drug of choice), physiological arousal (e.g. salivation) and behaviour needs to be understood, as this can lead the client to invalid conclusions, for example 'I am not craving, so I don't need to apply my coping skills' or 'I can have one drink because I am not really craving and will therefore not lose control'. This is a 'false negative', as the absence of craving is interpreted as absence of risk of lapse. Craving is neither necessary nor sufficient to produce drug-acquisitive behaviour. Because, however, it is commonly the only precursor of impulsivity that is available to introspection, it is accorded more credibility than perhaps it deserves. Craving thus provides limited, inconsistent and sometimes misleading insight into the cognitive and behavioural processes involved in addiction.

Field and Cox (2008, p. 14) proposed that a 'mutually excitatory relationship' exists between craving and attentional bias, particularly when there is an expectation that drugs are available. It appears that increased attentional focus on drug cues feeds forward into increased craving, which in turn narrows the focus of attention. Moreover, compromised inhibitory mechanisms are taxed by this and unable to disengage attention, or perhaps free capacity to deploy coping strategies acquired in therapy. At face value, this proposition does not appear to add much to existing accounts: a tendency to repeatedly focus on a given cue is invoked to account for the fact that that cue is salient. However, as discussed in Chapter 1 it is the *involuntary* or automatic nature of the preferential processing that is key. Cues ascribed motivational salience are selected very early in the cognitive processing cycle, before any cognitive control can be orchestrated. In the realm of selective attention only one thing really counts: access to the scarce processing resources that are available to conscious representation and manipulation.

Rapid primary appraisal of drug cues can also elicit psychophysiological arousal and craving that can further increase attentional bias (Franken, 2003; Field, Munafo and Franken, 2009). Referring back to the motoring analogy referred to above, this is the unwanted acceleration that occurs rapidly and before the driver is aware. The second striking finding is the distinctive pattern of neurocognitive deficits that have been detected in the context of substance misuse. At the risk of overstretching the motoring analogy, these go beyond simple brake failure and involve defects in the vehicle's computerized control system. In Chapter 4 I focused on deficiencies in error monitoring, but broader deficits in executive control have also been noted. It appears that, when attempting to resist drug-seeking impulses, the individual is not only assailed by rapidly detected cues but also impaired in his or her ability to inhibit the resulting cognitive representations and behavioural action tendencies. In the following sections the focus is on understanding impulse control and exploring how any insights gleaned can be used to accentuate existing cognitive-therapy procedures or point the way towards the development of novel therapeutic strategies. Thus, having identified the behavioural and cognitive processes using experimental approaches, the next step is to explore the potential for behavioural and cognitive change.

Cognitive Bias Modification

Fortuitously, laboratory paradigms such as the modified Stroop test and the visual probe that have been used to measure cognitive processing biases can be readily adapted as training procedures in therapeutic contexts, analogous to the manner in which measures of behavioural impulsivity such as the 'go/no go' task can be adapted. Using this cognitive bias modification paradigm (CBM), McLeod and colleagues (2002) were the first to modify the visual-probe paradigm from its original purpose as a measure of attentional engagement and disengagement to 'retrain' attentional priorities. In the visual-probe paradigm, participants are typically presented briefly with either a negative emotional stimulus (e.g. an angry face) or a benign cue (e.g. a smiling or neutral face) that quickly vanishes to be replaced by a 'probe' comprising say, one or two dots. The participant has to indicate via a keyboard whether there is in fact one or two dots, with faster responses revealing where attention was directed (because the participant was directing their attention to that location). Unbeknownst to the participants there is a preselected contingency with some probes linked to negative stimuli in 80–100% of presentations and others linked to positive or neutral images. If the probe replaces the nonthreatening stimulus all, or nearly all, of the time over many trials, attentional biases can be modified.

Using a nonclinical sample, McLeod and colleagues demonstrated that reducing attentional bias through repetitious practice appears to reduce experimentally induced anxiety. Subsequently, this 'cognitive bias modification' paradigm was used with emotionally disordered patients (see, e.g., Amir et al., 2009). Initial results appeared encouraging, providing support for the hypothesis that teaching cognitive control skills could yield therapeutic gain, even after relatively brief exposure to the putative therapeutic intervention. A recent meta-analysis (Hallion and Ruscio, 2011) suggests that claims of increased efficacy might be premature, at the very least. These findings were that effect sizes were smaller, for example $g = 0.29$ for attentional bias reduction following CBM with anxious patients, but statistically significant nonetheless. However, once publication bias (nonpublication of nonsignificant findings, known as the 'file-drawer' problem) was controlled for statistically, the degree of clinical gain indexed by lower levels of anxiety and depression appeared insignificant ($g = 0.13$). In the subset of the 45 studies included that assessed dysphoric symptoms after participants experienced a stressor such as a threatening video or upcoming exam following CBM training, the effect was larger ($g = 0.23$), albeit falling short of significance. This is consistent with the latency inherent in implicit cognitive biases.

Attentional Bias in the Context of Addiction

There are now several studies suggesting that the degree of attentional bias towards addiction-related stimuli observed during treatment has some predictive power in relation to treatment outcome. Cox *et al.* (2002), for example, found that some problem drinkers in an inpatient detoxification unit demonstrated an *increase* in attentional bias during their stay on the unit, as indexed by their performance on the modified Stroop test given at the start of treatment and just before discharge. These drinkers were more likely to be classified as unsuccessful three months hence, having either relapsed or been lost to follow-up. The 'successful' cohort, who were less likely to relapse, showed no change in attentional bias, in common with the control group, who were heavy social drinkers recruited from Treatment Unit staff. These findings suggest that patients who became increasingly focused on alcohol cues following detoxification proved to be more vulnerable to relapse. Consistent with these findings, Marissen *et al.* (2006) found that attentional bias measured by a modified Stroop test at the beginning of inpatient treatment predicted outcome for heroin-addicted recruits, again with a three-month follow-up period specified. These interesting findings did not address the question of whether systematically targeting cognitive biases in order to reverse them could enhance outcome.

More can be deduced about causality, with the added promise of therapeutic gain, by manipulating the degree of cognitive bias and assessing how this impacts on key components of addictive processes such as craving and drug seeking behaviour. To this end, Field *et al.* (2007) devised an attentional training procedure derived from the visual-probe paradigm designed to increase or decrease attentional bias for alcohol-related stimuli among a sample of 60 heavy social drinkers. Results indicated that it was possible to *increase* attentional bias, and this was associated with increased craving and desire for alcohol, at least among the majority of participants who recognized the contingency between the probe and the fact that it invariably replaced an alcohol-related image. This subset, manifesting higher levels of craving, did not consume more beer on a subsequent 'taste test'. Paradoxically, the group trained to shift their attention *away* from alcohol-related stimuli did show a reduction in attention towards the alcohol-related stimuli but an unpredicted *increase* in attentional bias for novel alcohol-related stimuli to which participants were subsequently exposed. Clearly, this would be a negative outcome should it occur in a clinical setting, given the findings reviewed above linking increased attentional bias at the beginning of treatment to poorer outcomes. However, the participants of Field *et al.* did not demonstrate increased attentional bias for alcohol-related stimuli at baseline, possibly due to an artefact of the recruitment procedure that was through media and Internet promotion. Moreover, there was no evidence that the effects of the attentional training procedure generalized to other tasks designed to measure attentional processing, such as the modified Stroop task. This suggests that participants were not acquiring more general cognitive control skills but were just becoming more efficient at the particular experimental task. In any event, the observed changes in attentional processing did not seem to be associated with reductions in subjective craving or subsequent drug-seeking behaviour.

Turning to research with smokers, Waters *et al.* (2003) recruited a sample of 158 smokers aiming to give up. They found those who again showed greater attentional bias were more susceptible to an early lapse. Thus, 49 who smoked within one week were 129 ms slower to colour name smoking-related words, whereas 73 who remained abstinent showed a 52 ms delay in responding to smoking versus neutral words. While causality cannot be inferred from these findings, it seems plausible to surmise that those who found it harder to ignore evocative smoking cues on the experimental task also have found it harder to distract themselves from smoking cues in naturalistic settings and thus became more susceptible to smoking once again.

The Alcohol Attention-Control Training Programme

The Alcohol Attention-Control Training Programme (AACTP; Fadardi, 2003; Fadardi and Cox, 2009) is a computerized programme designed to help problem drinkers override attentional bias that is deemed to instigate alcohol-seeking behaviour. This is a promising medium for delivering CBM, assuming access to personal computing facilities and a therapist familiar with the concept of the procedure. Having established a baseline of how much attention-grabbing power various alcohol cues have, feedback is given to the participant and personal goals set. Thus, this would involve reducing the degree of attentional bias and agreeing to participate in the practice sessions. After each training session participants are provided with visual feedback underperformance as indexed by the number of errors in the overall degree of attentional bias indicated by an 'interference score'. Interference is calculated by subtracting the mean reaction time to neutral stimuli from the mean reaction time to alcohol-related stimuli. An example of the procedure, which has varying levels of difficulty or challenge, is that participants would view either an alcoholic or a nonalcoholic beverage surrounded by one of four colours – red, yellow, blue, green. In keeping with the Stroop imperative, the participant is required to name the background or surrounding colour of the nonalcoholic stimulus as quickly and as accurately as possible. Over many repetitions, the participants' attention is thus directed towards the nonalcoholic image and away from the alcoholic one.

Fadardi and Cox (2009) subsequently evaluated the AACTP in a sample of hazardous drinkers (mean weekly drinking equals 44.6 units) and harmful drinkers (mean weekly drinking equals 71.5 units). Baseline measurements found that the harmful drinkers manifested more attentional bias than the hazardous drinkers. In turn, both of these groups showed higher levels of Stroop interference than a comparison group comprised of social drinkers drinking within recommended levels. The hazardous and harmful drinkers then went on to undergo four sessions of attentional training on a weekly basis. While only the drinkers classified as 'harmful' were followed up, they had reduced their attentional bias and alcohol consumption at the end of the four weeks of training, and these reductions were maintained at three-months. In addition, confidence in their ability to control the drinking had increased, as did their readiness to change. Fadardi *et al.* (2011) describe further work extending the AACTP to opiate-dependent people. Preliminary results suggest those receiving attentional training manifested decreased levels of attentional bias, drug temptations and supplementary drug use (i.e. acquiring and using illicit substances) at two- and six-month follow-up assessments. They also needed fewer doses of methadone, the standard opiate substitution drug.

A recent study in the Netherlands (Schoenmakers *et al.*, 2010) provided more encouraging findings, bolstered by a strong randomized design. Schoenmakers and co-workers recruited 43 abstinent alcohol-dependent clinic attendees and randomly assigned them to CBM or a control condition. Participants had all been detoxified and were engaged in CBT. A modified visual probe task was designed so that the probe always replaced a neutral as opposed to an alcohol-related picture over a series of five training sessions amounting to 2640 responses. Results indicated that the CBM procedure, compared with sham training, facilitated disengagement from alcohol cues but did not appear to impact on engagement or speeded detection. Importantly, the enhanced ability to disengage from cues generalized to new pictures of alcohol-related material. However, there was no post-test difference in self-reported craving between experimental and control groups. Neither was there a significant difference in clinical outcome, indexed by rates of relapse: 25% relapsed in the CBM condition and 21% in the control group, although the former took, on average, 1.25 months longer to relapse. Overall, the study does show that CBM can be used as an adjunct to standard treatments such as CBT and this seems to lead to meaningful changes in cognitive processing and at least short-term therapeutic gain. The clients did not appear to balk at the repetitious nature of the procedure, and were judged by their clinician to make a faster recovery than the control participants. In fact, the CBM group were discharged 28 days earlier on average than those in the control group. While convincing evidence of more manifest change in the parameters of addiction such as craving or ultimate vulnerability to relapse was lacking, the changes that were noted (early discharge and longer latency to relapse) appear clinically relevant.

Modifying Implicit Approach Tendencies

Addiction entails a very high frequency of response with regard to, say, smoking and consuming alcohol. As we have seen, instrumental behaviour becomes highly automated insofar as the necessary actions can take place with little or no conscious awareness. This is underpinned by changes at the neuronal level, whereby habitual behaviour is governed less by frontal or executive neural systems and more by dorsal domains of the striatum (see Robbins and Everitt, 2002, and Chapter 3 of this volume). For the habituated drug user, this transition is likely to be experienced as akin to finding oneself reaching for the drug of choice in a reflexive manner. Wiers et al. (2010) focused on the possibility that these implicit approach tendencies could be reversed through re-training. These researchers recruited 42 individuals designated as hazardous drinkers and randomly assigned them to a condition in which they were trained to either avoid or approach images of alcoholic beverages presented on a computer screen. Approach and avoidance were enacted by instructing the participants to either push (an avoidant response) or pull (an approach response) a lever depending on whether the image was either in 'landscape' or 'portrait' format. The participants were not told that in the majority of cases the avoid (push lever) response to landscape formats was also rejecting an alcoholic beverage. Conversely, the approach (pull lever) response was in the majority of cases enacting an approach to nonalcoholic beverages. The reason that the association between 'approach-nonalcohol' and 'avoid-alcohol' was not 100% was that participants would more readily recognize the link between the format, image and response if there was no variation or invalidity in trials. Those in the avoid-alcohol condition, instructed to shun the landscape format and embrace the portrait format, pushed most (90%) of the alcoholic drinks and pulled most (90%) nonalcoholic drinks towards them. Participants in the approach-alcohol condition were offered reverse contingencies, that is, predominantly pulling alcohol towards them and pushing soft drinks away. After the implicit training, participants performed a sham taste test, including beers and soft drinks. Participants in the approach-alcohol condition drank more alcohol than participants in the avoid-alcohol condition. Interestingly, no effect was found on subjective craving.

Demonstrating how rapidly experimental methods can migrate to the clinical arena, Wiers *et al.* (2011) allocated 214 alcohol-dependent inpatients to either four sessions of this behavioural analogue of CBM or a control training procedure. All patients also received treatment as usual based on one-to-one and group CBT. Participants in the experimental group showed a predicted reversal, from approach bias to avoidant bias, in response to alcohol pictorial stimuli. This was echoed by performance on an Implicit Association Test. The impact on craving (which tended to be low in any event) in response to alcoholic or nonalcoholic beverages presented after experimental and control training was less clear. When followed up one year later, 59% of the control group (63 of 106 participants) had relapsed compared with 46% (50 of 108), a finding that just fell short of statistical significance. An outcome was deemed successful if there was no relapse or a single episode of drinking lasting less than three days that was ended by the patient without further negative consequences. As pointed out by the authors, this binary outcome measure did not lend itself well to exploring the mediation effects of the CBM in what was primarily an experimental study rather than a clinical trial. Nonetheless, this brief augmentation to standard CBT appears to have altered core cognitive and behavioural processes in the desired direction and quite possibly contributed to sustained recovery.

Houben *et al.* (2011) recruited a sample of heavy-drinking students in the Netherlands. Using a standard procedure known as the go/no go task, the participants were trained to either respond or inhibit a response to an alcohol-related image such as a glass of beer or a control image such as a glass of water. Those trained to inhibit a response to alcohol (the no-go condition) were trained not to press a button when shown the alcohol image and always signalled to respond by pressing a button when shown the glass of water. The control group carried out the converse of this procedure, being trained to respond to the alcohol cue and inhibit a response to the nonalcoholic cue. Following 80 trials, the hypothesis that training in response inhibition would lead to an actual behavioural change, that is, a reduction in drinking, was supported.

Reversing the Bias: Conclusion

The above emerging technologies have the potential for modifying cognitive and behavioural processes associated with appetitive and potentially addictive behaviours. Some of the findings (see, e.g., Field *et al.*, 2007) highlighted problems with generalizability across stimuli and procedures for measuring or modifying cognitive processing, as well as anomalies such as reduced attentional bias with one set of stimuli apparently facilitating processing with alternative but semantically similar stimuli. A more fundamental problem with generalizability is that of drawing inferences from participants recruited from the community to the treatment-seeking, and indeed treatment-needing, population that this book is ultimately written for. Apart from the study by Schoenmakers *et al.* (2010), participants were not treatment seekers and did not meet the criteria for addictive disorders. Addicted individuals would have had much more intense and frequent exposure to drugs, alcohol and expressions of other compulsions such as gambling. Notwithstanding any direct cognitive deficits linked to neurotoxicity, they will have acquired a significantly higher degree of automaticity across cognitive and behavioural response systems. Insofar as CBM is a retraining procedure, I envisage that more repetitious practice would be required given the extant strength of processing bias that has to be overcome. The two complementary techniques aiming to modify cognitive and behavioural responding using implicit training procedures (i.e. procedures that do not, at face value, necessarily reveal their true purpose, although of course patients will be informed of this) can be adapted to run on computerized or Internet-based applications. They are a promising adjunct to existing approaches and merit more systematic and control evaluation in clinical settings.

Brain Training and Neurocognitive Rehabilitation Approaches

Attentional processing is a core component of cognitive control, requiring effortful suppression of prepotent responses. Plausibly, it is attentional capture, with or without conscious awareness, that ignites the impulsive behaviour that defines addiction. Procedures that enhance cognitive efficiency are therefore likely to improve control over habitual or automatic responses. Neurocognitive rehabilitation techniques, more recently popularized as 'brain-training' procedures, thus complement, or perhaps extend, the CBM techniques and behavioural approach–avoidance training discussed above. In practice, brain training aims to improve cognitive function through regular training, usually with computerized tests. This contrasts somewhat with CBM, where procedures are highly specific in terms of the chosen stimuli to which the individual is trained to attend/approach or not attend/avoid, but aims to foster a more generalized improvement in cognitive efficiency. The *generalizability* of any putative enhancements is therefore crucial. Somewhat disappointingly, some recent reviews suggest that individuals who engage in tasks aimed at improving cognitive efficiency or brain training show strong training effect with regard to the specific task but this does not appear to generalize to other tasks. This is problematic in the addiction context, as there is a potentially infinite variety of cues or combinations of cues that can prime impulsive approach behaviours.

A further challenge that has to be addressed is the *durability* of any cognitive gains associated with training. In this regard, it is important to emphasize that addiction is a chronic syndrome prone to reversal months or years after restraint is initially established. A 'quick-fix' is therefore unlikely to confer enhanced outcomes in the longer term. Owen *et al.* (2010) concluded on the basis of their review that modest effects have been observed with older individuals and preschool children, but that there was little if any empirical support suggesting that brain training conferred benefits across the wider population. Their own findings supported this when they assigned 11,430 participants recruited online to either a group engaged with training tasks that emphasized reasoning, planning and problem-solving or a group who practised a broader range of tasks aimed at enhancing short-term memory retention and visuospatial functioning. A third group was assigned to a control condition where they were tasked with answering obscure questions from six different categories using online sources. Findings indicated that participants improved significantly, indexed by large effect sizes, on tasks on which they were trained. However, performance on 'benchmarking' tests including short-term memory and reasoning improved only marginally over the six week training period, with effect sizes as low as 0.01. Moreover, the control group also improved on these tests, designed to capture generalized improvement in cognitive functioning. The authors concluded that the equivalent small gains observed across experimental and control groups could reflect practice effects because the tests were repeated, the adoption of new task strategies or possibly a combination of the two.

It would appear therefore that there is little to be gained, apart from improving performance on the training task, by normal individuals adopting general brain training. What, however if more focused training of core cognitive competencies is applied, perhaps where performance is compromised by factors such as ageing or indeed exposure to neurotoxic drugs? In the aptly named COGITO study, Schmiedek *et al.* (2010) examined whether there was a positive transfer subsequent to 100 days of one hour training sessions on tests of perceptual speed, WM and episodic memory with cohorts of 103 older and 101 younger participants. These researchers found reliable positive transfer for both individual tests and cognitive abilities represented as latent factors or constructs such as reasoning and cognitive control. Regarding the latter, for example Chein and Morrison (2010) found that a group of 21 undergraduates randomly assigned to an arduous WM training procedure showed significant improvement on a conventional colour-conflict Stroop task compared with untrained controls. The trained cohort also showed significant comparative gains with reading comprehension. This replicated earlier findings (see, e.g., Oleson *et al.*, 2004; Westerberg and Klingberg, 2007) showing enhanced performance on tasks or core cognitive competencies that were not on the training curriculum. In the latter study, improved performance was detectable for several months following the training. Moreover, these researchers found that enhanced WM performance was mirrored by increased activity in the dorsolateral prefrontal cortex and parietal regions as revealed by fMRI. These findings are consistent, albeit in a rather oblique manner, with one of the key predictions derived from the model in Figure 2.1. Thus, improving executive control or 'top-down' processes represents a relatively distinct therapeutic avenue through which the implicit 'bottom-up' mechanisms of impulse control can be modulated. This complements therapeutic interventions that target implicit processes more directly, such as CBM (see, e.g., Schoenmakers *et al.*, 2010) and reversing behavioural approach tendencies (see, e.g., Wiers *et al.*, 2010) referred to above. Assuming that cognitive control is impaired, efforts to restore or improve cognitive control should thus prove remedial, especially if any gains are generalizable and lasting. In particular, findings that fostering WM capacity can improve attentional control in a collateral manner (i.e., without directly targeting attentional processing *per se*) suggest a novel means of overcoming attentional bias, a process that is pivotal in the cycle of addictive behaviour. This also provides the therapist and client with a more flexible range of therapeutic strategies. For example, the client could be encouraged to do things that require the repeated utilization of WM or executive control competencies. This could include a wide range of activities, including reading a novel, doing crossword puzzles, computer gaming or simply engaging in more social interaction. This overlaps with the broader therapeutic inheritance of establishing and pursuing goals, not least because goal maintenance is itself a key component of cognitive control.

Physical exercise

For many clients with substance misuse and addictive behaviour problems, pursuing more 'intellectual' endeavours such as reading has not featured strongly in the history. Fortuitously, it appears that cardiovascular fitness training (CFT) can improve cognitive and behavioural functioning due to a putative neurogenerative process. Earlier (p. 69) I noted that exercise was associated with improved BDNF-dependent synaptic plasticity. While much of this work has been with laboratory animals, neuroanatomical evidence from older human participants shows comparable benefits in brain health to those observed in aging animals. In a cross-sectional study of people aged 55–79 (Colcombe *et al.*, 2003), frontal, prefrontal and parietal cortices showed a significantly reduced tendency towards age-related declines in cortical tissue density among those who engaged in significantly less aerobic exercise. Study 2 of Colcombe *et al.* (2004) consolidated these findings by randomly assigning a group of 29 high-functioning 58–78-year-olds to CFT or a nonaerobic control condition involving stretching and toning. Both conditions required participants to practice three times a week in 40–45 minute sessions over a six-month period. When required to complete a cognitively demanding task involving valid and invalid cues, those who received CFT training and were judged to have increased cardiovascular fitness demonstrated increased activity in areas associated with robust attentional control such as the middle frontal gyrus (MFG) and superior frontal gyrus (SFG). Moreover, there was less activation in areas such as the anterior cingulate cortex (ACC), interpreted by the investigators as evidence of less cognitive conflict and presumably of less effort required in error monitoring and inhibitory control. These findings echoed those found in a parallel cross-sectional study (Colcombe *et al.*, 2004, Study 1), which divided participants according to their level of cardiovascular fitness and associated training. Across both studies, either people who showed pre-existing levels of greater cardiovascular fitness, or those who were trained to acquire such fitness, performed significantly better on the experimental cognitive task.

Returning to the subject of addiction, there is a dearth of studies evaluating the potential benefits of exercise on outcome. However, in one of the few extant randomly controlled studies, Marcus *et al.* (1999) found that adding vigorous exercise to CBT made a significant contribution to improving outcome in a group of 281 female smokers attempting to give up. It emerged that 11.9% of those who were in the exercise condition were abstinent at 12 months follow-up compared with 5.4% of the control group. An added benefit was less weight gain (3.05 versus 5.40 kg) among the more aerobically active cohort.

Working memory and delay discounting

Excessive discounting of future rewards (delayed reward discounting or DRD) has been observed in a variety of disorders but appears to be emblematic of addiction insofar as it reflects the prioritization of immediate gratification and discounting or devaluing of deferred gratification. The addicted individual will consistently opt for immediate gratification associated with substance use or gambling and appears to devalue the longer-term rewards associated with restraint. It thus reflects a type of impulsive decision making that *discounts* the value of a reward based on its *delay* in time. DRD has been observed with a range of addicted populations. Converging, although not necessarily conclusive, evidence implicates DRD as a pre-existing vulnerability factor, possibly of genetic origin, for addictive disorders. In a prospective study, Audrain-McGovern *et al.* (2009) measured delay discounting in a cohort of 947 American 16–21-year-olds attending high school. They found that the standard deviation (SD = 1.41) increase in baseline delay discounting, measured by questionnaire, resulted in an 11% increase (OR = 1.11, 95% CI = 1.03, 1.23) in the odds of smoking uptake. It thus appeared that a tendency to 'want it now; not tomorrow' in a broader developmental context will prove something of a liability when drug-delivered rewards are encountered. Krishnan-Sarin *et al.* (2007) found that delay discounting predicted failure to give up in a group of treatment-seeking adolescents. MacKillop *et al.* (2011) conducted a meta-analytic review of DRD studies and concluded that there was sufficient evidence to implicate DRD as a vulnerability factor – and one that remains stable over time – for addiction to drugs and pathological gambling. These reviewers also concluded that drug exposure can itself engender or potentiate DRD, in effect acting as a recursive vulnerability factor for the endurance of patterns of addictive behaviour.

Clinical Implications of Delayed Reward Discounting

Bickel *et al.* (2011), in a ground-breaking study, focused on the interaction between WM and delay discounting. Bickel and his co-workers recruited 27 stimulant-dependent individuals, measured their propensity to discount delayed rewards and trained 14 of them on a range of WM tasks. Controls carried out comparable cognitive training but were not required to engage core WM processes. Those who engaged in WM training showed a significant decrease in delay discounting when re-evaluated, whereas controls showed no change. This was a highly specific outcome and groups did not differ significantly on any other pre- or post-training measure such as Letter Number Sequencing (Wechsler, 1997). Bickel and colleagues concluded that the findings potentially support a new strategy or intervention by which to decrease the discounting of delayed rewards. However, as this study appears to be the first to demonstrate that neurocognitive training of WM can decrease delay discounting, replication is important. Further, as pointed out by the authors, crucial questions relating to the durability of the reduced delay discounting remain unanswered pending further research.

The above findings validate the heuristic value of dual-processing models of addiction predicated on competing neural systems: an impulsive decision system associated with the acquisition of immediate gratification or reinforcement subserved by the limbic and paralimbic regions, and a more strategic, executive system embodied in the prefrontal cortex concerned with planning and deferred outcomes. Further, neuroimaging data indicates that prefrontal regions such as the dorsolateral prefrontal cortex are involved during WM activation *and* delay discounting tasks, suggesting that augmenting one core process should facilitate the related one, as in WM training apparently facilitating inhibition of impulsivity in the experiment of Bickel *et al.*. Thus McClure *et al.* (2007) found that greater limbic activation was observed when choices between an immediate reward and a delayed reward was required rather than for choices between two delayed rewards. Conversely, similar activity levels were observed in the posterior parietal cortex and the lateral prefrontal cortex regardless of whether the choice was between an immediate and a delayed reward or between two delayed rewards. Accordingly, the finding that augmenting WM functioning can have a measurable impact on delay discounting appears to validate these data as well as pointing the way bridging the gap between the neuroscience laboratory and the addiction clinic. This appears to be the first study demonstrating that neurocognitive training of WM decreases delay discounting. The authors concluded that the results offer evidence of a functional relationship between delay discounting and WM. In the absence of replication, these findings can be little more than indicative, but point to a hitherto unexplored arena for addressing a key component of addiction expressed as 'short-term gain = (probably) long term pain'. Ultimately, the utility of this procedure will depend on whether neurocognitive training such as this can improve outcomes in addictive disorders.

The approaches to WM training discussed above all focus on what has been termed 'core training': it involves repeated practice of demanding WM tasks designed to target core competencies or general WM mechanisms. Chein and Morrison (2010) distinguished core training from 'strategy training', for example using mnemonic techniques such as imagery, 'chunking' – devising a mental story within which the memory items are embedded, or simply rehearsal. Core training, by way of contrast, aims to

- limit the use of domain specific strategies
- minimize automatization
- include tasks or stimuli that span different modalities such as verbal or visual memory
- require maintenance despite interference
- oblige the trainee to conduct rapid encoding and retrieval operations
- adapt to trainees' varying degrees of proficiency with demanding cognitive workloads.

A different approach derives from the innovative work of Baumeister and his team (e.g. Baumeister *et al.*, 1998), who used the term 'ego depletion' to denote the fact that self-control apparently diminishes when repeatedly exercised, analogous to muscle fatigue following exertion. Self-control or willpower is thus seen as a limited resource: an individual will resist on the first, second or subsequent challenge, but eventually succumb to some degree. The analogy of a muscle also raises the possibility of training to increase strength or endurance, leading to an improvement in self-control performance. Muraven (2010) exploited this potential when he evaluated the hypothesis that self-control training would contribute to success in abstaining from smoking. He trained smokers aiming to give up to practice small acts of self-control such as squeezing a bar to the point of discomfort. Results suggested that augmenting self-control skills did indeed appear to facilitate abstinence. One month later, the enhanced self-control group had fared better than controls: 27% of the active 'self-control' group were verifiably abstinent from smoking compared with 12% of the controls, who were given a range of tasks that required some effort not particularly involving self-control.

Adopting a more cognitive approach, Jones et al. (2011) induced different mental sets in a cohort of 90 social drinkers by emphasizing either the importance of cautious responding and successful inhibition (Restraint group), the importance of rapid responding (Disinhibition group) or the equal importance of rapid responding and successful inhibition (Control group). Inhibition was measured by a standard measure of impulsivity, a Stop-Signal test. The groups appeared to respond to the experimental mandate, as the Restraint group responded more slowly and more cautiously (making fewer Inhibition Errors) than the Disinhibition group, and performance of the Control group falling in between the two experimental groups. Subsequently, when given the chance to drink beer in a spoof taste test, the Restraint group consumed less beer than the Disinhibition and Control groups, who both consumed similar quantities. The groups did not differ on measures of arousal or mood. Further, the experimental groups (restrained and disinhibited mindset) did not differ in self-reported alcohol craving after completing the stop-signal task, so beer consumption appears to have been unaffected by craving but more susceptible to variations in levels of cognitive control. The researchers concluded that regular practice or exercise of restraint might transfer to regulating intake of alcohol in individual problem drinkers. Table 7.1 outlines how different facets of impulsivity investigated in laboratory studies can generate 'real-world' applications aimed at boosting cognitive control.

Tried and Tested Techniques

There is a good conceptual case and an emerging, if inconsistent, empirical database to support the use of implicit cognitive and behavioural modification procedures. Currently, these reside within the laboratory apart

Table 7.1 'Real-world' analogues of experimental paradigms of impulsivity.

Facet of impulsivity	Experimental paradigm	'Real-world' example	Potential remedial procedures
Behavioural inhibition	Go/no go task or stop-signal task	Suppressing appetitive or acquisitive behaviour	Practising self-restraint; training in modifying implicit approach tendencies.
Attentional lapses and biases	Slower reaction to visual cues over longer time intervals; preferential processing of addiction-relevant stimuli	'Action slips' leading to default responses, temporarily "forgetting" goal is abstinence; distraction by addiction-related cues	Cognitive bias reversal; goal maintenance strategies such as rehearsal; aerobic exercise. Brain training focusing on sustaining attention.
Impaired (impulsive) decision making	Delay discounting task	Prioritizing immediate gratification via drug ingestion; devaluing longer-term benefits of restraint	Brain training with the aim of increasing WM capacity especially prospective memory; aerobic exercise.

from the occasional participation in a clinical trial as outlined above. The question arises as to whether these findings can inform current therapeutic transactions.

Educating the client about implicit cognitive and behavioural patterns

To illustrate how this might occur, I recorded the following from a session with Craig, a 37-year-old man with a 15-year history of escalating alcohol use, usually in tandem with cocaine. He was currently abstinent, having suffered a severe heart attack directly linked to his substance misuse. He was referred to the psychology clinic because of pre-existing and concurrent problems with anger management, although this had not been expressed as physical aggression for over a decade. I engaged in general conversation in order to establish rapport in advance of setting the agenda for the session, our third encounter. In accordance with the priority assigned to habit reversal in the *CHANGE* programme, every session addresses the client's status with regard to the addictive issues. If the client is abstinent or compliant with the treatment goal, this is reinforced; if not, the antecedents of the reported drug use are explored. The session begins thus:

THERAPIST: Hi Craig any problems getting to the clinic this morning, how did you travel here?

CLIENT: No I walked as it is only a mile and I would have needed to change trains. But I kept seeing small pieces of silver paper in corners and down alleyways. It made me think that I must still be craving crack, deep down.

T: That's very interesting. Recently researchers have found that when we stop using something addictive like cocaine or alcohol part of our subconscious mind doesn't quite get the message. It kind of goes like 'finding drugs (or things that point to where we can find of drugs) has been what the master (your conscious mind) wants for several years so I'll just carry on doing that'.

C: 'So are you saying that it's not just me and it doesn't necessarily mean I have some kind of secret longing for cocaine even though I know it nearly killed me and I really want to stay off it for the rest of my life?'

T: Yes. As far as I can see you've done all the right things since you started treatment and you're doing very well. Things like silver paper white powder or banknotes will continue to grab your attention whether you want them to or not: this is what happened when you were on your way here this morning. Basically, you're minding your own business making sure you'd be at the appointment on time but there was another hidden agenda which we could call the 'seek and find cocaine program'. This is like a program that runs in the background on your PC. You don't see it on the desktop although it occasionally makes its presence felt by maybe an irritating pop-up on your screen. It doesn't mean that you are not committed to continuing your recovery programme, although it can be tiring or even exhausting having to deal with these 'cocaine alerts'.

C: Thanks. I can certainly relate to what you said about the banknotes and when my girlfriend uses her make-up mirror. I also find that grabs my attention. It doesn't always trigger craving but it often distracts me from whatever I'm doing at the time. I must admit that my automatic thought was 'I'm still basically a crackhead at this rate I'm going to end up using at some stage'. Is there anything I should do to deal with this?

T: Yes there are a few things I can suggest to help you manage this. I think the first thing is to recognize that when you find yourself looking at bits of silver paper, white powder or whatever that is just your mind doing what it was trained to do over the many years you were using. Rationally, you've got the message but it takes a while to filter down to your subconscious. As I said earlier it does not mean you are not being fully honest with yourself or you are not fully committed to staying abstinent. So this means that the thought you shared with me about being a crackhead is not really true. In the light of what we've been discussing can you think of a more balanced way of interpreting the situation when you find yourself looking at cocaine cues or triggers?

C: Well. I guess you're saying that it's not really me swivelling around looking at silver paper and mirrors!

T: You're on the right track. It's part of you but something you're trying to move on from. So far, you've done really well – 18 months clean and sober! That's exceptional and shows how committed you are to the goal of abstinence, but you can't take your eye off the ball entirely, as shown by what can happen.

C: How about 'old habits die hard!'

T: I think that captures a key part of what is going on.

C: Yeah. I suppose really I should link this with some of the stuff we talk about in Cocaine Anonymous. I should just take things one day at a time.

T: Yes I agree. That's a very helpful rule. But in terms of the thought, it seemed to me it was saying something about your motivation, or perhaps more likely your lack of motivation.

C: I think I see what you're getting at. You could almost say that I was trying to set myself up for a fall. How about 'This is just a distraction. I genuinely want to stay clean and so far I seem to be doing things the right way'.

T: Good! I think that about sums it up.

Using behavioural experiments

The behavioural experiment is designed to bring about change at both an explicit or declarative level (e.g. 'I can enjoy myself at a party when staying sober at the same time') and at a more implicit or procedural level (e.g. It 'feels' natural to refuse alcohol and stay sober in social situations) (Bennett-Levy *et al.*, 2004). In the context of recovery from addictive disorders, this would entail challenging expectancies both about controlling addictive impulses and indications of choices made in a clearly defined forthcoming scenario. Astute clinical judgement is a prerequisite: it is important to carry out a thorough risk assessment before negotiating a behavioural experiment with a person aiming to remain abstinent. A lapse can have sometimes very serious consequences, for example if the person has parental responsibility or might be liable to impulsive behaviour when intoxicated. In these situations a behavioural experiment that may expose the client to what could prove to be irresistible cues might need to be deferred. This caution needs to be counterbalanced by an awareness of ubiquity of cues for alcohol, tobacco, gambling and illicit drugs. In addition, my emphasis on implicit processes such as attentional bias suggests that an individual will encounter potent triggers perhaps sooner rather than later, even if these are ambiguous or subtle cues. When this occurs drug-seeking behaviour can be mobilized automatically before coping strategies can be deployed. In contrast, the expectancy challenge accords with the principle 'forewarned is forearmed', meaning that anticipated challenges are easy to cope with them unexpected ones. Therefore, what is required is a calculated risk, balancing the risk associated with orchestrating cue exposure in a setting where there is an opportunity to engage in the addictive behaviour with the risk that cues will, almost inevitably, be detected at some other juncture. Again, there is a critical role for WM in preparing the client for an expectancy challenge experiment. Specifically, prospective memory, the capacity to remember to do something either at a particular time or in response to a particular future event, is recruited.

First, identify with the clients forthcoming situations where they are likely to encounter an opportunity to use or resume use of the substance they are trying to give up. The target cognitions refer to (a) self–mastery, for example a thought that is inimical to coping, or persistence of coping effort – 'If I am offered a cigarette I will be unable to say no' or (b) an outcome prediction or expectancy linked to possible outcomes. This is a template that can be completed in session and then given to the clients to take away and carry with them as a flash card.

Expectancy: 'now' or 'later'

Kober *et al.* (2010a) investigated the possibility that a very brief cognitive control strategy could modulate self-reported craving. To this end, they presented 62 participants, comprising a mixture of heavy smokers, light smokers and nonsmokers, with smoking- and food-related images, the latter essentially for control purposes. Participants were asked to focus either on the immediate consequences (NOW condition) or long-term consequences (LATER condition) of consuming the cigarette or food depicted. Subjective reports of craving for cigarettes were lower when cigarette-smoking participants considered the long-term consequences associated with smoking. These findings suggest that smokers can use cognitive strategies to reduce their craving for cigarettes. Kober and her colleagues (2010b) replicated the 'now, later' paradigm with the crucial addition of fMRI. Again, they found that the more remote cognitive appraisal reduced craving, with participants' ratings about a third lower when asked to focus on the long-term consequences of smoking the cue cigarette. Using contrast methods, areas associated with cognitive control including the dorsomedial prefrontal cortex, the dorsolateral prefrontal cortex and the ventrolateral prefrontal cortex were activated during the LATER condition. Crucially, the prefrontal–striatal pathway was also activated differentially when participants were engaging in the cognitive control required to focus on the long-term consequences of indulgence rather than the short-term gratification. This was accompanied by decreased activation in regions associated with craving such as the ventral striatum, the amygdala and the subgenual anterior cingulate. This pattern of neural activation is entirely consistent with the approach advocated in this text that relentlessly focuses on cognitive control. Table 7.2 depicts one of my client's responses to this task. The individual, George, had successfully

Table 7.2 Short-term and long-term consequences of resuming smoking.

	Immediate consequences: 'Now'	Long-term consequences: 'Later'
Positive expectancies	Feeling part of the crowd; sheer pleasure; less boredom	None really! I guess it means I won't have to worry about saying no to a cigarette!
Negative expectancies	Disappointment (I've put a lot of effort into quitting smoking); my breath will smell when I get home	Risk of illness. I may get cancer and die! Complete waste of money. Smoking is pointless

abstained from alcohol for three months. Two weeks prior to his review session with me he had also given up smoking but he reported experiencing strong urges and craving when he was in social situations mingling with smokers.

In the course of a subsequent review session George told me that he had coped successfully on two occasions by focusing on the longer-term consequences, which were markedly negative. He had smoked two cigarettes on another occasion, but had restrained himself since.

The Road to Recovery is Paved with Good Implementation Intentions!

Traditionally, approaches to human motivation have emphasized goal formation and definition, with less attention paid to implementation. Thus, an individual could commit to a goal along the lines 'I intend to apply for a new job' without anchoring the goal to a particular situation or context. An implementation intention (Gollwitzer, 1993; Prestwich *et al.*, 2006) entails making a commitment to act in a particular way in a given situation. Applied to the above example, this could be 'I will apply for the next job I see for which I am qualified'. This involves an individual deciding 'when, where, and how they will perform a behaviour' (Prestwich *et al.*, 2006, p. 455). The implementation intention is formed as an 'If, then' algorithm as follows: 'If I encounter Situation X, I will perform behaviour Y'. For example, 'If I am offered cocaine I will say no thanks, I've quit' or 'If I am offered an alcoholic drink I will say "No thanks, but I'd love a mineral water"'. Note that this links a behaviour with a particular response rather than simply stating a goal such as 'I will not smoke at the party'. The latter is of course important, but needs to be translated into action by the use of implementation strategies. According to Gollwitzer (1993), investing a forthcoming environmental event or situation with the power to elicit a coping response aims to harness *automatic* processes when the response is triggered. A response such as drug refusal is thus generated immediately, efficiently and with little conscious intent, attributes of automatic processing. Theoretically, this means that fewer demands are placed on the limited-capacity controlled processes necessary for inhibition of automatic cognitive biases and behavioural approach tendencies.

Implementation intentions can also be applied to other behaviours broadly linked to recovery and rehabilitation. Brandstatter *et al.*

(2001, Experiment 1) recruited 41 opiate-dependent attendees at a German detoxification unit and assigned them to relevant and irrelevant implementation conditions when tasked with composing a curriculum vitae (CV). About half of the group were still experiencing withdrawal symptoms; the other half were symptom free. In the relevant condition participants wrote a report specifying when and where they would draft their CV; in contrast the irrelevant group did the same but focused on where and when they wanted to have lunch and how they would start. All participants rated the degree of commitment they had to completing their CV. This did not differ across the groups and was at best modest in any event. Results showed a strong effect of the implementation intention, with 12 of the 21 in the relevant group submitting CVs compared with none of the 20 in the irrelevant. Interestingly, patients still manifesting withdrawal effects, deemed to be under a high cognitive load by the authors, seemed to benefit more from forming implementation strategies. Eight of the 12 who successfully completed CVs were still withdrawing from opiates. This is consistent with the assertion that implementation intentions do not demand much cognitive capacity because they are, at least partially, automatized.

In my clinic I developed the following implementation intention with a 61-year-old man who experienced strong impulses to drink excessively: 'If I feel an urge to have an alcoholic drink I will prepare herbal tea'. This was discussed in session and written on a note which the client took away with him. Two weeks later he reported this had proved successful on one occasion, although he had drunk excessively in other situations. A second example was with a 27-year-old individual using crack cocaine: 'When I get my benefit check next Thursday I will buy food in the local shop [before I do anything else such as visiting the dealer]'. More generally, I work with clients to form implementation intentions across a range of possibilities.

Contingency management

Contingency management (CM) interventions promote behaviour change by applying contingent reinforcement, usually positively valenced. This approach has been recently endorsed by the National Institute for Health and Clinical Excellence (NICE, 2007) in the UK following a comprehensive meta-analysis. One application is to reduce supplementary illicit drug use among methadone-maintained clinic attendees. The recommendation is that incentives should be offered (typically vouchers of escalating value) from £2 to £10 that can be exchanged for goods or services of the service user's choice, or 'privileges' such as take-home methadone doses. If the client is eligible for a voucher it is accompanied by praise and explicit restatement of the contingency. The client is also reminded of how the next contingent reward will be acquired, for example producing another drug-free urine sample and/or attending at the correct time. According to this guidance the frequency of screening should be initially set at three tests per week (for the first 3 weeks), two tests per week for the next 3 weeks, and one per week subsequently until stability is achieved. CM can be used to increase the frequency of a range of behaviours linked to engagement and treatment compliance such as punctual attendance and participation in therapeutic programmed activities. Conceptually, CM appears to have a number of crucial motivational and cognitive impacts. First, CM, despite relatively modest value rewards, appears to short-circuit highly motivated drug-seeking behaviour.

The efficacy of the CM can also be positively linked to the monetary value of the reward. Better outcomes indexed by abstinence rates were obtained for those attempting to give up cocaine when there was a higher-magnitude reward potentially available ($240 compared with $80) as a prize with entries to the draw earned contingently (Petry *et al.*, 2004). This suggests somewhat tantalisingly that a more rational metric for estimating value can co-exist along with the artificially inflated values ascribed to drug-derived rewards. This raises the question of why this rational decision making – receive £10 for taking only methadone or the chance to win $240 by not using cocaine – is apparently so rare outside the confines of the treatment centre. Those who regularly use legal or illicit substances or gamble repeatedly encounter very strong incentives to desist and often very intense punishment such as loss of liberty, health or even the opportunity to enjoy a normal lifespan.

Apart from the magnitude of the reward, the other key modulator is contingency, especially regarding the more rapid delivery of the reinforcer. Higgins *et al.* (2004) emphasized the power of the immediacy of reinforcement juxtaposed against the even more rapid positive and negative reinforcement provided by consumption of a drug to which one is habituated. Higgins and his colleagues contrast this with the delayed positive consequences, such as a cocaine-using pregnant woman delivering a healthy baby in several months' time, associated with restraint. Considering the tendency of those prone to addiction to discount delayed consequences, these reviewers proposed that providing contingent rewards served to bridge the gap between the undesirable short-term consequences of deferred gratification and the very meaningful but apparently very distant longer-term outcomes. More speculatively, I propose that the second, more cognitive, impact of contingency management interventions is reflected in WM processes as follows. For clarity, assume that the protocol used is in accordance with the NICE guidelines described above, which give up to three opportunities each week to deliver the intervention:

- The goal is clearly specified agreed and repeated.
- It is then encoded and maintained in WM, where it influences cognitive processing directly by guiding attention to goal-congruent stimuli, and less directly by capturing scarce cognitive processing resources in what is a limited-capacity system (see Chapter 4). According to the 'first past the post principle' this will restrict access by competing stimuli possibly associated with drug seeking and taking.
- If the target behaviour occurs it is quickly reinforced and the goal is maintained until the next scheduled clinic attendance.
- If the target behaviour has not occurred, the reinforcement is withheld but the individual is nonetheless reminded of the goal and given another opportunity to attain it.

The goal-maintenance process, a core executive function, is assumed to operate between sessions as a form of prospective memory. Without this ability to maintain a goal and inhibit competing goals it is likely that delay discounting would undermine the process: the prospect of a reward up to a week later would not necessarily have sufficient value to forestall the incentive of immediate gratification. However, as long as the goal, for example 'I need to provide a 'clean' urine specimen in order to get a £10 voucher', is encoded in WM, the operant conditioning process retains its potency.

One implication from the foregoing is that the efficiency of WM could influence outcome insofar as it is taxed with goal rehearsal and goal maintenance. Accordingly, those with less WM capacity or core WM skills as discussed above (Morrison and Chien, 2011) would be more challenged by cognitive control tasks such as goal maintenance and goal pursuit over extended periods, especially when assailed by distracters. Because there appears to be an overlap between goal maintenance and attention in that a common pool of neural resources seems to subserve both processes (see Lavie, 2005, for a review), intact WM functioning is crucial for filtering out irrelevant stimuli and the selection of relevant ones. This depends strongly on the availability of processing capacity or neural resources in WM systems. For example, individuals with a low WM capacity (e.g. as a result of brain damage) may be less able to select critical targets and to reject irrelevant distracters. In the context of addictive behaviours, what was previously the critical target (the drug-predictive cue) of course becomes the distracter once the goal of abstinence or restraint is set. This reversal of signals is cognitively demanding, especially on WM processes. Hester and Garavan (2005), for example, working with a nonclinical sample, showed that increasing the WM load by adding a secondary distracter task reduced control over attentional engagement and disengagement. Deficits in executive control, indexed by difficulty in task switching and inhibition, were particularly pronounced when stimulus items coincided with those in WM. These authors speculated that this could echo the experience of addicted people, who tend to maintain drug-related thoughts and images in WM. This means that attentional capture by drug-related cues will be greater if WM functioning is compromised and, at least on *a priori* grounds, enhanced WM functioning should increase attentional control.

As we have seen, procedures aimed at augmenting WM have been developed and deployed in clinical settings. The finding (Bickel *et al.*, 2011) that training aimed at bolstering WM processes contributes to reductions in DRD provides preliminary evidence that processing of the probability and value of future rewards relies in part on executive function. Recalling that DRD reflects impulsivity, this suggests that fostering cognitive control can enhance the capacity to defer gratification, a key target for therapeutic intervention in addiction.

In the following sections I shall look at other approaches that directly or indirectly target cognitive control. First, I shall briefly review recent findings using neurophysiological or neuromodulatory approaches. Next, I shall address emerging findings using pharmacological approaches aimed at accelerating deconditioning mechanisms in addiction. Finally, I shall return to the more familiar arena of cognitive behavioural approaches, selected because they are designed to facilitate a proactive, anticipatory stance that improves cognitive control.

Neurophysiological Techniques

Neural activity can be modulated using techniques such as transcranial direct current stimulation (tDCS) and transcranial magnetic stimulation (TMS) that generate transient but noninvasive interference with cortical activity. The process entails applying a low electric current to the scalp or inducing a magnetic field in order to modulate the resting potentials of underlying neural populations. Applied to areas such as the dorsolateral PFC and other PFC regions, brain stimulation has been explored as a means of reducing craving and associated impulsivity as well as enhancing core domains of cognitive control such as WM. For example, repetitive TMS to the PFC has been shown to transiently reduce cocaine craving (Camprodon *et al.*, 2007), and similarly tDCS applied to the PFC has proven effective to reduce smoking craving (Fregni *et al.*, 2008).

Interestingly, another study has shown that tDCS applied to the PFC can diminish risk-taking behaviour (Fecteau *et al.*, 2007), a finding that has implications for addiction. To date these electromagnetic techniques have been used more as investigative tools than therapeutic interventions, but a cluster of studies has shown that brain stimulation can attenuate craving and reduce nicotine or cocaine consumption at least transiently (see Feil and Zangen, 2010). tDCS has also been combined with training in WM competence, for instance with the *n*-back paradigm requiring the participant to recall, say, the second or third previous item from a list. Andrews *et al.* (2011) reported that that digit span forwards improved, but digit span backwards did not, when training using the *n*-back task was combined with tDCS with a sample of normal participants.

Prior work reviewed above has pointed to impaired function within attentional control areas in the PFC. Furthermore, there are reports of abnormal functioning in the orbitofrontal cortex (OFC), which is involved in regulating the reward value of stimuli (Roberts, 2006). It has been argued that reward systems are impaired during addiction, in that the reward value associated with the drug is far greater than the value associated with any other stimulus. Importantly, OFC has been shown to be hypoactive in addiction patients during withdrawal and hyperactive in cocaine individuals, with the degree of excitability proportional to the magnitude of their craving (Volkow *et al.*, 2001, 2004). While the current state of evidence does not justify implementing this in clinical practice, these techniques merit further evaluation and refinement. For the time being, the need to deploy the motivational, cognitive and behavioural strategies outlined here remains paramount.

Neuropsychopharmacological Approaches

There is an extensive and sometimes conflicting evidence base (see, for example Anton *et al.*, 2006) for conventional pharmacological approaches using combinations of agonists (drug-mimicking compounds such as methadone) and antagonists (compounds that blockade neuroreceptors and thus diminish the rewarding effect of self-administration of the problem drug) such as naltrexone. Compounds such as acamprosate are thought to target alcohol-related dysregulation of more than one neuroreceptor system by reducing excitatory glutamatergic processes and bolstering the neuro-inhibitory function of parts of the GABA system. Overall, the aim is to diminish the incentive of further drug use or, in the case of compounds such as disulfiram, trigger a severe aversive reaction following alcohol ingestion. These approaches can enhance outcome, particularly when deployed with the support of a life partner or significant other to ensure compliance. Conditioning accounts of habit acquisition and maintenance question overreliance on antagonists as, once acquired, habits can be relatively resistant to extinction or devaluation (see Chapter 3). The acquisitive behaviour has been 'stamped in' and will tend to maintain momentum even when anticipated reward fails to arrive. However, if blocking reward, augmenting inhibition or triggering aversion alters the computation of stimulus value in prefrontal systems, greater cognitive control could be deployed in subsequent cue exposure.

The use of compounds known to facilitate learning, in particular in areas such as habituation to or extinction of conditioned responses, resonates more closely with the cognitive control focus of this text. D-cycloserine (DCS) is a partial glutamatergic and N-methyl-D-aspartate (NMDA) receptor agonist originally developed as an antibiotic. DCS has been shown to facilitate extinction of learned fear in laboratory animals and clinically anxious people (see Norberg *et al.*, 2008, for a meta-analysis). Santa Ana *et al.* (2009), in a double-blind placebo-design pilot study, recruited 25 smokers from the general community and randomized them to DCS or placebo prior to cue-exposure therapy. Participants given DCS showed significantly reduced smoking-cue reactivity such as physiological arousal and subjective urge-to-smoke ratings following *in vivo* smoking cues. This cohort also produced significantly smaller expired carbon monoxide (CO) levels at the one-week follow-up compared with those given placebo. Somewhat disappointingly, however, exploratory analyses indicated no effect on smoking behaviour overall, although participants were not in fact trying to give up or reduce their smoking. Nonetheless, the impact on components of cue reactivity at least justifies further work in the area.

Kamboj *et al.* (2012) replicated this pilot study and found no robust reductions in cue reactivity indexed by subject ratings of craving, physiological measures of smoking behaviour. Note however that the participants were not in fact aiming to give up, instead indicating that they had an interest in cutting down or giving up, but were not currently taking steps to change their smoking behaviour. Attentional bias was measured before and after cue exposure but there was no significant reduction with either DCS or placebo. Kamboj et al. (2011), further investigated the potential of DCS to enhance habituation to alcohol cues and to reduce attentional bias in a community sample of heavy drinkers. In contrast to the work of Watson et al. (2011), significant cue reactivity and attentional bias to alcohol cues was apparent. Exposure to alcohol cues led to both within- and between-session habituation of cue reactivity, and a reduction in attentional bias to alcohol cues over time. However, there was no evidence of greater habituation in the DCS group compared with the group given a placebo in this randomized double-blind study. The DCS group showed mild subjective effects (increased contentedness and euphoria) apparently unrelated to exposure/response prevention following DCS. This raises the possibility that DCS could develop potential for misuse among clinical populations if this euphorigenic effect is robust. Watson et al. (2011), in another pilot study with a double-blind placebo design, investigated the cognitive-enhancing potential of DCS with a clinical cohort meeting the criteria for alcohol dependence. No significant difference was observed between the DCS and placebo groups on key outcome variables such as craving reports. As pointed out by the researchers, these ostensibly negative results need to be interpreted with caution, as some of the 16 participants showed low levels of cue reactivity in the first instance. It would thus have been difficult to demonstrate any added therapeutic impact of DCS as a putative cognitive enhancer.

Overall, the results from these small but well-controlled studies indicate that 'cognitive catalysts' such as DCS have not yet earned their right of passage from the laboratory to the addiction clinic. The fact that DCS did not impact on attentional processing is noteworthy, given the link between the strength of the eliciting power of drug cues and the degree of attentional bias they command (see Field and Cox, 2008). Alterations in attentional processes seem to be a reasonable criterion for by which the potency of a cognitive enhancer could be judged. By default, these essentially negative results emphasize that, for the foreseeable future, change strategies targeting cognitive and behavioural components of addiction retain their plausibility utility, if not their monopoly.

In the absence of proven neuropharmacological remedies, the focus on cognitive control as a skill that can be taught appears justified. The key proposition of this text is that WM, representing cognitive control both on a momentary and also more enduring basis, is a key target for therapeutic intervention. A corollary to this is that any therapeutic intervention that enhances or augments WM will steer the addicted individual towards recovery; conversely, those interventions that do not impact on WM will at best be neutral *apropos* outcome but could also serve to divert the client from possibly more-effective remediation. In addition to this theoretical stance, there are two further compelling reasons for focusing on controlled processes such as those subserved by WM. First, moving from the often obscure realm of the implicit and the automatic provides both therapist and client with more congenial (and accessible!) workspace. This is akin to saving an item to a desktop screen of a computer where it is readily accessible. Second, implementing and routinely using emerging techniques such as CBM or behavioural approach modification is not likely to be either rapid or widespread, judging from the generally poor performance in applying other empirically supported treatments such as CM. Here, I do not for an instant wish to discourage further development and evaluation of the techniques outlined in this chapter, whether behavioural, neurophysiological or pharmacological. In advance of such work, goal setting, rehearsal and maintenance are plausible and appear valid and acceptable to the client. The findings outlined here suggest that influencing WM processes can impact on implicit cognitive processes such as attention and, by inference, behaviour also.

8

Managing Mood

The Reciprocal Relationship Between Mood and Addiction

The *CHANGE* framework emphasizes the importance of addressing unregulated substance use as a prerequisite to addressing emotional disorder. This requires little justification, as active substance misuse renders therapeutic intervention futile. However, in the midst of longer-term therapeutic interventions addressing complex and enduring problems with compulsive substance use, emotional negativity and interpersonal relationships, both therapist and client can lose focus and direction. Mindful of this, in addition to providing a framework for assessment and formulation, the *CHANGE* algorithm provides a means of resetting the therapeutic agenda when needed. The *CHANGE* approach offers to integrate therapeutic intervention for the dual presentation of addictive and emotional disorders by focusing on cognitive control. The assumption is that impaired cognitive control contributes to the initiation and maintenance of both compulsive or addictive habits and persistent negative emotions (see Disner *et al.*, 2011). As outlined in Chapter 4, people with impulsive tendencies or personality characteristics are more liable to develop and sustain addictive behaviour patterns. However, impulsivity is a multifaceted construct and will influence cognitive and behavioural processes on a broad front. This provides added justification for bolstering cognitive control (see Chapter 7), as this could help people manage both addictive and emotional impulses. It appears at least plausible that the deficits in executive control associated with addictive disorders could also compromise efforts to regulate emotions. By implication, teaching affect regulation skills to people with addiction problems is likely to yield therapeutic gain. This input can of course be derived from extant treatment models (e.g. Witkiewitz and Marlatt, 2004). Nonetheless, the present focus on impulse control suggests that there could be a reciprocal, and beneficial, relationship between practicing self-control with regard to both appetitive impulses and emotionally driven cognitive and behavioural processes.

Within the *CHANGE* framework, habitual substance-seeking or gambling behaviour are addressed initially (see Table 6.1, an outline of the CHANGE/Four-M programme). Typically, this entails an element of repetition, given the involuntary and persistent nature of impulsivity and the rate of progress demonstrated by the client attempting to regulate this. This is why the client is always asked about episodes of substance use or impulsivity that may have occurred in the interval between sessions. By now the reader should recognize that the repetition of addictive behaviour is the norm, if not the default. Thus, even if emotional issues are top of the agenda, the status of the addictive disorder needs to be assessed and dealt with as necessary. The therapist's response to any reported lapses should be empathic and alert to the possibility of the attributional biases referred to in Chapter 5 undermining the therapeutic relationship.

In an effort to delineate the complex interactions between 'habits' and 'negative emotions' in terms of the model proposed here, this chapter will focus on three sources or pathways to negative affect associated with the development and persistence of addictive behaviours:

- pre-existing negative affect due to dispositional traits and/or exposure to adverse life events both historically and concomitant with recovery;
- negative emotions stemming from the after-effects of drug intoxication;
- negative emotions arising from setbacks or lapses when self-control fails.

These interact dynamically of course, but differentiation can inform the formulation and therapeutic intervention. As stated in the foregoing paragraphs, most or all those seeking help for addiction would benefit from an appropriate level of training in emotional control competencies. This would be regardless of whether the emotional dysregulation stems from dispositional traits of emotional negativity or exposure to adverse life experiences, both essentially pre-existing vulnerability factors on the one hand, or whether the negative affect is due to post-intoxication dysphoria (or negative affect following gambling losses), or negative emotions such as shame and guilt following a lapse to the proscribed addictive behaviour. Inevitably, this oversimplifies the situation, as these factors can interact. Rutter (2006), for example, pointed out that a genetic predisposition to antisocial behaviour can remain latent if parenting is nurturing, but become manifest if parenting or other environmental contingencies are punitive or adverse. Moreover, an individual predisposed to emotional negativity will also be prone to the negative impact of drug excess or the guilt associated with resumed drug use. There are thus compelling reasons to offer therapeutic intervention aimed at enhancing individuals' emotional control competencies, an outcome that cognitive therapy can deliver. However, the clinician and client need to correctly understand the sources of the negative affect according to the taxonomy presented here. To recap, a treatment seeker in an addiction clinic could manifest negative affect stemming from historical exposure to adversity, the presence of co-existing stress or personal problems, or the phasic impact of cycles of drug use, restraint or withdrawal cycles. Further, negativeemotions could be linked to negative self-evaluation or self-blame when restraint proves difficult or impossible and addiction re-asserts itself. Differentiating the interaction of these various sources of emotional negativity is not easy, but repeating standard measures of mood on a session-by-session basis can separate the more transient states from the more enduring ones.

Pre-existing Vulnerability to Emotional Distress

Those who have been exposed, perhaps repeatedly, to adverse or uncontrollable life events are prone to developing emotional disorders consequentially. These experiences are often linked historically to parental or familial substance misuse or mental health issues. This subgroup will typically present for treatment to a specialist addiction or mental health treatment facility as adults reporting a range of emotional, behavioural and interpersonal in addition to substance-related problems. Weaver *et al.* (2003), for example, found that, in drug-using clients in treatment for their drug (nonalcohol; $N = 216$) misuse, 75% met criteria for one or more co-occurring mental-health conditions in the year prior as follows:

- 8% psychotic disorder
- 19% severe anxiety
- 26% severe depression
- 37% personality disorder
- 40% minor or mild depression.

For people in treatment for alcohol dependence and related alcohol problems ($N = 62$), 86% met the criteria for one or more comorbid mental-health problems as follows:

- 19% psychotic disorder
- 32% severe anxiety
- 34% severe depression
- 40% minor depression
- 53% personality disorder.

Conversely, 44% of attendees at Community Mental Health facilities who were also screened for psychiatric and substance-related problems reported problematic drug and alcohol use within the previous year. Coincidentally, this epidemiological study was carried out in part in a London clinic where I worked at the time. Consistent with this, my current caseload (in another London clinic) includes individuals with social anxiety disorders, generalized anxiety, sleep disorders, posttraumatic stress disorder, obsessive–compulsive disorder, anger management problems and a spectrum of depressive conditions ranging from acute clinical depression to dysthymia. In a recent clinical audit using the *Personal Health Questionnaire-9* (PHQ-9; Kroenke *et al.*, 2001), 80% of 120 adults in local substance misuse clinics reported significant levels of anxiety and depression. 20% of these fell in the severe range as indicated by scores on the PHQ-9. These data from a locally recruited convenience sample are consistent with findings of the COSMIC study. Overall, the high level of concordance between mental-health problems and addictive disorders indicates that there is a need to offer empirically supported intervention to enable these patients to acquire emotional control strategies. The *CHANGE* model reflects the fact that these problems tend to become interdependent as part of a complex, self-perpetuating system. Accordingly, the care pathway needs to be integrated, with impulsivity and emotional distress addressed in sequence.

For example, I was recently referred Nigel, a 35-year-old man who had been sexually abused in childhood by an older sibling. His appraisal that he was complicit in this episode, which lasted over two years between the ages of 9 and 11, was associated with shame, guilt and self-loathing. As an adult in his 20s, Nigel formed a stable and loving relationship with another man who sadly died of natural causes. In the succeeding decade he did not become involved in any long-term relationships but on a weekly or near-weekly basis he engaged in brief sexual encounters with other men, invariably when he was intoxicated by alcohol and cocaine. This placed his health and personal safety at risk, as well as reactivating distorted beliefs associated with the historic sexual abuse. When intoxicated, he tended to engage in unhelpful reveries about his deceased partner, which led to depression and suicidal ideation. These problems occurred in the context of chronic insomnia. This contributed to an unhelpful dynamic whereby alcohol and cocaine were used as short-term palliatives. This led to continued mood disturbance and insomnia, but more worryingly contributed to Nigel engaging in risky sexual encounters. Nonetheless, Nigel's career went from strength to strength and over this period he was promoted to marketing manager for a multimedia company. After about 12 face-to-face sessions marked by some success but also setbacks I summed up as follows:

> I know that things have been particularly difficult for you over the past few weeks, even though you're working hard to move things on. You've also taken on an exciting but challenging role at work. So, while there are many positives I do also appreciate how complex and sometimes frustrating your emotions are. That said, I believe that we need to prioritize and focus on just two things, your willpower in the face of alcohol and cocaine and the negative feelings that often set the scene for problems in this regard.
> First, then, we need to look at ways to help you regain more control over your drinking. That really is the key because when the alcohol comes into the equation it sets the scene for more risky behaviour with cocaine and less control over the sexual impulses. It was concern about these risks that prompted you to seek out this referral a few months ago.
> Second, we need to look again at how you can manage your daily negative feelings such as shame and depression. If we agree on these priorities I am confident that we will see improvements in your quality of life, especially with regard to improved sleep. Along these lines, as an agenda for today's session I suggest we review the couple of situations you mentioned at the outset where you found yourself not really in control of your actions. I think one was your friend's birthday party and the other was that Friday night when you when you went out with the crew from work and partied until 3am.

More detailed discussion of the antecedents of Nigel's excessive use of alcohol and cocaine, which in turn were precursors to high-risk sexual behaviour, revealed the following:

- Nigel was very self-controlled for most of the week, exercising in the gym in the morning before work and meditating in the evening. Typically, he did not drink alcohol between Sunday and Thursday.

- He believed that he would be perceived as aloof or distant by his work colleagues if he did not participate in the Friday evening outings.
- He felt exhausted by the demands of his high-pressure job by the end of the week.

This exploration of the context and triggers of the problem behaviour led directly to an anticipatory coping strategy incorporating the following elements.

First, Nigel was encouraged to re-evaluate his somewhat austere lifestyle during the working week. Specifically, he identified opportunities for more social interaction during the week, for example agreeing to dine out with friends or simply go out alone to see a movie or a play in keeping with his well-developed cultural preferences.

Second, Nigel reappraised his beliefs about whether his absence from the Friday night sessions would be interpreted as some form of social exclusion. He considered that, if anything, his absence could be perceived as evidence of being socially engaged, but elsewhere! However, we agreed that occasionally, say once or twice a month, Nigel would join his colleagues for a drink. The goal was that he would only remain in the group and to have no more than two standard drinks. This was agreed in the form of an implementation intention as follows: 'If I decide to join my colleagues for a drink on a Friday evening I will make my excuses and leave after an hour'. The collateral goal of consuming no more than two alcoholic drinks was deemed to be implicit in this plan. In the course of the following six months Nigel found it easier to regulate his drinking and subsequent sexual impulsivity was reduced. There were only two episodes of alcohol excess reported, one of which was associated with risk although no harm subsequently occurred.

In keeping with the sequencing of the *CHANGE* programme, the initial focus on the management and reversal of habits paved the way to address the underlying emotional issues. As referred to above, these were associated with protracted inappropriate sexual interaction with a sibling, who was three years older than him, when he was aged 9–11. Consequential feelings of shame were mediated by Nigel's beliefs that he was complicit in this, together with guilt arising from the sensory pleasure he derived from the sexual activity. In turn, this appears to have made it more difficult for him to adjust the death of his partner, which occurred when Nigel was aged 27. Moreover, his single lifestyle created a more enabling context for the impulsive behaviour that ultimately proved to be the trigger for him to seek professional help. Nigel proved to be an excellent candidate for cognitive therapy designed to correct his faulty beliefs and attributions. For example, he re-evaluated his beliefs that assigned him culpability for what he now saw as unwanted sexual interaction that occurred in the absence of appropriate parenting or safeguarding. He recognized that this reflected a 'hindsight bias' based on the moral values of his adult persona rather than those he would have likely held as a child. The recurring episodes of sexual impulsivity served to reinforce Nigel's view of himself as morally deficient, providing further justification for targeting this as a therapeutic objective.

Negative Affect Due To Drug Effects

Individuals without pre-existing genetic or neurobiological predisposition to negative affect can nonetheless develop a prevailing negative affective state due to the effects of repeated self-administration of drugs on key neurotransmitters such as dopamine and serotonin. In Chapter 4 this was aptly characterized as 'the dark side of addiction' (Koob and Le Moal, 1997). This includes loss of motivation, dysphoria and irritability, probably rooted in alteration of function in the neurochemical systems mentioned above. Symptomatically, individuals presenting with this syndrome might be comparable to those with more established emotional comorbidity. A different formulation and treatment plan is needed in this case, with less intensive treatment required. Third, in addition to more enduring negative affect, negative emotional states can be triggered by setbacks on the road to recovery, that is, resuming drug use or emergence of compulsive behaviours such as gambling. Marlatt and Gordon (1985) described this as the 'abstinence violation affect' or 'rule violation affect'. Driven by negative attributions and cognitive errors such as labelling oneself as a failure, this negative emotional state containing elements of shame or guilt can motivate further addictive behaviour. A lapse or a slip, for example an abstinent smoker or drinker resuming smoking or drinking on one occasion, can thus spiral into a full-blown relapse. The following vignette illustrates the reciprocal relationship between affect and addiction.

Anthony is a 36-year-old man with a history of substance dependence dating back to his late teens. When I saw Anthony last month for initial assessment he was drinking alcohol episodically and excessively. He told me that two days prior to our meeting he had consumed the equivalent of 30 standard units of alcohol starting in a bar and continuing at home alone. As a child, Anthony recalled being regularly beaten by his father. He described feelings of dissociation whereby he felt 'like a piece of meat'. He said he was feeling anxious and depressed and scored 21 and 19 on the GAD-7 and PHQ-9 respectively. We agreed that the priority was for Anthony to resume abstinence from alcohol. When Anthony was seen again two weeks later his scores had reduced dramatically to 5 and 4 on the respective mood rating scales. He told me that he had stopped drinking several days after our first meeting. We explored potential targets for therapeutic intervention. Increasing self-esteem emerged as a priority. For example, Anthony tended to discount his achievements such as successfully acquiring a university degree through part-time study despite a negative emotional legacy from childhood and chronic substance misuse. This problem could be addressed using standard techniques such as maintaining a diary of positive events and attainments and correcting attributional bias that appeared to minimize his own considerable contribution to his achievements. Note that if high levels of alcohol consumption had continued an entirely different therapeutic objective – emotional regulation – would probably have been agreed. The primary anhedonic effects of substance misuse should not therefore be overlooked. In the above example the underlying vulnerability was not a primary deficit in emotional regulation skills but deficits in self-esteem and self-worth. Without doubt, these originated in the invalidating experiences of parental abuse and contributed to vulnerability to subsequent addiction.

Clearly, compromised self-esteem can contribute to emotional dysregulation but the more dramatic impact of current substance use on emotional tone should never be underestimated. Addressing underlying vulnerability will therefore be necessary but usually insufficient in pursuit of a good outcome. Negative emotional states accentuate cue reactivity and increase the incentive value of appetitive cues. Deficits in self-image or self-esteem can also engender vulnerability to substance use and dependence. Negative affect is often a precursor of resumed drug use and can also serve to exacerbate episodes of drug use by transforming a lapse into a relapse. Negative emotional states compromise cognitive control and increase competition for access to scarce resources such as working memory. Thus, an anxious individual will either perform less efficiently on a given task or have to apply more compensatory effort to obtain an outcome equivalent to that of the nonanxious performer. According to Eysenck *et al.* (2007; p. 336), 'anxiety impairs efficient functioning of the goal-directed attentional system and increases the extent to which processing is influenced by the stimulus-driven attentional system'. The cognitive-control perspective espoused here assumes that craving has a similarly compromising effect on cognitive control. Consequently, therapeutic intervention needs to reverse this, that is, increase the efficient functioning of the goal-directed attentional system and decrease the influence of the stimulus-driven system. In a word, negative emotions, and states such as craving, are taxing. In addition, craving can impair cognitive efficiency by capturing cognitive control systems such as working memory (Madden and Zwaan, 2001).

There is thus a strong case to be made for providing addicted people with an opportunity to learn emotional control strategies if they are aiming to overcome addiction. As a guide to terminology, the term 'mood' is used in the CHANGE model to signify a range of common mental-health problems where emotional distress combined with poor coping mechanisms is in evidence. While addiction is, of course, associated with a spectrum of co-morbid psychological and psychiatric disorders, anxiety and depression are either primary or secondary components in many cases. Accordingly, while the main focus of this chapter is on these common examples of negative affect, other emotions such as anger, shame or guilt are also implicated. In the following sections I shall outline a stepped-care framework for addressing emotional disorders and other mental-health problems. The rationale is that only a subset of clinic attendees will need formal or intensive psychological therapy such as CBT. Further, the decision on the level and intensity of any intervention can only be made once substance misuse has been addressed, as this is often accompanied by a significant reduction in dysphoria. Negative emotions interact dynamically with addictive behaviour.

For people recovering from addiction sudden or unexpected negative emotions can also increase liability to relapse. Anecdotally, I can think of several incidents where a parent who had made excellent progress during supervised treatment for an addictive disorder lapsed or relapsed immediately prior to a decision been made as to the suitability to resume parenting. Apprehension at facing a formal hearing about one's future as a parent is surely a candidate for triggering stress that made a lapse or relapse more likely at a critical time. Recall the study by Shiffman and Waters (2004), cited in Chapter 1, that indicated abstinent cigarette smokers were more likely to relapse after sudden upsetting incidents such as an argument with a partner rather than more enduring negative affect prevailing in the days prior.

Stuart, a 35-year-old man with a history of intensive alcohol use to the point of dependence who sustained abstinence for 10 weeks following detoxification in an inpatient unit is a case in point. He was also on extended leave from work in order to address his alcohol problems and appeared highly motivated and committed to remaining abstinent. Stuart did not report any adverse or traumatic events in childhood, adolescence and adulthood. He said he had enjoyed childhood and loved sports. There was no evidence of concurrent emotional or psychiatric disorder. He had separated from his girlfriend by mutual agreement because of his drinking. They met to discuss their future and an argument ensued. Joe thought that it was too early for them to resume the relationship and he felt pressured. He became angry and reported thoughts such as 'I'll show her' (Stuart explained that this meant he thought she did not realize how much of a struggle it was for him to remain abstinent and how vulnerable to relapse he was) and within the hour had purchased 24 cans of lager and proceeded to drink.

The next day, he awoke from an alcohol induced sleep on his sofa feeling physically and emotionally devastated. His thoughts on this occasion focused on failure: 'I've blown it; despite all my hard work I screwed things up again'. He described his mood as depressed, ashamed, angry (at himself) and anxious that he might have a neurological seizure of the type he had previously experienced. He felt too ashamed to contact the Treatment Centre to speak to me or his key-worker. He went to the refrigerator and retrieved one of the few remaining cans of beer and drank it. He then bought more lager and drank it but then stopped the following day. He continued to be negative and despairing and resumed drinking the following weekend. He became very fearful that he would have an alcohol withdrawal seizure. He contacted the emergency services claiming he was suicidal, although his main concern was acute alcohol withdrawal problems. He was admitted to hospital, where he received medical attention. He subsequently re-engaged with the Treatment Centre and the opportunity to reflect on the course of events arose. Clearly, a range of negative emotions influenced the course of events at critical stages. Anger was instrumental in the first lapse, with more negative affect such as depression, shame and anxiety being subsequently implicated.

So, bearing in mind that resources are always constrained, what is the best way to respond to the somewhat diverse needs of the community of treatment-seeking people with addictions? On the one hand, perhaps the majority of clinic attendees will have more transient emotional distress possibly linked to recent substance misuse and associated psychological and social problems. On the other hand, a significant minority will have more established and probably chronic emotional disorders that need more intensive psychological or pharmacological treatment. This will include individuals characterized as having personality disorders. In a substance-misuse setting, common problems that I have encountered include high levels of impulsivity or dissocial behaviour and chronic emotional instability, often accompanied by a propensity to self-harm and expression of suicidal impulses and actions. Here, I do not intend to focus particularly on these complex presenting problems. I would, however, point out that acquiring the emotional regulation skills profiled as part of the *CHANGE* programme is likely to confer some benefit on people with these more enduring difficulties.

In the UK, albeit in more general health and mental-health rather than substance misuse settings, the answer to this question has been to instigate a system of 'stepped care', which essentially attempts to calibrate the level and intensity of therapeutic intervention to the chronicity and severity of the presenting problem. A graduated response such as this will be familiar to many in the addiction-treatment community, as addictive disorders vary considerably in chronicity and intensity. As the *CHANGE* framework is designed for those with more severe addictive disorders but variable degrees of associated emotional or mental-health problems, the stepped-care approach is more relevant to the latter.

Stepped Care for Addiction

Stepped care is a cost-effective and parsimonious system that calibrates the level and intensity of intervention to the severity of the presenting problem. In the context of substance misuse, where emotional tone fluctuates widely, it is important to have a measured response, usually beginning with a less intensive intervention. Because of the dysphoria associated with excessive use of alcohol and other drugs, it is also important to assess emotional functioning longitudinally. This is of course one of the tenets of the *CHANGE* approach, which invariably addresses substance use in advance of emotional disorder. So when can an authentic judgement be made regarding an individual's mental health or emotional status? There is no simple cut-off point, but clinical judgement would suggest that, at the very earliest, any medication used for detoxification (such as benzodiazepines) should have been discontinued. In most cases however clinical judgement will inform the decision based on factors such as the personal history, for instance exploring vulnerability factors or a possible history of mental-health problems preceding any current substance issues. If it seems clear that substance misuse is the primary problem relatively little intervention is required to augment emotional control. For example, if there is a clear link between the experience of anger and alcohol use, anger management strategies need to be identified and implemented. What needs to be borne in mind however is that the primary therapeutic objective is to regulate the impulsive alcohol use in the first instance. Viewing the anger as the *primary* focus of therapy can detract from this.

Interventions aimed at improving emotional regulation should be routinely offered to those aiming to overcome addiction. The *CHANGE* model ensures that this is delivered as part of a formulated treatment plan, and consequential to tackling addictive impulses. A 'stepped-care' approach is proposed, in keeping with recent developments in the United Kingdom aimed at improving access to psychological therapies to the general population. The aim of stepped care is to apply the principle of optimal intervention. This means that the individual gets no less and indeed no more therapeutic intervention than required. In practice, this usually means that briefer, less intense interventions such as guided self-help procedures are deployed in the first instance. In the event of a good therapeutic response, this could be sufficient, but in many cases intervention would need to be 'stepped up', say to a more formal cognitive therapy protocol, or other approaches such as pharmacotherapy.

A guiding principle of the *CHANGE* approach is that restraint or stability needs to be attained in relation to substance misuse in advance of engaging in therapeutic intervention to address pre-existing or co-morbid mental-health problems. Some years ago, a 35-year-old woman had developed posttraumatic stress disorder (PTSD) stemming from experiences of being sexually abused as a child. She was also a daily excessive drinker with features of alcohol dependence. She was attending my clinic to address her alcohol problems but was seeing a clinical psychologist in a neighbouring mental-health team to address the psychological problems such as PTSD. It emerged from her weekly 'drink diaries' detailing alcohol consumption that her heaviest drinking days occurred following therapy for her PTSD. Her way of coping with the upsetting emotions evoked by revisiting her traumatic past in therapy was to drink excessively. While this perhaps illustrates uncoordinated care planning as much as anything else, it does serve to emphasize the importance of achieving stability or abstinence in the face of unregulated substance misuse before embarking on more intensive therapeutic intervention.

An Integrated Approach to Addressing Negative Emotion

Those who remain emotionally distressed following detoxification or stabilization, having been offered interventions such as guided self-help, could be considered for more intensive therapy based on cognitive behavioural principles. The unified protocol (UP; Allen *et al.*, 2008) is based on evidence that apparently diverse mood disorders such as depression and anxiety share elements of a common aetiology and similar latent structure. In the *CHANGE* model, with its emphasis on more generic negative affect, the UP approach slots neatly into a means of addressing the third 'M', managing mood. The UP model also shares common assumptions with the *CHANGE* account in relation to the complex origins of addictive disorders and associated emotional distress. Specifically, the UP model is based on the notion of 'triple vulnerability' (Suarez *et al.*, 2009) derived from the following interacting vulnerability factors or diatheses (See Figure 5.1):

- genetic loading contributing to neurobiological vulnerability;
- exposure to adversity in childhood and at early developmental stages;
- subsequent exposure to negative life events.

The development of emotional disorder in adulthood (in the present context presumed to be comorbid with addictive disorders) is at least partly influenced by interaction of genetic, developmental context and more specific environmental events, most likely occurring at a later developmental stage such as adulthood. According to Suarez *et al.*, the genetic predisposition is similar to emotional instability or neuroticism in classic personality trait theory. Opting for a trait or dimensional model of negative affect highlights common components of conditions where either anxiety or depression are the predominant emotion. Importantly, from a therapeutic standpoint a unified approach enables therapist and client to be guided by a common protocol regardless of the diagnostic label that could be applied. Accordingly, the UP is divided into four main components intended to be delivered sequentially. Treatment emphasizes emotional processing by, for example, exposure to situational, internal and somatic (interoceptive) cues designed to provoke emotion expression as well as by way of standard mood inductions. It is designed to be delivered within a maximum of 15 one-hour individual treatment sessions and in the following components.

1. *Psychoeducation* about emotions, emphasizing their intrinsic functional nature but tendency to become oversensitive in the face of adversity.

2. *Alteration of antecedent cognitive misappraisals*, of which there are two main categories. The first of type of misappraisal is 'probability overestimation', for example a socially anxious person predicting that it is highly likely that nobody would speak to them at a forthcoming birthday party. The second, linked, characteristic misappraisal serves to distort the impact of the negative prophecy, in effect catastrophizing the situation. In tandem, these evaluations promote avoidance and are key targets for cognitive reappraisal.

3. *Prevention of emotional avoidance*. Allen *et al*. refer to three general categories of emotional avoidance strategies, viewed as any technique used by patients to reduce or prevent emotional arousal:

- *Subtle behavioural avoidance*, such as procrastination or avoiding eye contact. 'Self-medication' with substances such as alcohol or psychoactive drugs such as diazepam can also be a means of emotional avoidance. In the *CHANGE* model the assumption is that this substance-based emotional avoidance would be revealed early on in the therapeutic intervention along with other habitual behaviours.
- *Cognitive avoidance* such as thought suppression; a person with PTSD distracting themselves from reminders of the trauma; a depressed person ruminating.
- *Safety signals* such as carrying a bottle of water or anxiolytic medication to possibly forestall dryness of the mouth in the event of anxious arousal.

4. *Modification of emotion-driven behaviours*. Emotion-driven behaviours (EDBs) are action tendencies associated with particular emotions. Ultimately, EDBs serve to avoid complete processing of the emotion with which they are associated. For example, an individual with

exaggerated fear of criticism in the event of making a mistake would engage in perfectionistic behaviour at work, or a socially phobic individual would contrive to leave a social situation in advance of any anxious arousal. Hypervigilance for repeatedly seeking medical advice for trivial unexplained symptoms can also be classified as EDBs. The therapeutic response entails working with the patient to identify EDBs and replace them with incompatible responses. Thus, the hypervigilant individual would be taught how to focus attention or to relax or meditate, and the depressed person whose EDB is social withdrawal would be encouraged to engage in behavioural activation.

Throughout any intervention aimed at alleviating emotional distress, the therapist needs to be aware of the risk of relapse, and needs to closely monitor the first component of the *CHANGE* model: changing habits and ensuring that this is sustained. The therapist also needs to be alert to the possibility that emotions evoked in the therapeutic space might themselves act as precursors to addictive impulses. A few minutes spent at the end of each session evaluating the emotional impact is a good investment. The UP model described above is one of many tried and tested approaches to helping people overcome emotional disorder. Therapists and treatments therefore have considerable choice in this regard. In the following section I provide examples in order to illustrate typical presenting problems in therapeutic responses of varying focus and intensity.

Example 1

Jerry, a 36-year-old man, acquired the alcohol dependence syndrome. His alcohol problems caused him significant problems at work and in his relationships. When I saw him after he completed a detoxification there were no sensitizing or vulnerability factors in his background. He described a happy and well-adjusted childhood with loving parents, a happy school life and enthusiasm for sports. When referred for routine psychological review he was three weeks abstinent from alcohol and scoring moderately on the standard measure of anxiety. He attributed this to financial worries and uncertainty about returning to his job. He had mild sleeping difficulties and occasionally felt frustrated and mildly depressed when he experienced strong craving for alcohol. In this case, about four to six sessions of CBT (Jerry was also attending a relapse prevention group) was considered sufficient to address his emotional concerns and sleep-related difficulties. This was augmented by use of a guided self-help internet resource.

Example 2

I recently assessed Tracey, a 28-year-old woman who appears to have developed an anxiety disorder following repeated episodes of excessive alcohol consumption. Initially, she would wake following heavy drinking bouts with a feeling of intense dread and no recall of what she had done or said the previous evening. Once or twice she had caused disturbances, and on one occasion been arrested by the police, but not charged, apparently for her own safety. In this case exploration of her personal history revealed nothing of note, with an apparently happy, emotionally secure childhood, subsequent completion of further education and embarking on a career that has, thus far, been successful. The formulation we devised suggested that mild-to-moderate withdrawal effects of alcohol, combined with rumination on what might have happened while intoxicated, led to Tracey acquiring an anxiogenic cognitive style. This led her to interpret previously neutral situations, such as meeting her colleagues or her boss, as potentially very threatening. To complete the circle, Tracey would fantasize about when she could have her next drink, as she knew that this would alleviate her distress. Further assessment revealed issues such as unrelenting standards, perfectionism and sensitivity to criticism that may have contributed to Tracey's difficulties. While this does not detract from the very clear link between acute intoxication and the development of an anxiety disorder in the absence of other risk factors, in terms of stepped care it suggests that further cognitive restructuring would be beneficial. This could elicit underlying assumptions perhaps bearing on the implications of being criticized or core beliefs focusing on being perfect.

Example 3

Next is an example from another typical clinical encounter, this time with Patrick, a 58-year-old man describing intense emotions such as anger, anxiety and depression in the context of alcohol dependence. Here, as well as a more established history of alcohol dependence, there is also clear evidence of vulnerability to the point of emotional trauma in the personal history. This is an outline of the formulation.

Patrick 58	Situational or developmental	Substance specific
Origins (family and developmental)	Father died when Patrick was 11. Mother depressed and unable to cope. Died when Patrick was 16, making him homeless. Onset of social anxiety disorder.	Father heavy drinker (possible genetic loading). Culture (Ireland).
Origins (adult traumas and experiences)	Becoming homeless as adult; brother and sister seeing him in dishevelled homeless state.	
Mechanisms	Safety behaviours; avoidance; rumination; NATs*: 'They know I'm homeless' > anger and shame; '40 years on and I've nothing to show for it' > depression	Inhibiting effects of alcohol on social and general anxiety. NATs/expectancies: 'Alcohol helps me sleep; alcohol helps me cope with social situations'.
Problem	General anxiety and social anxiety disorder. Isolation.	Alcohol dependence; chronic daily alcohol excess.
Problem	Depression, self-loathing, frustration.	Salience of alcohol seeking; reinforced both positively and negatively.

*NATs, negative automatic thoughts.

Summary of formulation. Childhood was spent in rural Ireland. Patrick's father worked away from home, leaving him in the care of his mother, who appears to have been depressed. His father died when Patrick was 11 and his mother found it even harder to cope. She was not apparently a loving parent and it is possible that Patrick encoded these experiences of emotional deprivation as evidence of failure and inadequacy on his part. His mother died when he was 16, leaving him alone in the family house, being five years younger than his closest sibling. He remembered being lonely and unable to cope for a year or two before he moved to London and got a clerical job. At work and in his shared accommodation Patrick believed he was regarded as an 'outsider' and 'different' in some way. He recalled a friend looking at him almost 40 years earlier and looking away, which he interpreted as rejection and evidence that he was unwanted. Patrick felt unable to commit to intimate relationships and progressively isolated himself from others unless he was drinking alcohol. He became dependent on alcohol, lost his job and became episodically homeless throughout his life. Currently, Patrick's tendency to isolate himself and avoid social interaction, often involving alcohol excess, is preventing him from taking advantage of efforts to provide him with independent accommodation outside the hostel setting.

When I first saw Patrick he had completed a residential detoxification but had resumed drinking, albeit at a much more reduced level. His self-monitoring sheets indicated that he was drinking about 10 units of alcohol three to four times per week. These episodes were associated with meeting other residents at the hostel where Patrick had lived for about a year. He described a pervasive sense of anxiety that did not appear linked to any obvious triggers, although this reduced when he continued alcohol and when he isolated himself in his room. Patrick was overtly self-critical and disparaging about himself. In session he said 'look at me: nearly 60 years of age and I'm living in a hostel. I've just worried and drank all my life, I'm a failure. I've never been happy'. It was impossible not to be moved by this dignified, amiable and pleasant man discounting his entire adult life, and blaming himself for the misfortune he had experienced.

From a more clinical perspective, it is clear that Patrick would benefit from a reappraisal of the grossly distorted beliefs that appear to be fuelling his negative emotion and in turn motivating his drinking. In session, it proved relatively easy to guide Patrick to re-evaluate some of his self-critical beliefs. Thus, he was able to recall periods of his life when he was happy: for instance, in his early 20s he spent a year travelling in India. Even though this enabled him to remain somewhat reclusive, he readily embraced the peripatetic lifestyle. Patrick also conceded that he had recently made some good decisions, such as agreeing to a detoxification and engaging in the follow-up programme. By the end of the session he said he felt better, having found it helpful to express his feelings and reflect on things. He agreed to keep a record of more intense negative emotions in the coming week, paying particular attention to the thoughts that accompanied these experiences.

We next looked at setting realistic goals for Patrick's alcohol consumption in the coming week. Note that, given the history of dependent-type drinking, abstinence from alcohol was indicated, but Patrick did not consider this attainable. The first step was to identify an alternative behavioural goal that could compete with drinking or at least reduce the likelihood of seeking and consuming alcohol. Two options emerged. First, Patrick was an avid moviegoer and had located a small cinema that offered reduced rates to benefit claimants. However, he tended to go to the cinema in the afternoons, leaving the evenings free and increasing the likelihood of drinking. Second, I was already aware that Patrick tended to go for long walks lasting an hour or more. He began to do this years earlier as a means of managing his pervasive anxiety. Again, Patrick did not tend to drink alcohol before beginning these walks. In the coming week we agreed that Patrick would attend the cinema in the evenings rather than the afternoons. This cost slightly more but we calculated that it was just a little more than a can of his favourite lager. We then formulated the plan in the form of an implementation strategy: 'When I go to the cinema on Tuesday and Thursday I will go in the evening rather than the afternoon'. Next, it was agreed that Patrick would take a long walk on the evenings that he did not go to the cinema. This was not formulated as an implementation strategy but as a straightforward behavioural goal. This was in an effort to ensure that Patrick would be able to focus on the primary implementation strategy.

None of this is a departure from conventional cognitive behaviour therapy, involving cognitive reappraisal within session, self-monitoring and behavioural goals or assignments between sessions. However, the rationale for providing explicit goals is clarified and amplified. According to the model outlined in this text, what occupies working memory influences attentional deployment in a top-down manner. By default, goals linked to substance satiation will prevail in working memory (see p.58 above) and need to be supplanted by alternative goals. Accordingly, investing time and effort in identifying and rehearsing goals in session is an important means of influencing the downregulation of cognitive biases. As we have seen, cognitive biases, given free rein, will ensure that appetitive cues are detected and escorted to working memory. Concluding a session with an agreed, attainable and memorable goal that is inimical to substance procurement for the client is a good ending.

9

Maintaining Change

Relapse Prevention Strategies from a Neurocognitive Perspective

Automatic or implicit tendencies, specifically the acquisitive responses at the core of addiction, take time to develop but are slower to decay. Moreover, because of their capacity to operate without conscious awareness or insight, these action tendencies and cognitive biases can be latent vulnerability factors to the reinstatement of addictive behaviour months or years after cessation. In this chapter, I shall first explore the chronicity of addiction from a neurocognitive perspective. As will be seen, addiction casts a long shadow because of the enduring nature of changes to neural reward circuitry linked to a highly repetitive cycle of reward seeking. The following sections explore the implications for treatment planning in a context where on the one hand automatic processing of motivational cues is facilitated, and on the other executive – in particular inhibitory – control is compromised in the longer term.

The chronic nature of cognitive deficits

Clearly, in phases of active substance use, intoxication and withdrawal, inhibitory control is compromised. However, findings that changes to PFC connectivity and structure can endure for periods ranging from 6–9 months to 6 years in, for example, alcohol-dependent people who are largely abstinent have direct implications for the delivery of treatment. Thus, detoxified men with an average of over 26 weeks abstinence and with otherwise good psychosocial functioning can nonetheless register loss of grey matter in neural structures involved in higher cognitive function (Chanraud *et al.*, 2007). Morphological changes were highest in the DLPFC (up to 20%), but were noted also in the temporal cortex, insula, thalamus and cerebellum. Makris *et al.* (2008) used a broadly similar approach, except that the alcohol-dependent cohort had been abstinent for almost 6 years. They noted volumetric reductions in neural regions associated with reward processing including the right DLPFC, right anterior insula, right nucleus accumbens and left amygdala. These correlated with performance on a working memory task (Wechsler, 1997), suggesting a functional deficit linked to observed structural changes, while amygdala volume correlated with general memory (Wechsler, 1997). Furthermore, nucleus accumbens and anterior insula volumes improved in alcoholic subjects with increasing length of abstinence, suggesting some potential recovery of structural deficits. This coheres with findings from one of the few studies that followed up a community sample of men, over a quarter of whom met the DSM-111 criteria for alcohol abuse at some point in their lives. Vaillant (1996) found that between 28 and 59% of these men, representing a lesser-educated 'core-city' and Harvard-educated cohort respectively, were still abusing alcohol at age 60 after up to 20 years biennial follow-up interviews. 11 and 30% of each group was abstinent. Notwithstanding the interesting finding that the 'city men' appeared to recover at a much higher rate than the 'college men', Vaillant noted that after abstinence had been maintained for five years relapse was rare. It seems plausible that, over several years, increasingly effective cognitive control was both supported by and in turn benefitted from recovering brain function.

Volumetric reductions in grey matter, in the region of 5–11%, have also been observed with other addictions such as cocaine (Franklin *et al.*, 2002) and heroin (Yuan *et al.* 2009). These structural changes in temporal and cingulate cortical regions were observed, it should be noted, after several months of abstinence. The cohort of 30 long-term heroin users of Yuan *et al.* had been verifiably abstinent when the density of their grey matter was measured and compared with healthy controls. Moreover, the duration of heroin use inversely correlated with reductions in grey matter indicated by voxel-based morphometry. The ecological or 'real-world' impact of the subtle loss of function associated with these morphological changes is open to further investigation. However, given the need for executive control when habits are reversed, any loss of function does not bode well for recovery. In addition to the inhibitory mechanisms vital to overcoming addictive impulses, 'prefrontal' processes also include

- emotion regulation
- motivation, indexed by persistence and sustained effort

- insight and interoceptive awareness
- flexible deployment of attention
- decision making and encoding of value (including impaired reward devaluation)
- working memory and goal maintenance
- learning and memory processes such as stimulus–response learning and reward.

Existing cognitive and behavioural approaches to overcoming addiction do not acknowledge the likely negative impact of enduring cognitive impairment on the capacity of the client to process information within session and between sessions. Relapse prevention skills training and allied coping skills approaches proceed, no doubt with the best of intentions, to teach those aiming for abstinence or restraint a range of complex skills. In predominantly cognitive approaches, the person seeking help for addiction is expected to engage and collaborate in the complex process of change at the same level expected of an anxious or depressed individual. While anxiety and depression clearly interfere with cognitive processing, the affected individual does not have the possible pre-existing or consequential range of cognitive control deficits associated with addiction. Many of the procedures that form the basis of CBT are heavily reliant on executive functioning. Anticipating 'high-risk' situations and deploying problem-solving strategies require key 'prefrontal' competencies such as flexibility in response to changing task requirements, monitoring and updating progress in terms of goal pursuit and suppressing or inhibiting distractions. Granted, extant cognitive and behavioural approaches might compensate for possible cognitive deficiencies insofar as they embody a coaching or mentoring function. However, clients with more intensive or lifelong histories of substance use might struggle to acquire and apply new ways of thinking and behaving, particularly if this is not acknowledged by the therapist and remains unknown to the client.

Apart from directly affecting the ability to acquire and deploy new skills, underlying problems in the cognitive control domain could serve to undermine the therapeutic alliance. In common with implicit cognitive processes, it is the latency of these deficits that challenges the maintenance of change. The cohort of 31 detoxified alcohol-dependent men of Chanraud et al. (2007) were apparently functioning normally in the psychosocial domain. However, they displayed deficits on some neuropsychological tests and of course manifested volumetric reductions in grey matter primarily in the DLPFC and other cortical structures. It should also be recalled that pre-existing deficits in executive control could have been reflected in the anatomical or neuropsychological findings in this study, but the design does not allow for this to be revealed. In sum, maintaining change, here involving repeated suppression of impulses previously given free rein, is undermined by the perseverance of deficits in cognitive control. It appears that cognitive-control deficits that may have increased liability to addiction in the first instance do not simply go away once the treatment plan is signed.

The Importance of Goal Maintenance in the Long Term

In Chapters 3 and 4, I emphasized how exposure to drug-associated rewards can grossly distort the pursuit and valuation of normal rewards in two ways. First, the intensity and contingency of substance-derived gratification competes with, and often achieves ascendancy over, natural rewards such as eating, drinking, sex and social affiliation. However, recalling the experience of Gerald, when drugs such as cocaine become associated with sexual gratification the latter can become compulsive also. Second, even when the initial euphoria no longer ensues, strong stimulus–response learning ensures that the cue will still tend to elicit the response.

The more neurobiological emphasis here is based on evidence of the relatively enduring changes in neural processes as addiction becomes less outcome driven and more stimulus driven. In other words, choice and volition play less of a role as addiction becomes more established. A partial answer is revealed in the following anecdote recounted by one of my clients, Craig, the 37-year-old man with a history of addiction to cocaine and alcohol introduced on p. 120, who described the following episode that occurred after 20 months of abstinence from alcohol and cocaine: 'I found myself on my bike like I was possessed, cycling along the road where the house I used to go to [to buy cocaine] was'. I asked Craig if he could recall anything else was going through his mind at the time. He recalled the following thoughts: 'what am I doing'; 'this is dangerous'; 'this feels almost nostalgic'. One striking feature of these statements is the passive or observer-like status of the statements. It seemed as if Craig was watching himself carrying out a complex sequence of behaviours that he was unable to disrupt. Moreover, the rather dissociated sequence of thoughts did not seem to fulfil any functional role in mediating behaviour. For example, Craig did not recall thinking that he might feel better, worse or even differently if he used. Predictably, the episode of drug use that ensued left

Craig impoverished financially and bereft emotionally. He had, as he saw it, left himself down after sustaining abstinence for almost two years. In an effort to reassure and empathize with him I responded as follows:

> You have done really well with your recovery programme so far. What happened to the weekend is unfortunately a common occurrence when we try to overcome in addiction to a drug like cocaine. What seems to happen is that, while the rational and sensible part of you fully recognizes the need to abstain, another part of you, let's say the more impulsive or emotional parts of your brain, still has not got the 'quit' message. This is not a particularly clever part of your brain but what it lacks in intellect it makes up for in persistence! If you're feeling tired or stressed, which I know you were because of your forthcoming job interview, your impulsive brain can take advantage and get in the driving seat. What I suggest we do next in the session is a debrief about what was happening with you before you found yourself on the way to the crack house....

Craig engaged with the task of identifying the antecedents of his lapse and the session progressed well. He did not have any difficulty with the idea that impulsivity could be expressed behaviourally even though he was fully committed to overcoming his addiction. I believe that invoking a role for involuntary mental processes enabled me to provide a more nuanced version of the lapse reported by Craig. First, more accurate empathy was possible by acknowledging the existence of an impulsive system that remained influential despite his commitment to abstinence. Second, Craig was less likely to make the attributional error of blaming himself for the lapse. Finally, it is worth noting that Craig was reporting incidents of attentional bias, for example the 'silver paper' incident described in Chapter 7, even though he had been abstinent for 18 months at this point. As one of his between session tasks I asked Craig to read a copy of the Six Tips relapse prevention handout (see Appendix). The extent to which this cognitive bias subsequently contributed to the lapse into cocaine use remains a matter of speculation. However, it is consistent with the findings of Cox et al. (2002) that the strength of attentional bias following detoxification predicted liability to relapse.

A Neurocognitive Perspective on Relapse

Steve, a 37-year-old builder, was one of my clients who had sustained abstinence from alcohol for five months when attending a day programme and individual sessions of cognitive therapy, recently returned to work after an absence of six months. In the week prior to his return to work he reported only one episode of craving or compulsion. Two weeks following his return to work he attended for the scheduled follow-up session. He described experiencing high levels of craving and compulsion on his return from work each evening. Steve lived alone, having agreed on a temporary separation from his partner while he addressed his alcohol and related problems. He described the recurring compulsions as 'exhausting'. His coping strategy was to retire to bed about 9 p.m., shortly after eating his evening meal. Prior to returning to work he was maintaining a good daily routine involving exercise such as swimming, running and attending a local gym. Steve also enjoyed cooking and watching DVDs, especially at weekends. After a day at work he believed that he did not have the energy for this, hence the early bedtime. Steve was also heavily indebted due to his alcohol problems.

As his recovery progressed he duly returned to work. His creditors increased their demands for payment and Steve was particularly angry about one demand for rapid payment from a utility company. He described being preoccupied with this, especially when he returned home and opened his mail. Looking at Figure 4.3, Steve appears to be in the top right quadrant with low working-memory capacity and low perceptual load. This is because he was ruminating about his debts (thus absorbing available working-memory capacity) and not engaging in any pursuits that might be stimulating (approximating to a low perceptual load). This provides a formulation for the resurgence of craving and compulsion in the absence of any available triggers or cues in his workplace or in his apartment, which was devoid of alcohol. It also provides a rationale for agreeing on a coping strategy. In the session, we agreed that Steve could accept a ride home from work with a colleague, thus avoiding a 40-minute walk that was his normal routine. This meant that he would be at home earlier, feel less tired and thus be able to either attend the gym or go jogging. The combined effect of these activities would be to free working-memory capacity and increase perceptual loading, in effect moving Steve to the top left quadrant. At a recent six-month review I was delighted to learn that Steve had been abstinent from alcohol since this episode, apart from a relatively minor lapse. He also told me that he had left his job as a building worker and was getting help with longstanding literacy difficulties and planning a career in the personal-fitness industry. Clearly, it is impossible to attribute his progress to any particular factor, but the example illustrates that successful recovery needs to proceed on a number of fronts and at different levels. And it takes time.

Any competent therapist would doubtless derive a similar or comparable strategy. However, the cognitive, formulation-based approach outlined here provides a rationale not immediately apparent from existing CBT or other approaches. More generally, working-memory function could be facilitated by strategies such as goal maintenance or goal rehearsal and implementation intentions. Perceptual loading can be augmented by identifying activities, for example computer games; reading; creative pursuits, that 'soak up' attentional capacity that might otherwise be diverted to process addictive cues. But what if there are constraints such as being at work or sitting on a train? Mindfulness meditation appears to be a plausible option insofar as it presumably increases perceptual load. For example, consider this segment from the *Awareness of Seeing* mindfulness exercise from Bowen et al. (2011; p. 102) and derived from Segal et al. (2002):

> Sit or stand in a way that you can comfortably see out the window. Take a few moments to look outside, noticing all the different sites. The colours, the different textures, the shapes. For the next few minutes just see if you can let go of trying to make sense of things in the way that we usually do instead, see if you can see them as merely patterns, shapes, and movement.

According to the theoretical account proposed here, one way in which mindfulness can increase focus and reduce distraction is by increasing the vibrancy and texture of the perceptual world by simply paying attention. Mindfulness training can help individuals become more aware of these processes. The acronym RAIN (recognize, accept, investigate and note) can be applied to foster detached mindfulness of cravings, and as a way to encourage individuals to disengage from habitual or automatic responding. Meditation techniques are addressed in more detail on p.168.

Twelve-Step Facilitation Therapy

The defining feature of the Twelve-Step doctrine must surely be the repetition of the same message followed by sequential recovery steps. Commonly, an individual participating in the 12 steps would attend a meeting with perhaps 20 or more individuals attempting to manage their addiction on a daily basis. Some attend more than one meeting each day. Pursuit of this recovery pathway can begin with 90 meetings in 90 days and continue, on a daily or near daily basis, for many years. Throughout, participants acknowledge the chronicity of their addiction and the requirement to address this on a daily basis or, in the terminology of the Fellowship, 'one day at a time'. Viewed through a cognitive-control prism, one is again struck by the repetitious nature of the message. This robust goal maintenance, reinforced by rehearsal, is likely to guide cognitive processing and behavioural governance.

Implicit Denial

Consider the following anecdote from a recent clinical encounter. The client was Simon, a 46-year-old man with a 20-year history of intensive alcohol consumption. Simon was a highly educated man with a PhD in history. Unfortunately, his successful academic career was undermined by his escalating alcohol consumption over the years. This had also had a negative effect on his health and interpersonal relationships. He had, somewhat reluctantly, accepted that abstinence from alcohol was the best option for him. In the course of our fourth session he announced that he had been invited to spend a week with some friends in France. The following section illustrates how Simon had rationalized his addiction to alcohol as a matter of choice, negating the implicit assumptions that guided his decision making. At this stage he had maintained abstinence from alcohol for over nine weeks following the completion of an inpatient detoxification. My aim was to encourage him to select goals other than alcohol consumption. This is what he said next:

SIMON: I think it's going to be very difficult for me not to drink when I'm in France. I keep thinking of a cold glass of Chardonnay. Ultimately, despite what they say in AA, I think it is a matter of free choice. I have chosen not to drink for over two months therefore I should be able to choose to have a drink when I go to France. I then intend to choose not to drink when I return to London.

THERAPIST: I am glad that you brought this issue to today's session. You've done very well not drinking for the past couple of months or so. We agreed last week that there had been significant improvements in your mood, health and general wellbeing. But I can well understand that thoughts about drinking are never too far away, especially when you are reminded of times when maybe drinking seemed more like fun. Can you tell me a little bit more about your dilemma about drinking?

S: Well, when I received the invitation to spend some time in France, I started thinking about wine. You see, I don't really buy into the idea that alcohol, or any other addiction for that matter, is a disease involving loss of willpower. I chose not to drink a while ago and I fully accept that I needed to, but equally I feel I should be able to choose to have a drink, especially when I am in a different environment, and with friends who drink sensibly.

T: I see. Your point is that you have chosen not to do something so by the same token you should be able to choose freely to do it again.

S: Yeah, something like that.

T: My view is that in general we can exercise free choice in many areas, for example deciding what to wear or where to go to lunch. The picture with addictive drugs such as alcohol is more complicated. It appears that once we've been overexposed to alcohol, as we know you have in the past, it seems to bias or distort how we view the world. This can alter the way we make decisions, specifically guiding us back to further drinking.

S: In what way?

T: What actually happened here is that you were invited to spend a week in France with some old friends. Your response, or what seems to be the most obvious response, was to reflect on the remembered pleasures of alcohol and re-evaluate your decision to quit drinking. I know that in the minds of many France is associated with fine wines but there is much more to France than wine! For the sake of argument, can you mention something else about France?

S: Of course, France is the home of haute cuisine and a centre of culture and the arts. It is a large country with beautiful cities and landscapes. It also has a range of climate – which helps make such good wine! Seriously, I think I'm beginning to see what you're getting at. I'm also meeting up with old friends who I haven't seen for years, so perhaps there is more to this trip than just wine after all.

T: I fully agree. My point is how quickly you interpreted this invitation as an opportunity to resume drinking. By planting that thought or goal in your mind, the likelihood of you drinking again is increased. Going back to the issue of free will I would say that, while you are still a free agent, the range of options you have arrived at has at the very least

	restricted your free will. Instead of a wide range of options it seems to have narrowed down to a question of 'to drink or not to drink'. I would suggest that, paradoxically, choosing to drink when you visit France demonstrates a *lack* of free will rather than the expression of free choice.
S:	You mean that I reduced my options and my room for manoeuvre. But what should I do now?
T:	First, you need to recognize that you have not made a mistake or done anything wrong: it's just your mind doing what it is trained to do, or what you have become used to doing! For many years seeking out alcohol was the thing to do, so that is the 'default'. The best way to manage the situation now is to identify other goals, especially ones that you will find engaging or rewarding. Any ideas?
S:	Well, I've never been to the top of the Eiffel tower, and I will be only a hour away from Paris by train. I also want to see some modern art in Paris, and of course check out some restaurants.

COMET: continuous outcome monitoring while engaged in treatment

In the *CHANGE* model, outcome is continuously monitored (i.e. session by session) across two central domains: addiction and emotional wellbeing or absence of distress. The latter domain is clearly the more diverse and likely to encompass numerous specific indicators of therapeutic gain such as improved quality and quantity of sleep, less anger or more harmonious relationships. For the most part these issues are linked to, or indeed index, emotional dysregulation. For example, recall Kevin, the 47-year-old man introduced in Chapter 6, who reported chronic problems with low mood, worrying and insomnia. He initially progressed with a significant decrease in frequency and intensity of excessive alcohol binges. From a baseline of 20–30 units two to three times a week, with examples of more restrained drinking in evidence also, Kevin constrained himself to about 3–5 units daily with one or two days alcohol free. Sleep and mood improved (anxiety ratings reduced to 'mild' from 'severe' and depression reduced to 'moderate' from 'severe'), although Kevin did not meet the criteria for major depressive disorder in any event. Sleep had also improved insofar as Kevin reported two or three good nights' sleep each week and less worrying about the perceived negative consequences of insomnia. After 20 sessions spread over 14 months it was agreed to pause, and a follow-up date agreed for three months hence. The continuous monitoring served two purposes. First, and most obviously, it enabled both Kevin and I to evaluate progress and be better able to adjust the intensity and focus of therapy. Second, and perhaps more subtly, it fostered goal maintenance in working memory (in fact for both parties!). By anticipating that he would be asked about his drinking, in particular, Kevin had a rationale for maintaining his goal of moderation.

Rationale for continuous feedback

Consider this statement and the ensuing discussion with a client who I saw recently:

CLIENT: I failed again, I simply was not able to stop drinking. Of course when I was drinking last weekend I phoned my dealer and got 2 g of cocaine. That took care of the weekend and I had to phone in sick to work on Monday.

THERAPIST: I'm glad to see you in the clinic today. It's important that you make it along to these appointments whether things have gone well or not so well between sessions. It sounds like you have had problems at least some of the days in keeping to the goal we talked about earlier on. Was that the time that you used?

CLIENT: I shared a bottle of wine with my partner at home on Wednesday, but it was last Friday when I went out after work that I drank more heavily.

T: Okay. So, including the weekend scene that you just mentioned, on how many days did you have any alcohol or cocaine in the past week?

C: Let me think – on Friday I had four or five beers and then I phoned Gary because I knew he would have some coke. We met in the bar, had a few lines [of cocaine] and carried on drinking until about midnight. We then went to a club, had some more coke and a few shots of vodka. I think I got back home about 5 a.m. I stayed in bed most of Saturday but when I got up I drank some wine and had some more cocaine. I then went out to the bar and had some more beers. This wasn't such a late night but I was due to pick up Jason, my little boy, from my ex-girlfriend's on Sunday and spend the day with him. I really didn't feel able to do that. Joanne, my ex, has warned me that she does not want me

T: looking after Jason if I've been partying at the weekend. So I had to phone her and say I wasn't feeling well enough on Sunday to look after Jason. I'm sure she knows that it was all self-inflicted, although she didn't accuse me directly of using.

T: In the circumstances, you didn't really have much choice but to cancel Sunday, although I know this would not have made you feel good about yourself. But just staying with the substance issue for the moment, it seems that you used only three days of the past seven. I appreciate that things didn't go well at the weekend but you're getting it right more days than you're getting it wrong.

C: It just doesn't feel like I'm getting it right most of the time! I seem to have no control when it matters the most.

T: I agree that it does seem in particular situations you seem to reach a stage where there is no going back. I think it would be helpful to go back over the lead-up to last Friday's episode. The aim here would be to help you to anticipate and be more prepared to cope if you find yourself in a similar situation again. One simple technique that has been proved useful in research trials and in practice is to plan in advance precisely what to do if you are in a situation where there is a risk of using, based on past experience. For example if someone often drank too much wine before dinner, they would come up with something like: 'If I really want a drink then I will prepare dinner a bit earlier and have a glass of wine with the meal'.

Providing feedback in a neurocognitive framework

In a situation where the client has been unable to maintain the goal of abstinence or restraint it is helpful to restate that addiction is essentially a disorder of impulse control, for example

THERAPIST: In one sense, what happened to you at the weekend was almost inevitable: in a particular situation, such as being in a bar and consuming alcohol, wanting to have cocaine is bound to happen. It's a bit like seeing the red stop signal too late to give yourself a chance to stop. That is why your treatment programme here emphasizes looking ahead or forward planning. This means that there is little point in playing the blame game but that doesn't mean you are 'completely off the hook'! What I'm saying here is that once there was a real prospect of getting your hands on some cocaine it would have taken more willpower than you, or most other people for that matter, would be able to summon up. But that makes it all the more important for you to scan the horizon well in advance so you have more time to avoid situations like this altogether, or cope with them when they occur. With the benefit of hindsight, is there anything you could have done differently to maintain your agreed goal: not using cocaine?

CLIENT: Going to that particular bar and drinking that amount of beer was a big mistake. I actually did a deal with myself, telling myself that I somehow 'deserved' a few drinks because I worked hard all week and I was staying away from the coke. But after four or five beers I really felt like a line or two.

T: It sounds as if at that stage you had forgotten your earlier resolve and your goal of not using cocaine. As I said a moment ago, it would have been especially difficult to put the brakes on at that stage. But the question is what can you do that's different when, say, you finish work next Friday?

C: Well, it's a no-brainer, I could go straight home! But that would make me miserable, I mean going back to an empty apartment. Since I separated from Joanne it seems quite lonely and of course I miss Jason a lot although he would usually be in bed by the time I get home.

T: I know. That must be one of those times when you feel that you have lost a lot over the past few months. But I remember when Joanne came to one of the sessions early on she seemed be keeping an open mind about your future together. She said that the main problem in the relationship was your drug-using lifestyle, which I suppose is a reminder that we have work to do. As we agreed last week the best way forward is for you to gain more control over your drug use. So, looking ahead to Friday are there any options other than a possibly lonely night in or a night out in the pub where you might be made an offer you can't refuse?

C: I got an e-mail out of the blue from an old school friend the day before yesterday and he suggested that it would be good to meet up and maybe go for something to eat.

T: It sounds like a good idea. Might I ask whether your friend was part of your cocaine using network or was that before you started using?

C: You're right, Steve was never into any of the clubbing party scene.
T: Right. So what did you say in your reply to Steve's e-mail?
C: He e-mailed me his number and I said I would phone him.

Meditation techniques

Meditation techniques aim to enhance the regulation and monitoring of attention. In this text, with its emphasis on cognitive control, I have attempted to create a coherent framework within which meditation can be practised. Lutz et al. (2008) outlined a neuroscientific framework for the practice of meditation, which they conceptualized as 'a family of complex emotional and attentional regulatory strategies developed for various ends, including the cultivation of well-being and emotional balance' (Lutz et al., 2008, p. 163). They proposed two broad styles of meditation, *focused attention* (FA) and *open monitoring* (OM). These styles, found in several meditation traditions such as Zen and Vipassana, are often combined either within a given session or perhaps in the course of a practitioner's learning processes. FA meditation techniques include

focusing and sustaining attention, for example on the breath
gently disengaging attention from distracters back to the focused object
cognitive reappraisal of distracter, for example 'it's just a thought'.

OM meditation techniques include

no explicit focus or selective attention
nonreactive metacognitive monitoring such as labelling of experience
nonreactive awareness of implicit aspects of mental life.

In addiction-treatment settings, mindfulness has been integrated with traditional relapse prevention skills training approaches and packaged as mindfulness-based relapse prevention (MBRP; Bowen et al., 2011). It thus followed the development of the prototype, mindfulness-based stress reduction (MBSR: Kabat-Zinn, 1990) and subsequent development of mindfulness-based cognitive therapy (MBCT: Segal et al., 2002). In the *CHANGE* programme, elements of MBRP are important at three of the four stages or Four Ms (see Table 9.1). First, components of mindfulness practice such as 'urge-surfing', a metacognitive or acceptance-based means

Table 9.1 Mindfulness practice at different stages of the Four Ms.

Managing impulses	Urge surfing
Managing mood	Mindful acceptance
Maintaining recovery	Maintaining a balanced lifestyle

of dealing with urges or craving, are potentially helpful as a means of managing impulses.

Second, drawing on MBSR and MBCT, detached mindfulness can help those in treatment acquire more effective emotional-control strategies. Third, in the longer term a mindful approach to living would appear to offer a means of counterbalancing the impulsivity that is the hallmark of addiction.

Indirect support for this is provided by findings (Farb et al., 2010) that training in mindfulness reduces emotional reactivity at the neuronal level when sadness is provoked. The neural responses of those trained in mindfulness were less active in areas associated with 'self-referential' processing and autobiographical memory retrieval, while areas associated with inhibiting emotion and interoceptive awareness such as the insula showed less deactivation. In contrast, those untrained in mindfulness displayed neural activation patterns associated with *more* self-referential processing accompanied by apparently more strenuous attempts at suppression of interoceptive sensory integration. Both groups reported similar levels of sadness in response to the dysphoric challenge, suggesting a more fundamental change in regulatory response to emotion rather than an artefact of experimental design such as demand characteristics. This suggests that a mindful stance would be helpful in countering the spectrum of impulsivity, craving, urges or 'wanting' that defines addiction. Considering also the evidence that subtle cognitive deficits are linked to impaired self-regulation in the context of substance misuse, the upshot is that an approach such as mindfulness that promotes a 'pause, reflect, notice' strategy appears eminently suitable to those who tend to 'act first and reflect later'.

In summary, the *CHANGE* approach aims to promote long term recovery by acknowledging the enduring influence of deficits in cognitive control and cognitive biases. These can be addressed by psychoeducational techniques, guided self-help, careful goal selection and nuanced therapeutic feedback. Mindful acceptance can complement or supplement these approaches.

10

Future Directions

Neurocognitive Therapy

It is 9.30 a.m. and your first client has arrived. In the light of the foregoing, what could be done differently in terms of formulation ad treatment now than, say, a decade ago? In an effort to elaborate on this issue I shall highlight key reference points on a typical treatment journey consistent with the Four M structure. The chapter will conclude with a scan of the horizon in an effort to identify key areas for research and how this might be translated into practice. To recap, the key theme in applying the model thus far is that addiction endures because cognitive control is compromised by repeated drug seeking and taking or the pursuit of overvalued rewards associated with gambling. This contributes to the enduring nature of addiction because cognitive control is vital when the challenge is to overcome these highly motivated habits. Executive control is weakened and impulsivity is given free rein, more or less.

This emphasis on cognitive control has important implications for how addictive disorders and associated mental health problems are conceptualized, formulated and managed. For instance, in Chapter 1, I described how cognitive therapy has, in effect, ascribed addiction a rather utilitarian role insofar as the goal is to manage or compensate for unbearable emotions linked to extreme or distorted beliefs. Further, cognitive therapy has historically addressed addiction by encouraging the client to either supplant irrational beliefs about addiction such as 'I need cocaine to be sociable; people find me boring unless I have a few drinks; I can't cope without a tranquilizer'; or discover and modify core beliefs about self, others and the world. Targeting these cognitions is, I propose, often necessary but rarely sufficient in combating addiction. This is because, in addition to the accessible thoughts and beliefs cited above, cognitive processes that evade introspection, operating in parallel with or in advance of deliberation, can lead to the recurrence of addictive behaviour by default. Of course, targeting implicit cognitive and behavioural processes requires considerable

Cognitive Therapy for Addiction: Motivation and Change, First Edition. Frank Ryan.
© 2013 Frank Ryan. Published 2013 by John Wiley & Sons, Ltd.

ingenuity. However, ignoring their existence and influence is not an option for empirically supported therapy such as cognitive therapy.

Increasing Cognitive Control is the Goal

This serves to create a rather different therapeutic dynamic than specified or implied by the extant accounts referred to in Chapter 1. It is less about core beliefs, schemata or spirituality and more about engaging with competing neural systems that generate a 'valuation malfunction', in computational parlance (Rangel *et al.*, 2008). This provides a focus for therapeutic intervention along these lines: components that enhance cognitive control are good; those that do not are less good, or perhaps a waste of time. In the earlier chapters I explored the implications of this idea across the phases of typical therapeutic encounters. The balancing act that was required was to maintain the robust, proven format of cognitive therapy while at the same time incorporating innovations such as WM training or cognitive-bias modification. I surmised that, while explicit or specified, these elements of therapeutic intervention are usually embedded in otherwise diverse approaches such as Twelve-Step or CBT. Goal setting or regular attendance at Twelve-Step meetings directly act on WM, the engine of executive control. However, no intervention is 'process pure' with regard to cognitive enhancement, so the therapist has to accentuate these particular levers of change.

My hope is that this text provides a rationale and a guide to translate cognitive-neuroscience concepts and applications to the addiction clinic. Targeting cognitive control by the diverse techniques outlined in this text offers both patient and therapist a coherent and accepting, if prototypical, framework to understanding and modifying harmful habits. The components of *CHANGE* are all individually supported by experimental findings, preclinical or clinical outcome studies. However, the package *per se* has not yet been subject to formal evaluation. In due course, innovative techniques such as cognitive-bias modification, modifying behavioural approach tendencies and more explicit neurocognitive interventions such as WM enhancement might well feature prominently in the addiction-therapist's toolkit. Researchers and clinicians are currently refining and evaluating these interventions. In one treatment centre where I worked clients readily took advantage of internet access, spending much time on social networking sites! Steering these computer-literate individuals, or encouraging those less computer literate, towards programmes aimed at reversing cognitive and behavioural biases seems entirely plausible. Pending the likely wider dispersal of these interventions, the question is how to apply the findings detailed in the foregoing chapters. In this concluding chapter I shall briefly revisit the major phases of the therapeutic journey, cycling through the Four Ms.

Do We Know Anything New?

Converging findings with both community and clinic-based populations have accorded cognitive control a key role in the persistence, cessation and resumption of addictive behaviour. Further, insights into the component processes of cognitive control of addictive impulses have also been gleaned from a diverse range of methodologies employed by a wide range of research teams. The task I embraced in the foregoing chapters was to create a psychotherapeutic framework that could accommodate these findings and perhaps create a platform for evaluation and refinement. Throughout, I have endeavoured to remain focused on the therapeutic alliance, the importance of case formulation and the scope this provides for addressing the more dysfunctional component processes of cognitive control.

Motivation: the First M

Initially, using the first component of the Four-M structure, I emphasized the need for both therapist and treatment seeker to grasp the challenge posed in addressing a disorder that has an implicit motivational and cognitive substrate that leads to either spurious or unreliable insight. Combined with the resistance to change that is emblematic of addiction, the resulting interpersonal dynamics can undermine the therapeutic alliance and increase the risk of poor compliance and disengagement. Case formulation also needs to be re-appraised given the distinct learning mechanisms that shape addictive behavior, as outlined in Chapter 3. Addiction is viewed as an acquired dysfunction of neural reward mechanisms.

Managing impulsivity: the Second M

Progressing on to the next 'M', managing impulsivity, enables the therapist and client to engage more directly with the essential feature of addiction: impaired impulse control. In a sense, this brings us back to Bill, the man addicted to alcohol whose attention was grabbed and held by the word 'binge' as described on p. xi. This relatively involuntary capture of attention is a cognitive precursor to impulsivity: the tendency to act in haste and often repent in leisure. This combination of preferential processing of appetitive cues with impaired inhibition of the ensuing thoughts, images and longings provides a plausible account of the preoccupation that often haunts those on the path to recovery. It is not, as clients sometimes suggest, a sign of weakening resolve or less than complete commitment. It is a sign of a normally functioning cognitive system – albeit one likely to be compromised by substance misuse and its attendant hazards. The *CHANGE* account places impulse control at the centre of therapeutic intervention. First, the model acknowledges that impulsivity is a dimensional and multifaceted variable: individuals can vary along this dimension and in whether it is expressed in impaired decision making, high levels of risk taking or lack of perseverance. The young man with a history of antisocial behaviour, poor school record and substance-misuse problems can thus benefit from recognizing that there might be a common factor that not only accounts in part for his historical and current problems but also can help sculpt a treatment plan that is more likely to deliver a good and lasting outcome. In terms of formulation, this enables client and therapist to produce a more granulated account of the presenting problems and construct a treatment plan that builds on strengths (e.g. openness to new experiences) rather than combating weaknesses (e.g. low threshold for boredom when doing rote tasks). *CHANGE* recognizes that addiction is fundamentally a disorder of reward processing. It is thus more focused on motivation than on emotion, albeit according the latter a major collateral role.

Cognitive therapy is remedial and any knowledge accrued is valued only insofar as it can change maladaptive patterns of thought or behaviour. In this regard surely the most exciting knowledge to emerge in recent years is reflected in first the development of methods to measure cognitive processes and then the evolution of these into techniques that show promise in reversing these cognitive and behavioural habits. The power of the cognitive-neuroscience paradigm is shown by the success of several groups of researchers translating diverse experimental methods into the 'real world' of the clinic or treatment centre. Much of this work could not be conceived, let alone implemented, without the conceptual advances of cognitive neuroscience. The finding, for instance, that training in core WM skills led to a reduction in impulsivity as measured by delayed discounting of rewards (Bickel *et al.*, 2011) links cognitive control to impulse control.

While needing further testing and refinement, there are examples of emerging therapeutic strategies that promise to reduce salience attribution and improve impulse control.

In Chapter 3, I pointed out that information retained in WM appeared to influence the allocation of attention in a top-down fashion. A recent study found evidence that food-related stimuli, stored in WM, did appear to strongly influence the allocation of attention. The reader will recall the findings of David Soto and his colleagues summarized in Chapter 3, suggesting that what is encoded in WM can influence the deployment of attention. If, for example, an image of an apple is stored in WM, subsequently presented images of apples will gain an advantage in capturing scarce attentional resources. These images are more likely to be rapidly detected to exert a distracting influence if they are not the searched-for target. Higgs *et al.* (2012) evaluated this theory further and found that the speed of detection of targets was increased by 33.9 ± 26.5 ms when the participants, who were normal-weight, apparently untroubled undergraduates, were cued by food-related stimuli they were required to store in WM for a subsequent categorization challenge (the WM condition). This was significantly improved performance compared with a more marginal 9.9 ± 23.5 ms when the anticipatory cue was merely primed (the priming condition), and not required for subsequent processing. These findings appear to suggest that any top-down process represented by WM activation can influence attentional deployment in a robust manner when compared with a bottom-up process such as priming.

Applied to the clinical domain, these findings suggest that influencing what goes on in WM through discussion, dialogue and counselling can indeed increase control over cognitive biases that would otherwise have free rein. Recent work cited in Chapter 7 shows how willpower, the persistence of effort in pursuit of goals, can be augmented by practice but also depleted by overuse. Calibrating this is surely a task that therapists and clients should embrace. Identifying the optimal level of practising and sustaining cognitive control while remaining alert to the possibility of willpower depletion appears to me a very good use of a therapeutic hour. As 'Plan B', (or perhaps 'Plan A' for some!) the client could be reminded of the practice of mindfulness, as at some stage implicit cognitive and behavioural processes will overwhelm all but the most resourceful client. Acknowledging the relentless nature of automatic, bottom-up processes gives a rationale for this, and enables the clients to see their wavering motivation in more naturalistic terms. A mindful stance thus emerges as a way to move on from the intrusion and compulsion that characterize the addictive experience.

Managing mood: the Third M

Negative emotions provide the context within which many seek help for addictive disorders. In the foregoing I emphasized the importance of case formulation in an effort to disentangle the relationship between addiction and affect. Even if I have discounted default assumptions that emotional vulnerability is either necessary or sufficient for addiction to emerge, emotional control is nevertheless crucial for two reasons. First, exposure to adversity can render individuals more susceptible to *both* emotional dysregulation and addiction. Accordingly, some will have primary emotional disorders and other mental health problems that either precede or occur in tandem with addiction. Second, even in those, albeit perhaps a minority of clinic attendees, who are not predisposed to emotional vulnerability, negative emotions will have occurred, perhaps consequential to substance misuse. For example, a 29-year-old woman referred to me recently described the onset of an anxiety disorder following the distressing experience of amnesia and 'blacking out' while intoxicated. The personal history did not reveal any obvious vulnerability factors or traumagenic experiences.

Another source of dysphoria is the 'carryover' effects of drugs that stimulate key neurotransmitter pathways, referred to as the darker side of addiction. More generally, the process of overcoming drug addiction is itself fraught with emotional challenges, whether the transient euphoria that comes from initial success or the guilt and shame arising from setbacks. The present focus on self-regulation suggests a somewhat ironic source of relapse: successful coping with urges and craving. Thus, the mentally exhausting effect of suppressing impulses over extended intervals, labelled 'ego depletion' (Baumeister *et al.*, 1998), can prime impulsivity: a case, perhaps, of a surfeit of success contributing to failure. The ego-depletion model, of course, proposes that willpower can be drained by any task requiring cognitive or behavioural suppression. This further justifies the Four M account insofar as it reaffirms the importance of addressing emotional-control skills as a core component of the treatment package. The aim is to protect and nurture the scarce cognitive resources subsumed under the headings WM or executive control functions. This is aimed at resetting or 'rebooting' WM, which can influence attentional engagement and guide behaviour.

Maintaining change: the Fourth M

If investigation of cognitive biases has shown that milliseconds matter in the competition for attention for reward-predictive cues, neurobiological approaches to understanding compulsive habits (see, e.g., Robinson and Berridge, 2003; Everitt and Robbins, 2005) have outlined how the ensuing behavioural response retains potency for many years. Whether regarded as compulsive wanting or aberrant learning, these accounts highlight the enduring nature of the learned response. As reputedly said of the Bourbon dynasty by the French eighteenth-century statesman Talleyrand, these processes 'have learned nothing and forgotten nothing'. There are several lines of evidence and reasoning that point to the intransigence of addiction. First, and most pragmatically, high relapse rates following completed episodes of treatment attest to the precarious nature of recovery for many. Second, the converging findings on which this book is reliant show that cognitive vulnerability factors, specifically processing biases and inhibitory or executive failure, can last well beyond the date of the discharge summary, or indeed the planned follow-up: unless, that is, they are targeted directly and indirectly by therapeutic interventions modifying implicit processes or boosting inhibitory control. In the absence of longer-term follow-up studies the long-term impact of these interventions remains conjectural, but preliminary findings offer some promise in this regard. Based on extant findings, my conclusion is that many of those who meet the criteria for addictive disorders need to be monitored and supported for longer than is likely to be the case currently. This suggests that follow-up care, perhaps of low intensity and frequency, needs to be extended accordingly. Automatic or internet-based alerts or prompts may also be useful and cost efficient.

The enduring nature of addiction also accords with the material in Chapter 3 describing the relative immunity to devaluation displayed by cues associated with substance-derived reward. Note that these response tendencies are latent and often not available to introspection. This means that the therapist needs to compensate for the limited insight of the recovering person by urging caution even months or years after abstinence is attained. Conventional relapse-prevention approaches are of course helpful in this regard, differentiating a lapse or slip from a relapse and applying a damage-limitation approach.

Cognitive therapy is an evolving system and further refinement and testing of the approach described here is essential. The overarching theme in the foregoing is that cognitive factors have been overlooked in two important respects. The first stems from the fact that repetitious behaviour, especially if subjected to powerful motivational forces as in addiction, is increasingly governed by automatic cognitive processes. Second, the controlled processes that ordinarily restrain automaticity are compromised. The upshot is that cognitive control is impaired. It is thus a prime target for remediation. This rather abstract target is in fact amenable to change both by modifying implicit cognitive and behavioural processes and by teaching self-regulation skills. To echo the theme of the book, that whatever occupies working memory guides attention and behaviour, I hope that focusing the readers' minds on cognitive control will guide their therapeutic interventions accordingly.

Appendix
Self-Help Guide Six Tips
A Pocket Guide to Preventing Relapse

Introduction: Why Six Tips?

We are all creatures of habit. We often do not realize how hard it is to change a habit until perhaps we have to. Then, we need not just willpower but also some tips to help us cope. The reason that it is often difficult to give up alcohol, cigarettes or other drugs is that they are habits, and habits do not go away easily or quickly. Like old computer programs they lurk about on your personal computer – your brain! Another problem with habits is that when we do anything a lot of times, perhaps over many years, we learn to do it 'robotically', that is without knowing we are doing it. This can be very helpful when we are carrying out routine things such as brushing our teeth, getting dressed or even driving a car on a quiet, familiar stretch of road. However, when the habits involve reaching for that drink, or the cigarette we have decided we no longer really need, the sometimes helpful habit can place us in harm's way.

The *Six Tips* are *not* a short version of the *Twelve-Step* approach, although the first of the Twelve Steps about recognizing powerlessness or lack of willpower is important here as well. If you are involved with a Twelve-Step programme or attend Alcoholics Anonymous this is not in any way a substitute! There is one important difference in emphasis in the way powerlessness is regarded: the approach in this brief guide suggests that *sometimes* we are powerless, but only when the 'autopilot' has taken over. The example of the autopilot is that it is programmed to keep a plane at a certain height and course without the pilot having to constantly attend to it. While the pilot can take control at the push of a button, it is not so easy for us to switch off our own autopilot; in fact sometimes we do not even

---

Cognitive Therapy for Addiction: Motivation and Change, First Edition. Frank Ryan.
© 2013 Frank Ryan. Published 2013 by John Wiley & Sons, Ltd.

know when it is in charge! A key aim of the Six Tips approach is to *help you to recognize when you are operating in this automatic pilot or habit mode.* Unlike an airline pilot however, we do not have an indicator that flashes 'autopilot engaged'. In order to reverse or control habits such as problem drinking you need to learn to recognize when you are in 'habit -mode'. The following six tips are intended to help you do this.

1. Don't Always Trust Your Memory!

Your memory can play tricks with you when you recall your drinking days by conveniently not drawing your attention to the bad times and the unpleasant consequences: you have good reasons for wanting to change your drinking or to abstain altogether and the reasons are even more compelling now that you have got over the most difficult bit and have something to lose. Your mind can also provide you with a similarly biased view of the positive consequences of resuming drinking. Some of these might seem reasonable in the short term, but how would things appear in, say, six months or so? Remind yourself of some of the reasons that brought you into treatment here.

2. Beware of the 'Booze Bias'!

The world is not full of bars and off-licences – it's just that wherever there is one it grabs your attention! This is another trick that your mind can play you by being selective. It is really trying to be helpful, as in your drinking days this was what was required. The danger is that this 'booze bias' can automatically trigger behaviour patterns that are only too familiar, such as ordering and consuming an alcoholic drink. (However, it is not *just* your mind: pubs do often occupy prominent positions – but then again so do churches, and they can remain invisible to all but the most devout!) The serious point here is that it takes a while for the change of priorities to filter down from the command-and-control centre to the troops on the ground, so the commanders are advised to be very vigilant. This is bit like the saying 'your left hand doesn't know what your right hand is doing', and is a telling reminder of how even with loads of willpower we still find ourselves doing precisely what we earlier decided not to. As an exercise, try and imagine your locality (sketch out a map if you like). How frequently do pubs, for example, appear? Now try the same exercise but deliberately concentrate on *other* significant features: prominent buildings, landmarks or other features.

3. Separate Thoughts from Actions

But what do you do when you find yourself face to face with a source of alcohol? In many cases this will lead to thinking about having a drink. *Thinking* about doing something is not the same as *doing* something. This might sound pretty obvious, but sometimes we assume that thinking about something makes it almost inevitable. If you are aiming to abstain from drinking, it is inevitable that your thoughts will turn to alcohol. This does not mean that you are weak-willed or that it is inevitable you will act on your thoughts.

4. Learn How to Distract Yourself

Thoughts about drinking can be upsetting and need to be dealt with. Sometimes you can simply leave the situation which has triggered the thoughts. Or you could practice trying to distract yourself. Like most things this is easier said than done, but you will be surprised how you can improve with practice. Effective distraction is a bit like changing the TV channel — like TVs we can really only properly focus on one thing at a time, so if the programme you are watching ends with the central character (you) having a drink, you need to change it! It helps to know in advance what is available, and now is a chance for you to think ahead.

The first option is to switch to something distracting in the environment. Other people can be genuinely interesting, especially when they are in social situations. If you are not talking with anybody in particular you can focus your mind on something positive such as a holiday, which can be anything from a day trip to an ocean cruise. While this might not always be feasible, it can always be planned for, which is something you can do *immediately*. The trick is to distract yourself with something that is absorbing enough to capture your attention and might also require effort. A useful tip is to work towards your strengths or interests. You may not of course be able to actually carry out the activity there and then but you could *talk about* your interest. Remember one of the key points of relapse prevention training – urges are usually *short* periods of temptation and they can disappear almost as quickly as they arrive. For a moment look ahead to the coming week or so

5. Willpower Is Sometimes Not Enough

Oscar Wilde said this with more wit: 'I can resist everything except temptation'. Of course temptation is, by definition, difficult to resist – that's why you need to be prepared in advance. Drawing up a list of people, activities or places to go that can offer support or distraction when you are feeling vulnerable to relapse or if you experience a lapse is a start. As mentioned above, changing well-established habits leads to conflict. An example of this is driving a car in a country where they drive on the 'wrong' side of the road. Fortunately, this is something most of us manage to do safely most of the time. Often though, it is when things happen too fast for the driver, or due to factors such as being tired, that the new rule ('drive on the right') loses out to the familiar rule of driving on the left. The key then is knowing your limits and staying alert.

You will by now have probably been told about the difference between a lapse and a relapse. *If at first you don't succeed, don't blame yourself*. What helps turn one into another is often the belief that it is a result of our own failings or weakness in the willpower department. Deciding to change a habit such as heavy drinking does signal the start of a deep conflict in our motivational system: resuming drinking even when we have undertaken not to happens a lot, but it is pointless blaming ourselves. It is useful to look closely at what led up to the lapse so we can be better prepared if it reoccurs. What we need to do also is to implement our damage-limitation plan. This should include some of the strategies such as getting in touch with understanding friends, relatives or carers that you listed above.

6. Beware of the Dog that Doesn't Bark . . .

In the Sherlock Holmes story, the fact that the dog did not bark provided a vital clue. Sometimes, after giving up drinking people experience little or no craving, in a way a bit like the curious case of the silent hound! This can of course be a good thing: it could mean that you are coping well with the events that used to trigger the familiar desires for a drink. It could also lead you to be a bit too relaxed and not ready with the coping skills you have learned. The sixth tip is therefore to be on your guard even if you are not aware of any craving or desire, especially in situations where you would have had alcohol in your drinking days.

References

Allen, L.B., McHugh, R.K. and Barlow, D.H. (eds) (2008) *Clinical Handbook of Psychological Disorders: a Step-by-Step Treatment Manual*, 4th edn, Guilford, New York, pp. 216–249.
American Psychiatric Association (1994) *Diagnostic and Statistical Manual of Mental Disorders*, 4th edn, American Psychiatric Association, Washington, DC.
Amir, N., Beard, C., Burns, M. and Bomyea, J. (2009) Attention modification program in individuals with generalized anxiety disorder. *Journal of Abnormal Psychology*, 118 (1), 28–33.
Amrhein, P.C., Miller, W.R., Yahne, C.E. et al. (2003) Client commitment language during motivational interviewing predicts behavior outcomes. *Journal of Consulting and Clinical Psychology*, 7, 862–878.
Andrews, S.C., Hoy, K.E., Enticott, P.G. et al. (2011) Improving working memory: the effect of combining cognitive activity and anodal transcranial direct current stimulation to the left dorsolateral prefrontal cortex. *Brain Stimulation*, 4, 84–89.
Annis, H. and Davis, C.S. (1988) Self-efficacy and the prevention of alcoholic relapse: initial findings from a treatment trial, in *Assessment and Treatment of Addictive Disorders* (eds T.B. Baker and D.S. Cannon), Praeger, New York, pp. 88–112.
Anthony, J.C., Warner, L.A. and Kessler, R.C. (1994) Comparative epidemiology of dependence on tobacco, alcohol, controlled substances, and inhalants: basic findings from the National Comorbidity Survey. *Experimental and Clinical Psychopharmacology*, 2, 244–268.
Anton R., O'Malley S., Ciraulo D. et al. (2006) Combined pharmacotherapies and behavioural interventions for alcohol dependence. The COMBINE study: a randomized controlled trial. *Journal of American Medical Association*, 295, 2003–2017.
Aron, A.R., Dowson, J.H., Sahakian B.J. and Robbins, T.W. (2003) Methylphenidate improves response inhibition in adults with attention-deficit/hyperactivity disorder. *Biological Psychiatry*, 54, 1465–1468.

Cognitive Therapy for Addiction: Motivation and Change, First Edition. Frank Ryan.
© 2013 Frank Ryan. Published 2013 by John Wiley & Sons, Ltd.

Audrain-McGovern, J., Rodriguez, D., Epstein, L.H. *et al.* (2009) Does delay discounting play an etiological role in smoking or is it a consequence of smoking? *Drug Alcohol and Dependence*, 103, 99–106.

Baler, R.D. and Volkow, N.D. (2006) Drug addiction: the neurobiology of disrupted self-control. *Trends in Molecular Medicine*, 12, 559–566.

Baumeister, R.F., Bratslavsky, E., Muraven, M. and Tice, D.M. (1998) Ego depletion: is the active self a limited resource? *Journal of Personality and Social Psychology*, 74, 1252–1265.

Bechara, A., Noel, X. and Crone, E.A. (2006) Loss of willpower: abnormal neural mechanisms of impulse control and decision-making in addiction, in *Handbook of Implicit Cognition and Addiction* (eds R.W. Wiers and A.W. Stacy), Sage, Thousand Oaks, CA, pp. 215–232.

Beck, A.T. (1967) *Depression: Clinical, Experimental and Theoretical Aspects*, Harper & Row, New York.

Beck, A.T., Wright, F.D., Newman, C.F. and Liese, B.S. (1993) *Cognitive Therapy of Addiction*, Guilford, New York.

Beck, D.M. and Kastner, S. (2009) Top-down and bottom-up mechanisms in biasing competition in the human brain. *Vision Research*, 49, 1154–1165.

Bennett-Levy, J., Butler, G., Fennell, M. *et al.* (2004) *Oxford Guide to Behavioural Experiments in Cognitive Therapy*, Oxford University Press, Oxford.

Berridge, K.C. and Robinson, T.E. (1995) The mind of an addicted brain: neural sensitization of wanting versus liking. *Current Directions in Psychological Science*, 4 (3), 71–76.

Berridge, K.C., Robinson, T.E. and Aldridge, W.J. (2009) Dissecting components of reward: 'liking', 'wanting', and learning. *Current Opinion in Psychopharmacology*, 9, 65–73.

Bickel, W.K., Yi, R., Landes, R.D. *et al.* (2011) Remember the future: working memory training decreases delay discounting among stimulant addicts. *Biological Psychiatry*, 69 (3), 260–265.

Bolla, K. I., Brown, K., Eldreth, D. *et al.* (2002) Dose-related neurocognitive effects of marijuana use. *Neurology*, 59, 1337–1343.

Bolla, K., Ernst, M., Kiehl, K. *et al.* (2004) *Journal of Neuropsychiatry and Clinical Neuroscience*, 16 (4), 456–464.

Bowen, S., Chawla, N. and Marlatt, G.A. (2011) *Mindfulness-Based Relapse Prevention for Addictive Behaviours: a Clinician's Guide*, Guilford, New York.

Brandstatter, V., Lengfelder, A. and Gollwitzer, P.M. (2001) Implementation intentions and efficient action initiation. *Journal of Personality and Social Psychology*, 8 (5), 946–960.

Brevers, D., Cleeremans, A., Tibboel, H. *et al.* (2011) Attentional blink for gambling-related stimuli in problem gamblers. *Journal of Behavior Therapy and Experimental Psychiatry*, 42 (3), 265–269.

Brewer, J.A., Mallik, S., Babuscio, T.A. et al. (2011) Mindfulness training for smoking cessation: results from a randomised controlled trial. *Drug and Alcohol Dependence*, 119, 72–80.

Burke, B.L, Arkowitz, H. and Menchola, M. (2003) The efficacy of motivational interviewing: a meta-analysis of controlled clinical trials. *Journal of Consulting and Clinical Psychology*, 71, 843–861.

Camprodon, J.A., Martinez-Raga, J. Alonso-Alonso, M. et al. (2007) One session of high frequency repetitive transcranial magnetic stimulation (rTMS) to the right prefrontal cortex transiently reduces cocaine craving. *Drug and Alcohol Dependence*, 86, 91–94.

Carter, B.L. and Tiffany, S.T. (1999) Meta-analysis of cue-reactivity in addiction research. *Addiction*, 94 (3), 327–340.

Carter, C.S. and van Veen, V. (2007) Anterior cingulate cortex and conflict detection: an update of theory and data. *Cognitive, Affective, and Behavioral Neuroscience*, 7 (4), 367–379.

Castellani, B. and Rugle, L. (1995) A comparison of pathological gamblers to alcoholics and cocaine misusers on impulsivity, sensation seeking, and craving. *The International Journal of the Addictions*, 30 (3), 275–289.

Chambers, C.D., Garavan, H. and Bellgrove, M.A. (2009) Insights into the neural basis of response inhibition from cognitive and clinical neuroscience. *Neuroscience and Biobehavioural Reviews*, 33, 631–646.

Chanraud, S., Martelli, C., Delain, F. et al. (2007) Brain morphometry and cognitive performance in detoxified alcohol-dependents with preserved psychosocial functioning. *Neuropsychopharmacology*, 32, 429–438.

Chein, J. and Morrison, A. (2010) Expanding the mind's workspace: training and transfer effects with a complex working memory span task. *Psychonomic Bulletin and Review*, 17 (2), 193–199.

Childress, A.R., Ehrman, R.N., Ze Wang et al. (2008) Prelude to passion: limbic activation by 'unseen' drug and sexual cues. *PloS ONE*, 3, e1506.

Colcombe, S. J., Erickson, K. I., Raz, N. et al. (2003) *The Journals of Gerontology. Series A. Association of Biological Sciences and Medical Sciences*, 58, 176–180.

Colcombe, S.J., Kramer, A.F., Erickson, K.I. et al. (2004) Cardiovascular fitness, cortical plasticity, and aging. *Proceedings of the National Academy of Sciences USA*, 101, 3316–3321.

Conklin, C.A. and Tiffany, S.T. (2002) Applying extinction research and theory to cue exposure addiction treatments. *Addiction*, 97, 155–167.

Conrod, P.J., Castellanos-Ryan, N. and Strang, J. (2010) Brief, personality-targeted coping skills interventions prolong survival as a non-drug user over a two-year period during adolescence. *Archives of General Psychiatry*, 67 (1), 85–93.

Copello, A., Williamson, E., Orford, J. and Day E. (2006) Implementing and evaluating Social Behaviour and Network Therapy in drug treatment practice in the UK: a feasibility study. *Addictive Behaviors*, 31, 802–810.

Corbetta, M. and Shulman, G.L. (2002) Control of goal-directed and stimulus-driven attention in the brain. *Nature Reviews: Neuroscience*, 3 (3), 201–215.

Costa, P.T., and McCrae, R.R. (1992) *Personality Inventory (Short Form): Neuroticism, Extraversion and Openness (NEO: Revised NEO Personality Inventory [NEOPI-R] and the NEO Five-Factor Inventory [NEO-FFI]): Professional Manual*, Psychological Assessment Resources, Odessa, FL.

Cox, W.M., Hogan, L.M., Kristian, M.R. and Race, J.H. (2002) Alcohol attentional bias as a predictor of alcohol abusers' treatment outcome. *Drug and Alcohol Dependence*, 68, 237–243.

Cox, W.M. and Klinger, E. (1988) A motivational model of alcohol use. *Journal of Abnormal Psychology*, 97, 168–180.

Cox, W.M. and Klinger, E. (2011) Systematic Motivational Counselling: from motivational assessment to motivational change, in *Handbook of Motivational Counselling: Goal-Based Approaches to Assessment and Intervention with Addiction and Other Problems* (eds W.M. Cox and E. Klinger), John Wiley & Sons, Ltd, Chichester, pp. 274–302.

Crits-Christoph, P., Siqueland, L., Blaine, J. et al. (1999) Psychosocial treatments for cocaine dependence. National Institute on Drug Abuse collaborative cocaine study. *Archives of General Psychiatry*, 56, 493–502.

Desimone, R. and Duncan, J. (1995) Neural mechanisms of selective visual attention. *Annual Review of Neuroscience*, 18, 193–222.

Deutsch, R. and Strack, F. (2006) Reflective and impulsive determinants of addictive behaviour, in *Handbook of Implicit Cognition and Addiction* (eds R.W. Wiers and A.W. Stacy), Sage, London, pp. 45–57.

de Wit, H. (2009) Impulsivity as a determinant and consequence of drug use: a review of underlying processes. *Addiction Biology*, 14, 22–23.

Dijksterhuis, A. and Aarts, H. (2010) Goals, attention, and (un)consciousness. *Annual Review of Psychology*, 61, 467–490.

Disner, S.G., Beevers, C.G., Haigh, E.A.P. and Beck A.T. (2011) Neural mechanisms of the cognitive model of depression. *Nature Reviews: Neuroscience*, 12, 467–477.

Dutra, L., Stathopoulou, G., Shawnee, L.B. et al. (2008) A meta-analytic review of psychosocial interventions for substance use disorders *American Journal of Psychiatry*, 165, 179–187.

Eldreth, D.A., Matochik, J.A., Cadet, J.L. and Bolla, K. (2004) Abnormal brain activity in prefrontal brain regions in abstinent marijuana users. *Neuroimage*, 23, 914–920.

Ersche, K.D., Jones, P.S., Williams, G.B. et al. (2012) Abnormal brain structure implicated in stimulant drug addiction. *Science*, 335, 601–604.

Evans, K.K. and Treisman, A. (2005) Perception of objects in natural scenes: is it really attention free? *Journal of Experimental Psychology: Human Perception and Performance*, 31 (6), 1476–1492.

Everitt, B.J., Belin, D., Economidou, D., Pelloux, Y., Dalley, J.W. and Robbins, T.W. (2008) Review. Neural mechanisms underlying the vulnerability to develop compulsive drug-seeking habits and addiction. *Philosophical Transactions of the Royal Society London. Biological Science*, 3 (63), 3125–3135.

Everitt, B.J. and Robbins, T.W. (2005) Neural systems of reinforcement for drug addiction: from actions to habits to compulsion. *Nature Neuroscience*, 8 (11), 1481–1489.

Eysenck, M.W., Derakshan, N., Santos, R. and Calvo, M.G. (2007) Anxiety and cognitive performance: attentional control theory. *Emotion*, 7. 336–353.

Fadardi, J.S. (2003) Cognitive–motivational determinants of attentional bias for alcohol-related stimuli: implications for a new attentional-training intervention. PhD thesis. Bangor University.

Fadardi, J.S. and Cox, W.M. (2009) Reversing the sequence: reducing alcohol consumption by overcoming alcohol attentional bias. *Drug and Alcohol Dependence*, 101, 137–145.

Fadardi, J.S., Shamloo, Z.S. and Cox, W.M. (2011) Cognitive and motivational retraining: reciprocal effects, in *Handbook of Motivational Counselling: Goal-Based Approaches to Assessment and Intervention with Addiction and Other Problems* (eds W.M. Cox and E. Klinger), John Wiley & Sons, Ltd, Chichester, pp. 395–411.

Farb, N.A.S., Anderson, A.K., Mayberg, H. *et al.* (2010) Minding one's emotions: mindfulness training alters the neural expression of sadness. *Emotion*, 10, 25–33.

Fecteau, S., Knoch, D., Fegni, F. *et al.* (2007) Diminishing risk-taking behavior by modulating activity in the prefrontal cortex: a direct current stimulation study. *The Journal of Neuroscience*, 27 (46), 12500–12505.

Feil, J. and Zangen, A. (2010) Brain stimulation in the study and treatment of addiction. *Neuroscience and Biobehavioural Reviews*, 34, 559–574.

Field, M. and Cox, W.M. (2008) Attentional bias in addictive behaviors: a review of its development, causes, and consequences. *Drug and Alcohol Dependence*, 97 (1/2), 1–20.

Field, M., Duka, T., Eastwood, B. *et al.* (2007) Experimental manipulation of attentional biases in heavy drinkers: do the effects generalize? *Psychopharmacology (Berlin)*, 192, 593–608.

Field, M., Munafo, M.R. and Franken, I.H.A. (2009) A meta-analytic investigation of the relationship between attentional bias and subjective craving in substance abuse. *Psychological Bulletin*, 135 (4), 589–607.

Forman, S.D., Dougherty, G.G., Casey, B.J. *et al.* (2004) Opiate addicts lack error-dependent activation of rostral anterior cingulate. *Biological Psychiatry*, 55, 531–537.

Franken, I. H. A. (2003) Drug craving and addiction: Integrating psychological and neuropsychopharmacological approaches. *Progress in Neuro-Psychopharmacology and Biological Psychiatry*, 27, 563–579.

Franklin, T.R., Acton, P.D., Maldjian, J.A. *et al.* (2002) Decreased gray matter concentration in the insular, orbitofrontal, cingulate, and temporal cortices of cocaine patients. *Biological Psychiatry*, 51, 134–142.

Fregni, F., Liguori, P., Fecteau, S. *et al.* (2008) Cortical stimulation of the prefrontal cortex with transcranial direct current stimulation reduces cue-provoked smoking craving: a randomized, sham-controlled study. *Journal of Clinical Psychiatry*, 69 (1), 32–40.

Fumagalli, F., Caffino, L., Racagni, G. and Riva, M.A. (2009) Repeated stress prevents cocaine-induced activation of BDNF signaling in rat prefrontal cortex. *European Journal of Neuropsychopharmacology*, 19, 402–408.

Fumagalli, F., Molteni, R., Racagni, G. and Riva, M.A. (2007) Stress during development: impact on neuroplasticity and relevance to psychopathology. *Progress in Neurobiology*, 81, 197–217.

Garavan, H., Kaufmann, J.N. and Hestor, R. (2008) Acute effects of cocaine on the neurobiology of cognitive control. *Philosophical Transactions of the Royal Society*, 363 (1507), 3267–3276.

Garavan, H., Ross, T.J., Kaufman, J. and Stein, E.A. (2003) A midline dissociation between error-processing and response-conflict monitoring. *NeuroImage*, 20, 1132–1139.

Garavan, H. and Stout, J.C. (2005) Neurocognitive insights into substance abuse. *Trends in Cognitive Science*, 9, 195–201.

Garland, E.L., Franken, I.H.A. and Howard, M.O. (2012) Cue-elicited heart rate variability and attentional bias predict alcohol relapse following treatment. *Psychopharmacology*, 272, 17–26.

Goldstein, R.Z., Craig, A.D.B., Bechara, A., Garavan, H., Childress, A.R., Paulus, M.P. and Volkow, N.D. (2009) The neurocircuitry of impaired insight in drug addiction. *Trends in Cognitive Science*, 13, 372–380.

Goldstein, R.Z. and Volkow, N.D. (2002) Drug addiction and its underlying neurobiological basis: neuroimaging evidence for the involvement of the frontal cortex. *American Journal of Psychiatry*, 159, 1642–1652.

Goldstein, R.Z. and Volkow, N.D. (2011) Dysfunction of the prefrontal cortex in addiction: neuroimaging findings and clinical implications. *Nature Reviews: Neuroscience*, 12 (11), 652–669.

Gollwitzer, P.M. (1993) Goal achievement: the role of intentions, in *European Review of Social Psychology*, Vol. 4 (eds W. Stroebe and M. Hewstone), Wiley, Chichester, pp. 141–185.

Grant, S., London, E.D., Newlin, D.B. *et al.* (1996) Activation of memory circuits during cue-elicited cocaine craving. *Proceedings of the National Academy of Sciences of the USA*, 93, 12040–12045.

Gray, J.A. (1991) Neural systems, emotion and personality, in *Neurobiology of Learning, Emotion and Affect* (ed. J. Madden IV), Raven, New York, pp. 273–306.

Greenwald, A.G. and Banji, M.R. (1995) Implicit social cognition: attitudes, self-esteem, and stereotypes. *Psychological Review*, 102, 4–27.

Gross, T.M., Jarvik, M.E. and Rosenblatt, M.R. (1993) Nicotine abstinence produces content-specific Stroop interference. *Psychopharmacology*, 110 (3), 333–336.

Gustavsson, A., Svensson, M., Jacobi, F. et al. (2011) Cost of disorders of the brain in Europe 2010. *European Neuropsychopharmacology*, 21, 718–779.

Hallion, L.S. and Ruscio, A.M. (2011) A meta-analysis of the effect of cognitive bias modification on anxiety and depression. *Psychological Bulletin*, 137 (6), 940–958.

Hester, R. and Garavan, H. (2005) Working memory and executive function: the influence of content and load on the control of attention. *Memory and Cognition*, 33, 221–233.

Higgins, S.T., Heil, S.H. and Lussier, P.L. (2004) Clinical implications of reinforcement as a determinant of substance use disorders. *Annual Review of Psychology*, 55, 431–436.

Higgs, S., Rutters, F., Thomas, J.M. et al. (2012) Top-down modulation of attention to food cues via working memory. *Appetite*, 59, 71–75.

Hiroi, N. and Agatsuma, S. (2005) Genetic susceptibility to substance dependence. *Molecular Psychiatry*, 10, 336–344.

Hodgins, D. C., el Guebaly, N. and Armstrong, S. (1995) Prospective and retrospective reports of mood states before relapse to substance use. *Journal of Consulting and Clinical Psychology*, 63, 400–407.

Houben, K., Nederkoorn, C., Wiers, R.W. and Jansen, A. (2011) Resisting temptation: decreasing alcohol-related affect and drinking behavior by training response inhibition. *Drug and Alcohol Dependence*, 116 (1–3), 132–136.

Ingjaldsson, J.T., Thayer, J.F. and Laber, J.C. (2003) Craving for alcohol and pre-attentive processing of alcohol stimuli. *International Journal of Psychophysiology*, 49, 29–39.

Irwin, J.E., Bowers, C.A., Dunn, M.E. and Wang, M.C (1999) Efficacy of relapse prevention: a meta-analytic review. *Journal of Consulting and Clinical Psychology*, 67, 563–570.

Jones, A., Cole J., Goudie, A. and Field, M. (2011) Priming a restrained mental set reduces alcohol-seeking independently of mood. *Psychopharmacology*, 218, 557–565.

Jonides, J., Lewis, R.L., Nee, D.E. et al. (2008) The mind and brain of short-term memory. *Annual Review of Psychology*, 59, 193–224.

Kabat-Zinn, J. (1990) *Full Catastrophe Living: Using the Wisdom of your Body and Mind to Face Stress, Pain, and Illness*, Delacorte, New York.

Kahneman, D. (2003) A perspective on judgment and choice: mapping bounded rationality. *American Psychologist*, 58 (9): 697–720.

Kamboj, S.J., Joye, A., Das, R.K. *et al.* (2012) Cue exposure and response prevention with heavy smokers: a laboratory-based randomised placebo-controlled trial examining the effects of D cycloserine on cue reactivity and attentional bias. *Psychopharmacology*, 221, 273–284.

Kamboj, S.K., Massey-Chase, R., Rodney, L. *et al.* (2011) Changes in cue reactivity and attentional bias following experimental cue exposure and response prevention: a laboratory study of the effects of D-cycloserine in heavy drinkers. *Psychopharmacology*, 217, 25–37.

Kane, R.W and Engle, M.J. (2003) Executive attention, working memory capacity, and a two-factor theory of cognitive control. *Psychology of Learning and Motivation*, 44, 145–199.

Kaufman, J.N., Ross, T.J., Stein, E.A. and Garavan, H. (2003) Cingulate hyperactivity in cocaine users during a go no-go task as revealed by events related functional magnetic resonance imaging. *The Journal of Neuroscience*, 23 (21), 7839–7843.

Kavanagh, D.J., Andrade, J. and May, J. (2005) Imaginary relish and exquisite torture: the elaborated intrusion theory of desire. *Psychological Review*, 112, 446–467.

Kennerley, S.W., Behrens, T.E.J. and Wallis, J.D. (2011) Double dissociation of value computations in orbitofrontal and anterior cingulate neurons. *Nature Neuroscience*, 14, 1581–1589.

Kessler, R.C., Berglund, P., Demler, O., Jin, R. and Walters, E.E. (2005) Lifetime prevalence and age-of-onset distributions of DSM-IV disorders in the National Comorbidity Survey Replication. *Archives of General Psychiatry*, 62, 593–602.

Klinger, E. and Cox, W.M. (2011) The Motivational Structure Questionnaire, Personal Concerns Inventory and their variants: psychometric properties, in *Handbook of Motivational Counselling: Goal-Based Approaches to Assessment and Intervention with Addiction and Other Problems* (eds W.M. Cox and E. Klinger), John Wiley & Sons, Ltd, Chichester, pp. 1–47.

Kober, H., Ethan, F., Kross, E.F. *et al.* (2010a) Regulation of craving by cognitive strategies in cigarette smokers. *Drug and Alcohol Dependence*, 106, 52–55.

Kober, H., Mende-Siedlecki, P., Kross, E.F. *et al.* (2010b) Prefrontal–striatal pathway underlies cognitive regulation of craving. *Proceedings of the National Academy of Sciences*, 107 (33), 14811–14816.

Koch, C. and Tsuchiya, N. (2006) Attention and consciousness: two distinct brain processes. *Trends in Cognitive Science*, 11, 16–22.

Kohut, H. (1971) *The Analysis of the Self*, International University Press, New York.

Koob, G.F. and Le Moal, M. (1997) Drug abuse: hedonic homeostatic dysregulation. *Science*, 278, 52–58.

Koob, G.F. and Le Moal, M. (2005) Plasticity of reward neurocircuitry and the 'dark side' of drug addiction. *Nature Neuroscience*, 8, 1442–1444.

Koob, G.F. and Le Moal, M. (2008) Addiction and the brain anti-reward system. *Annual Review of Psychology*, 59, 29–53.

Krishnan-Sarin, S., Reynolds, B., Duhig, A.M. et al. (2007) Behavioral impulsivity predicts treatment outcome in a smoking cessation program for adolescent smokers. *Drug and Alcohol Dependence*, 88, 79–82.

Kroenke, K., Spitzer, R.L. and Williams, J.B.W. (2001) The PHQ-9: validity of a brief depression severity measure. *Journal of General Internal Medicine*, 16, 606–613.

Kuyken, W., Padesky, C.A. and Dudley, R. (2009) *Collaborative Case Conceptualization: Working Effectively with Clients in Cognitive Behavioural Therapy*, Guilford, New York.

Lavie, N. (2005) Distracted and confused?: Selective attention under load. *Trends in Cognitive Science*, 9, 75–82.

Leventhal, A.M., Waters, A.J., Breitmeyer, B.G. et al. (2008) Subliminal processing of smoking-related and affective stimuli in tobacco addiction. *Experimental and Clinical Psychopharmacology*, 16 (4), 301–312.

Libet, B., Gleason, C.A., Wright, E.W. & Pearl, D.K. (1983) Time of conscious intention to act in relation to onset of cerebral activities (readiness-potential); the unconscious initiation of a freely voluntary act. *Brain*, 106, 623–642.

Linehan, M.M. (1993) *Cognitive Behavioural Treatment of Borderline Personality Disorder*, Guilford, New York.

Litt, M.D., Kadden, R.M. and Cooney, N L. (2003) Coping skills and treatment outcomes in cognitive behavioural interactional group therapy for alcoholism. *Journal of Consulting and Clinical Psychology*, 71. 118–128.

Livesley, W.J., Jang, K.L. and Vernon, P.A. (1998) Phenotypic and genetic structure of traits delineating personality disorder. *Archives of General Psychiatry*, 55, 941–948.

Lutz, A., Slagter, H.A., Dunne, J.D. and Davidson, R.J. (2008) Attention regulation and monitoring in meditation. *Trends in Cognitive Sciences*, 12, 163–169.

Lynam, D.R. (2011) Impulsivity and deviance, in *Inhibitory Control and Drug Abuse Prevention: from Research to Translation* (eds M.T. Bardo, D.H. Fishbein and R. Milich), Springer, New York, pp. 145–175.

MacKillop, J., Amlung, M.T., Few, L.R. et al. (2011) Delayed reward discounting and addictive behavior: a meta-analysis. *Psychopharmacology*, 216, 305–321.

Madden, C.J. and Zwaan, R.A. (2001) The impact of smoking urges on working memory performance. *Experimental and Clinical Psychopharmacology*, 9 (4), 418–424.

Makris, N., Oscar-Berman, M., Jaffin, S.M. et al. (2008) Decreased volume of the brain reward system in alcoholism. *Biological Psychiatry*, 64, 192–202.

Marcus B.H., Albrecht, A.E., King, T.K. et al. (1999) The efficacy of exercise as an aid for smoking cessation in women: a randomized controlled trial. *Archives of Internal Medicine*, 159 (11), 1229–1234.

Marlatt, G.A. and Gordon, J.R. (eds) (1985) *Relapse Prevention: Maintenance Strategies in the Treatment of Addictive Behaviors*, Guilford, New York.

Marissen, M.A.E., Franken, I.H.A., Waters, A.J., Blanken, P., van den Brink, W. and Hendriks, V.M. (2006) Attentional bias predicts heroin relapse following treatment. *Addiction*, 101, 1306–1312.

Maslow, A.H. (1943). A theory of human motivation. *Psychological Review*, 50 (4), 370–396.

Matthews, G., Deary, I.J. and Whiteman, M.C. (2009) *Personality Traits*, 3rd edn, Cambridge University Press, Cambridge.

McClure, S.M., Ericson, K.M., Laibson, D.I. *et al.* (2007) Time discounting for primary rewards. *Journal of Neuroscience*, 27, 5796–5804.

McDougal, W. (1925). A great advance of the Freudian psychology. *The Journal of Abnormal and Social Psychology*, 20.1, 43–47.

McGinty, J.F., Whitfield, T.W. Jr and Berglind, W.J. (2010) Brain-derived neurotrophic factor and cocaine addiction. *Brain Research*, 1314, 183–193.

Miller, G.A. (1956) The magical number seven, plus or minus two: some limits on our capacity for processing information. *Psychological Review*, 63 (2), 81–97.

Miller, W.R. and Rose, G.S. (2009) Toward a theory of motivational interviewing. *American Psychologist*, 64 (6), 527–537.

Mitcheson, L., Maslin, J., Meynen, T., Morrison, T., Hill, R. and Wanigaratne, S. (2010) *Applied Cognitive and Behavioural Approaches to the Treatment of Addiction: a Practical Treatment Guide*, Wiley-Blackwell, Chichester.

Miyake, A.,. Friedman, N.P., Emerson, M.J. *et al.* (2000) The unity and diversity of executive functions and their contributions to complex 'frontal lobe' tasks: a latent variable analysis. *Cognitive Psychology*, 41, 49–100.

Munafo, M.R. and Flint, J. (2011) Dissecting the genetic architecture of human personality. *Trends in Cognitive Sciences*, 15 (9), 395–400.

Muraven, M. (2010) Practicing self-control lowers the risk of smoking lapse. *Psychology of Addictive Behaviors*, 24 (3), 446–452.

Naqvi, N.H., Rudrauf, D., Damasio, H. and Bechara, A. (2007) Damage to the insula disrupts addiction to cigarette smoking. *Science*, 315 (5811), 531–534.

National Institute for Health and Clinical Excellence (NICE) (2007) *Drug Misuse: Psychosocial Interventions*, CG51, NICE, London.

Noel, X., Van Der Linden, M., Verbanck, P., Pelc, I. and Bechara, A. (2003) Attentional bias and inhibitory control processes in substance-dependent individuals with alcoholism. *Journal of Psychophysiology*, 17, S8.

Norberg, M.M., Krystal, J.H. and Tolin, D.F. (2008) A meta-analysis of D-cycloserine and the facilitation of fear extinction and exposure therapy. *Biological Psychiatry*, 63, 1118–1126.

Norman, D.A. and Shallice, T. (1986) Attention to action: willed and automatic control of behaviour, in *Consciousness and Self-regulation*, Vol. 4 (eds R.J. Davidson, G.E. Schwartz and D. Shapiro), Plenum, New York, pp. 1–18.

O'Brien, C. (2011) Addiction and dependence in DSM-V. *Addiction*, 106 (5), 866–867.

O'Doherty, J.P., Deichmann, R., Critchley, H.D. and Dolan, R.J. (2002) Neural responses during anticipation of a primary taste reward. *Neuron*, 33, 815–826.

O'Farrell, T.J. and Fals-Stewart W. (2006) *Behavioral Couples Therapy for Alcoholism and Drug Abuse*, Guilford, New York.

Office for National Statistics (ONS) (2011) *Alcohol-Related Deaths in the United Kingdom, 2000–2009*, HMSO, London.

Oleson, P.J., Westerberg, H. and Klingberg, T. (2004) Increased prefrontal and parietal activity after training of working memory. *Nature Neuroscience.* 7 (1), 102–106.

Orford, J. (2008) Joining the queue of dissenters. *Addiction*, 103 (5), 706–707.

Owen, A.M., Hampshire, A., Grahn, J.A. *et al.* (2010) Putting brain training to the test. *Nature*, 465 (7299), 775–776.

Patton, J.M., Stanford, M.S. and Barratt, E.S. (1995) Factor structure of the Barratt Impulsiveness Scale. *Journal of Clinical Psychology*, 51, 768–774.

Perkins, K.A., Karelitz, J.L., Conklin, C A. *et al.* (2010) Acute negative affect relief from smoking depends on the affect situation and measure but not on nicotine. *Biological Psychiatry*, 67 (8), 707–714.

Persons, J.B. (1989) *Cognitive Therapy in Practice: a Case Formulation Approach*, Norton, New York.

Persons, J.B. (2008) *The Case Formulation Approach to CBT*, Guilford, New York.

Pessoa, L., McKenna, M., Gutierrez, E. and Ungerleider, L.G. (2002) Neural processing of emotional faces requires attention. *Proceedings of the National Academy of Sciences*, 99, 11458–11463.

Pessoa, L., Padmala, S. and Morland, T. (2005) Fate of unattended fearful faces in the amygdala is determined by both attentional resources and cognitive modulation. *Neuroimage*, 28 (1), 249–255.

Petry, N.M., Tedford, J., Austin, M. *et al.* (2004) Prize reinforcement contingency management for treating cocaine users: how low can we go, and with whom? *Addiction*, 99, 349–336.

Phillips, P.E.M., Stuber, G.D., Heien, M.L.A.V. *et al.* (2003) Subsecond dopamine release promotes cocaine seeking. *Nature*, 422, 614–618.

Pickering, A.D., Diaz, A. and Gray, J.A. (1995) Personality and reinforcement: an exploration using a maze-learning task. *Personality and Individual Differences*, 18, 541–558.

Posner, M.I. and Petersen, S.E. (1990) The attention system of the human brain. *Annual Review of Neuroscience*, 13, 25–42.

Powell, J., Bradley, B. and Gray, J. (1992) Classical conditioning and cognitive determinants of subjective craving for opiates: an investigation of their relative contributions. *British Journal of Addiction*, 87, 1133–1144.

Prendergast, M., Podus, D., Finney, J. and Greenwell, L. (2006) Contingency management for treatment of substance use disorders: a meta-analysis. *Addiction*, 101 (11), 1546–1560.

Prestwich, A., Conner, M. and Lawton, R.J. (2006) Implementation Intentions: can they be used to prevent and treat addiction? in *Handbook of Implicit Cognition and Addiction* (eds R.W. Wiers and A.W. Stacy), Sage, Thousand Oaks, CA, pp. 455–469.

Project MATCH Research Group (1997) Matching alcoholism treatment to client heterogeneity: Project MATCH posttreatment drinking outcomes. *Journal of Studies on Alcohol*, 58, 7–29.

Rangel, A., Camerer, C. and Montague, P.R. (2008) A framework for studying the neurobiology of value-based decision making. *Nature Reviews: Neuroscience*: 9 (7), 545–556.

Raymond, J.E.; Shapiro, K.L. and Arnell, K.M. (1992) Temporary suppression of visual processing in an RSVP task: an attentional blink? *Journal of Experimental Psychology: Human Perception and Performance*, 18 (3), 849–860.

Reason, J.T. (1984) Lapses of attention in everyday life, in *Varieties of Attention* (eds R. Parasuraman and R. Davies), Academic, New York, pp. 515–549.

Robbins, T.W. and Everitt, B.J. (2002) Limbic–striatal memory systems and drug addiction. *Neurobiology of Learning and Memory*, 78 (3), 625–636.

Roberts, A. (2006) Primate orbitofrontal cortex and adaptive behaviour. *Trends in Cognitive Science*, 10, 83–90.

Robinson, T.E. and Berridge, K.C. (1993) The neural basis of drug craving: an incentive-sensitization theory of addiction. *Brain Research Reviews*, 18, 247–291.

Robinson, T.E. and Berridge, K.C. (2003) Addiction. *Annual Review of Psychology*, 54, 25–53.

Rose, J. E., Mukhin, G.A., Lokitz, S.J. *et al.* (2010) Kinetics of brain nicotine accumulation in dependent and nondependent smokers assessed with PET and cigarettes containing 11C-nicotine. *Proceedings of the National Academy of Sciences, USA*, 107 (11), 5190–5195.

Rutter, M. (2006) *Genes and Behaviour: Nature–Nurture Interplay Explained*, Blackwell, Malden, MA.

Ryan, F. (2002a). Attentional bias and alcohol dependence: a controlled study using the modified Stroop paradigm. *Addictive Behaviors*, 27, 472–482.

Ryan, F. (2002b). Detected, selected, and sometimes neglected: cognitive processing of cues in addiction. *Experimental and Clinical Psychopharmacology*, 10 (2), 67–76.

Ryan, F. (2006) Appetite lost and found: cognitive psychology in the addiction clinic, in *Cognition and Addiction* (eds M. Munafo and I. Albery), Oxford University Press, Oxford, pp. 279–302.

Santa Ana, J.E., Rounsaville, B.J., Frankforter, T.L. *et al.* (2009) d-Cycloserine attenuates reactivity to smoking cues in nicotine dependent smokers: a pilot investigation. *Drug and Alcohol Dependence*, 104, 220–227.

Schmiedek, F., Lövdén, M. and Lindenberger, U. (2010) Hundred days of cognitive training enhance broad cognitive abilities in adulthood: findings from the COGITO study. *Frontiers in Aging Neuroscience*, 2, 27.

Schoenmakers, T.M., Marijn de Bruin, M., Irja, F.M. *et al.* (2010) Clinical effectiveness of attentional bias modification training in abstinent alcoholic patients. *Drug and Alcohol Dependence*, 109, 30–36.

Schultz, W. (2002) Getting formal with dopamine and reward. *Neuron*, 36 (2), 241–263.

Segal, Z.V., Williams, J.M.G. and Teasdale, J.D. (2002) *Mindfulness Based Cognitive Therapy for Depression: a New Approach to Preventing Relapse*. Guilford, New York.

Shiffman, S. and Waters, A.J. (2004) Negative affect and smoking lapses: a prospective analysis. *Journal of Consulting and Clinical Psychology*, 72, 192–201.

Shriffin, R.M. and Schneider, W. (1977). Controlled and automatic human information processing: II. Perceptual learning, automatic attending and a general theory. *Psychological Review*, 84, 127–190.

Sinha, R. (2009) Stress and addiction: a dynamic interplay of genes, environment, and drug intake. *Biological Psychiatry*, 66, 100–101.

Solms, M. and Nersessian, E. (1999) Freud's Theory of Affect: questions for neuroscience. *Neuropsychoanalysis*, 1, 5–14.

Solomon, R.L (1980) The opponent-process theory of acquired motivation: the costs of pleasure and the benefits of pain. *American Psychologist*, 35 (8), 691–712.

Soto, D., Humphreys, G.W. and Rotshtein, P. (2007) Dissociating the neural mechanisms of memory based guidance of visual selection. *Proceedings of the National Academy of Sciences, USA*, 104, 17186–17191.

Soto, D., Wriglesworth, A., Bahrami-Balani, A. and Humphreys, G.W. (2010) Working memory enhances visual perception: Evidence from signal detection analysis. *Journal of Experimental Psychology: Learning, Memory, and Cognition*, 36 (2), 441–456.

Stacy, A.W. and Wiers, R.W. (2010) Implicit cognition and addiction: a tool for explaining paradoxical behavior. *Annual Review of Clinical. Psychology*, 6, 551–575.

Stockwell, T., Hodgson, R., Edwards, G. *et al.* (1979) The development of a questionnaire to measure severity of alcohol dependence. *British Journal of Addiction*, 74, 79–87.

Strack, F. and Deutsch, R. (2004) Reflective and impulsive determinants of social behaviour. *Personality and Social Psychology Review*, 3, 220–247.

Suarez, L.M., Bennett, S.M., Goldstein, C.R. and Barlow, D.H. (2009) Understanding anxiety from a 'triple vulnerability' framework, in *Oxford Handbook of*

Anxiety and Related Disorders (eds M.M. Antony and M.B. Stein), Oxford University Press, Oxford, pp. 153–172.

Talmi, D., Seymour, B., Dayan, P. and Dolan, R.J. (2008) Human Pavlovian–instrumental transfer. *The Journal of Neuroscience*, 28 (2), 360–368.

Tarrier, N. and Calam, R. (2002) New developments in cognitive–behavioural case formulation. Epidemiological, systemic and social context: an integrative approach. *Behavioural and Cognitive Psychotherapy*, 30, 311–328.

Thoenen, H. (1995) Neurotrophins and neuronal plasticity. *Science*, 270 (5236), 593–598.

Thome, S.L., Malarcher, A., Maurice, E. and Caraballo, R. (2009) Cigarette smoking among adults – United States, 2007. *Journal of the American Medical Association*, 301, 373–375.

Tiffany, S.T. (1990) A cognitive model of drug urges and drug-use behavior: role of automatic and nonautomatic processes. *Psychological Review*, 97, 147–168.

Tversky, A. and Kahneman, D. (1974) Judgement under uncertainty: heuristics and biases. *Science*, 185, 1124–1130.

Ungless, M.A., Argilli, E. and Bonci, A. (2010) Effects of stress and aversion on dopamine neurons: implications for addiction. *Neuroscience: Biobehavioural Reviews*, 35, 151–156.

United Kingdom Alcohol Treatment Trial (UKATT) Research Team (2005) Effectiveness of treatment for alcohol problems: findings of the randomised United Kingdom Alcohol Treatment Trial (UKATT). *British Medical Journal*, 331, 541–544.

United Nations Office on Drugs and Crime (UNODC) (2009) *World Drug Report*.

Vaillant, G. (1996) A long-term follow-up of male alcohol abuse. *Archives of General Psychiatry*, 53 (3), 243–249.

Volkow, N.D., Chang, L., Wang, G.J., Fowler, J.S., Ding, Y.S., Sedler, M., Logan, J., Franceschi, D., Gatley, J., Hitzemann, R., Gifford, A., Wong, C. and Pappas, N. (2001) Low level of brain dopamine D2 receptors in methamphetamine abusers: association with metabolism in the orbitofrontal cortex. *American Journal of Psychiatry*, 158, 2015–2021.

Volkow, N.D., Fowler, J.S. and Wang, G.J. (2002) Role of dopamine in drug reinforcement and addiction in humans: results from imaging studies. *Behavioural Pharmacology*, 13 (5/6), 355–366.

Volkow, N.D., Fowler, J.S. and Wang, G.J. (2004) The addicted human brain viewed in the light of imaging studies: brain circuits and treatment strategies. *Neuropharmacology*, 47 (Suppl. 1), 3–13.

Wagner, F.A. and Anthony, J.C. (2002) From first drug use to drug dependence: developmental periods of risk for dependence upon marihuana, cocaine and alcohol. *Neuropsychopharmacology*, 26, 479–488.

Waters, A.J., Heishman, S.J., Lerman, C. and Pickworth, W. (2007) Enhanced identification of smoking-related words during the attentional blink in smokers. *Addictive Behaviors*, 32, 3077–3082.

Waters, A.J., Shiffman, S., Sayette, M.A. et al. (2003) Attentional bias predicts outcome in smoking cessation. *Health Psychology*, 22 (4), 378–387.

Watson, B.J., Wilson, S., Griffin L. et al. (2011) A pilot study of the effectiveness of D-cycloserine during cue-exposure therapy in abstinent alcohol-dependent subject. *Psychopharmacology*, 216, 121–129.

Weaver, T., Madden, P., Charles V. et al. (2002) Co-morbidity of substance misuse and mental illness in community mental health and substance misuse services. *British Journal of Psychiatry*, 183, 304–313.

Wechsler, D. (1997) *Wechsler Memory Scale – III*, Psychological Corporation, San Antonio, TX.

West, R. (2001) Theories of addiction. *Addiction*, 96, 3–15.

Westen, D. and Morrison, K. (2001) A multidimensional meta-analysis of treatments for depression, panic and generalised anxiety disorder: an empirical examination of the status of empirically supported therapies. *Journal of Consulting and Clinical Psychology*, 69 (6), 875–899.

Westerberg, H. and Klingberg, T. (2007) Changes in cortical activity after training of working memory – a single-subject analysis. *Physiology and Behavior*, 92, 186–219.

Whiteside, S.P. and Lynam, D.R. (2001) The Five Factor Model and impulsivity: using a structural model of personality to understand impulsivity. *Personality and Individual Differences*, 30, 669–689.

Whiteside, S.P., Lynam, D.R. and Reynolds, S.K. (2005) Validation of UPPS impulsive scale: a four factor model of impulsivity. *European Journal of Personality*, 19, 559–574.

Wiers, R.W., Cox, W.M., Field, M. et al. (2006) The search for new ways to change implicit alcohol-related cognitions in heavy drinkers. *Alcoholism: Clinical and Experimental Research*, 30, 320–331.

Wiers, R.W., Eberl, C., Rinck, M. et al. (2011) Retraining automatic action tendencies changes alcoholic patients' approach bias for alcohol and improves treatment outcome. *Psychological Science*, 22, 490–497.

Wiers, R., Rinck, M., Kordts, R. et al. (2010) Retraining automatic action-tendencies to approach alcohol in hazardous drinkers. *Addiction*, 105 (2), 279–287.

Wikler, A. (1948) Recent progress in research on the neurophysiologic basis of morphine addiction. *The American Journal of Psychiatry*, 105, 329–338.

Wilde, O. (1893; 1999) *Lady Windermere's Fan*, Dover, London.

Williams, J.M.G., Watts, F.N., MacLeod, C. and Matthews, A. (1988) *Cognitive Psychology and Emotional Disorders*, John Wiley & Sons, Ltd, Chichester.

Willutzki, U. and Koban, C. (2011) The Elaboration of Positive Goal Perspectives (EPOS): an intervention module to enhance motivation, in *Handbook of Motivational Counselling: Goal-Based Approaches to Assessment and Intervention with Addiction and Other Problems* (eds W.M. Cox and E. Klinger), John Wiley & Sons, Ltd, Chichester, pp. 437–459.

Wise, R.A. (1988)).The neurobiology of craving: implications for the understanding and treatment of addiction. *Journal of Abnormal Psychology*, 97, 118–132.

Wise, R.A. and Kiyatkin, E.A. (2011) Differentiating the rapid actions of cocaine. *Nature Reviews: Neuroscience*, 12, 479–484.

Witkiewitz, K. and Marlatt, G.A. (2004) Relapse prevention for alcohol and drug problems: that was Zen, this is Tao. *American Psychologist*, 59, 224–235.

Witkiewitz, K. and Villarroel, N.A. (2009) Dynamic association between negative affect and alcohol lapses following alcohol treatment. *Journal of Consulting and Clinical Psychology*, 77 (4), 633–644.

World Health Organisation (WHO) (1992) *International Classification of Diseases. Tenth Revision, Classification of Mental and Behavioural Disorders: Clinical Descriptions and Diagnostic Guidelines*, WHO, Geneva.

Yin, H.J. and Knowlton, B.J. (2006) Addiction and learning in the brain, in *Handbook of Implicit Cognition and Addiction* (eds R.W. Wiers and A.W. Stacy), Sage, London, pp. 167–183.

Yuan, Y., Zhu, Z., Shi, J. *et al.* (2009) Gray matter density negatively correlates with duration of heroin use in young lifetime heroin-dependent individuals. *Brain and Cognition*, 71 (3), 223–228.

Yucel, M., Lubman, D.I., Harrison, B.J., Fornito, A., Allen, N.B., Wellard, R.M., Roffel, K., Clarke, K., Wood, S.J., Forman, S.D. and Pantelis, C. (2007) A combined spectroscopic and functional MRI investigation of the dorsal anterior cingulate region in opiate addiction. *Molecular Psychiatry*, 12, 691–702.

Index

Note: Page references in *f* refer to Figures; those in *t* refer to Tables

AA. *see* Alcoholics Anonymous (AA)
AACTP (Alcohol-Control Training Programme)   108–10
Aarts, H.   53–4
aberrant learning   41
absence of consciousness
　purposeful behavior in   53–4
ACC. *see* anterior cingulate cortex (ACC)
action(s)
　control of   51–2
　vs. thoughts   181
action slips   52–3
action–outcome (A–O) association in addictive behaviour   39
addiction. *see also* substance misuse
　in absence of awareness 16–17
　ACC effects of   9–11
　attentional bias in context of 106–8
　avoiding pain *vs.* seeking reward in   33–4
　BDNFs and   69–70
　"biopsychosocial" framework for   2
　case example   75–6

CBT for. *see* cognitive behavioural therapy (CBT)
　changing habits in management of 14–15
　cognitive control compromised in 8–9
　cognitive developmental model of 22–3, 22*f*
　compulsive nature of   45–61
　core motivational processes in 33–44
CT for. *see* cognitive therapy (CT)
　"dark side" of   34
　defined   2
　denial in   77
　described   13–14
　diagnostic criteria for   15
　endurance and relapse proclivity in 33–4
　engagement in   75–97
　equivocal findings from research trials   16
　existing cognitive behavioural accounts of   21–31
　factors in overcoming   17
　features of   88–90
　formulation gone astray   34–5

Cognitive Therapy for Addiction: Motivation and Change, First Edition. Frank Ryan.
© 2013 Frank Ryan. Published 2013 by John Wiley & Sons, Ltd.

Index

addiction (continued)
 implicit cognition and   6–9
 impulse control in   99–133. *see also*
  impulse control
 incentive-focused models of   54
 incentive theories of   35–6
 introduction to   1–5, 5f
 learning mechanisms in   36–40
 liability for   63–73
 mindfulness in control of   18
 mood management in   135–53. *see also* mood
 motivation in   75–97
 motivational enhancement strategies for   18–19
 neuropsychological findings in   9–11
 overview of   1–5, 5f
 personality disorders and   66–7
 reciprocal relationship between mood and   135–7
 from research to practice   72–3
 scope of   2–3
 stepped care for   145–7
 tenacity of   1–20
 terminology related to   1–2
 towards integration in   15–16
 vulnerability factors in   63–73
addiction clinic
 findings from   71–2
 "wanting and liking" in   41–2
addiction liability
 individual differences in   63, 64f
 personality traits in   63–6
addictive behaviour   11–14
 "ABC" convention of   21
 craving and   103–4
 dopamine neurons in   68
 learning mechanisms in   36–40
 liability for   63, 64f
 maintaining change related to   155–69

 pathways to negative affect and   136
 routes to   24, 25f
 urge and   103–4
addictive personality
 defined   64
advice
 in motivation building   84–5
affect
 negative   136, 141–5
affect regulation
 in overcoming addiction   17
affective vulnerability factors   67–9
Agatsuma, S.   12
agreeableness
 in addiction liability   65
Alcohol Attention-Control Training Programme (AACTP)   108–10
alcohol dependence
 case example   138–41, 144
 mental-health problems with   137–8
 PTSD and   146–7
Alcoholics Anonymous (AA)   179
 "loss of control" accounts by   15
alliance
 therapeutic   88–90
ambivalence
 dual-processing approach to   85–6
 as systemic problem with systemic solution   76
anankastic (compulsivity) personality disorder   66
anchoring and adjustment bias   89–90
anchoring heuristic   89–90
Andrews, S.C.   130
antecedent(s)
 in addictive behaviour and addiction   21
antecedent cognitive misappraisals
 alteration of   148

Index

anterior cingulate cortex (ACC) 77, 115
  addiction effects on 9–11
  dorsal 36
  rostroventral 36
anti-social (dissocial behavior) personality disorder 66
anticipation
  core motivational processes and 38–9
"antireward" 34
A–O association
  in addictive behaviour 39
appetitive behaviours
  compulsive 3–4
  cortical structure damage effects on 9
appetitive cues
  competitive advantage of 52–3
approach
  as behavioural signature of addictive disorders 14
asthenic (emotional dysregulation) personality disorder 66
attention
  in control of action 51–2
  focused 168
  theories of 46–7
  volition and 51–2
attentional bias 7
  in context of addiction 106–8
  craving and 54–6, 104–5
  reversing 112
attentional bias research
  in implicit cognition approaches in addictive behaviour field 7
attentional blink 49
attentional template 50
attributional bias 90–1
Audrain-McGovern, J. 116
autobiographical memory
  bias in 34–5

automatic
  meanings of 51
automatic processes 28–31, 30t
  limitlessness of 48
  top-down influences as 47–8
availability heuristic 89
avoidance
  cognitive 148
  emotional 148
  pain 33–4, 43–4
avoidance (inhibitedness) personality disorder 66
awareness
  absence of 16–17
Awareness of Seeing mindfulness exercise 161

Baler, R.D. 45
Barratt Impulsiveness Scale 67
BAS. *see* behavioural activation system (BAS)
Baumeister, R.F. 118
BDNFs. *see* brain-derived neurotrophic factors (BDNFs)
Bechara, A. 29
Beck, A.T. 18, 22
Beck, D.M. 50
behavioral patterns
  educating client about 120–2
behaviour(s). *see also specific types, e.g., appetitive behaviours*
  addictive, 21. *see* addictive behaviour
  compulsive appetitive 3–4
  emotion-driven 148–9
  implicit cognition and 56
  impulsive 67
  purposeful 53–4
behavioural activation system (BAS) 65
behavioural avoidance
  subtle 148

Behavioural Couples Therapy 24–5, 25*f*
behavioural experiments
  in impulse control 123
behavioural inhibition system (BIS) 65
behavioural techniques 24
Bennett-Levy, J. 20
Berridge, K.C. 41–2, 44
between-session change 83
"beyond the pleasure principle" 43–4
bias(es)
  anchoring and adjustment 89–90
  attentional 7, 54–6, 104–8, 112
  attributional 90–1
  in autobiographical memory 34–5
  "booze" 180–1
biased competition 50–1
Bickel, W.K. 117
"biopsychosocial" framework for addiction 2
BIS. *see* behavioural inhibition system (BIS)
blame game 90–1
blink
  attentional 49
Bolla, K.I. 10
"booze bias" 180–1
bottom-up attentional strategies 47
Bowen, S. 161
brain-derived neurotrophic factors (BDNFs) 69–70
brain training
  in impulse control 112–17
Brandstatter, V. 125–6
Brewer, J.A. 23

Calam, R. 93
capacity
  overload and 60*f*, 61

cardiovascular fitness training (CFT)
  in impulse control 115
Carter, B.L. 49, 103
Carter, C.S. 77
case formulation 91–7, 96*t*
Castellani, B. 3
CBM. *see* cognitive bias modification (CBM)
CBT. *see* cognitive behavioural therapy (CBT)
CFT. *see* cardiovascular fitness training (CFT)
Chambers, C.D. 8
change
  between-session 83
  maintaining 155–69
  in motivation building 85
  within-session 83
CHANGE approach 145, 146
  described 135
CHANGE framework 135–6, 145
CHANGE model 13, 138, 143, 146, 147, 149, 164, 172, 174
  in addiction management 16–17
  formulation for co-occurring addiction and emotional disorder according to 96*t*
  vs. existing approaches to addiction 19–20
CHANGE model/Four-M Model 78*t*–9*t*
CHANGE programme 140, 145, 168
changing habits 14–15
Chanraud, S. 157
Chein, J. 114, 118
Childress, A.R. 6, 61, 80
classical (stimulus–stimulus) learning mechanisms
  in addictive behaviour 36–40
clinic(s)
  findings from 71–2
  "wanting and liking" in 41–2

CM. *see* contingency management (CM)
cocaine users
　neuropsychological findings in　10
COGITO study　114
cognition
　discovering　5–6
　implicit　56. *see* implicit cognition
cognitive algebra　83
cognitive avoidance　148
cognitive behavioural accounts
　of addiction and substance misuse 21–31
cognitive behavioural therapy (CBT) 172
　for addiction　16
　behavioural approaches to　24–5, 25*f*
　definitive features of　21
　dual-processing framework for 28–31, 30*t*
　evidential basis of　23
　mechanisms of change in　26–7
　meta-analytic findings in　23–4
　missing variable in　27–8
cognitive bias modification (CBM)
　in impulse control　105–6
cognitive bias modification (CBM) paradigm　105–6
cognitive control
　addiction effects on　8–9
　in addiction management　18
　dynamics of　45, 46*f*
　Four Ms in　173–8
　increasing　172–3
　neurocognitive therapy in 171–2
cognitive control mechanisms
　in understanding compulsive nature of addiction　45–61
cognitive control skills
　in overcoming addiction　17

cognitive cycle of preoccupation 56–61, 57*f*, 60*f*
cognitive deficits
　chronic nature of　155–8
cognitive developmental model of addiction　22–3, 22*f*
cognitive processes
　craving and　104–5
cognitive processing
　competitive nature of　50
　in impulse control　104–5
cognitive therapy (CT)
　for addiction　16
　mindfulness-based　23
　in neurobiological framework　18
　overall strategy of　20
Colcombe, S.J.　115
COMBINE study　26
COMET　164
competition
　biased　50–1
compulsion
　emergence of　41
compulsive appetitive behaviours 3–4
compulsive nature of addiction
　cognitive approach to understanding 45–61
compulsivity personality disorder　66
conditioned response　38
conscientiousness
　in addiction liability　65
consciousness
　absence of　53–4
consequence(s)
　in addictive behaviour and addiction 21
contingency management (CM) 24–5, 25*f*
contingency management (CM) interventions
　in impulse control　126–9

continuous feedback
  rationale for   165–6
control of action
  attention in   51–2
controlled processes   28–31, 30t
controlled processing   28–31, 30t
core motivational processes
  in addiction   33–44
  anticipation and   38–9
core training
  goals of   118
COSMIC study   138
counselling
  motivational   87–8
Cox, W.M.   7, 42, 104, 107, 109, 159
craving(s)
  in addictive behaviour   103–4
  attentional bias and   54–6, 104–5
  cognitive processes and   104–5
  fostering detached mindfulness of   161
  impulses and   104–5
CT. see cognitive therapy (CT)
cue(s)
  appetitive   52–3
  motivationally relevant   48–9
current concern   58

D-cycloserine (DCS)
  in impulse control   131–2
dACC. see dorsal anterior cingulate cortex (dACC)
"dark side of addiction"   34
DCS. see D-cycloserine (DCS)
decision making
  heuristics impact on   89
  in MI session   86
delay discounting
  WM and   116–17

delayed reward discounting (DRD)   116–17
  clinical implications of   117–19, 120t
denial
  in addiction   77
  implicit   162–9, 169t
dependence
  term description   3
Desimone, R.   50
Deutsch, R.   28
Dijksterhuis, A.   53–4
Disner, S.G.   18
dissocial behavior personality disorder   66
distraction
  learning   181–2
DLPFC. see dorsolateral prefrontal cortex (DLPFC)
Dodd   3
doing
  vs. thinking   181
dopamine
  gambling related to   3
dopamine neurons
  in addictive behaviours   68
dopamine reuptake
  drug effects on   35–6
dorsal anterior cingulate cortex (dACC)   36
dorsal prefrontal cortex (PFC)   36, 37f
dorsolateral prefrontal cortex (DLPFC)   36, 77, 155–6, 158
DRD. see delayed reward discounting (DRD)
drug abuse
  case example   138–42
drug effects
  negative affect due to   141–5

dual-processing approach
  to ambivalence   85–6
dual-representation theories   29–30, 30t
Duncan, J.   50
Dutra, L.   23

EDBs. *see* emotion-driven behaviours (EDBs)
ego depletion   118–19, 176
Eldreth, D.A.   10
emotion(s)
  negative   147–53, 151t
  psychoeducation about   148
emotion-driven behaviours (EDBs)
  modification of   148–9
emotional avoidance
  prevention of   148
emotional distress
  pre-existing vulnerability to 137–41
emotional dysregulation
  issues related to   92
emotional dysregulation personality disorder   66
emotional stability
  goal selection related to   87
empathy
  in motivation building   85
empirically supported therapy (EST)   93
engagement   75–97
Ersche, K.D.   70
EST. *see* empirically supported therapy (EST)
Evans, K.K.   48
Everitt, B.J.   36, 40, 42, 77
exercise(s)
  mindfulness   161
  physical   115–16

expectancy
  in impulse control   124–5, 124t
extraversion
  in addiction liability   65
  Eysenckian construct of   65–6
Eysenck, M.W.   142–3
Eysenckian construct of extraversion 65–6

FA. *see* focused attention (FA)
Fadardi, J.S.   109
feedback
  continuous   165–6
  in motivation building   84
  in neurocognitive framework 166–8
Field, M.   42, 55, 104, 107
Five-Factor Model (FFM)   65–7
fMRI. *see* functional magnetic resonance imaging (fMRI)
focused attention (FA)   168
focusing illusion   90
Forman, S.D.   8
formulation
  addiction effects on   34–5
Four M Model   4, 5f, 78t–9t
  in cognitive control   173–8
  mindfulness practice at different stages of   168–9, 169t
FRAMES
  in MI   84–8
Franken, I.H.A.   66
Freud, S.   43
Fumagalli, F.   68, 69
functional magnetic resonance imaging (fMRI)
  in exploring neural signature of very briefly presented appetitive stimuli   6

GAD-7   142
gambling   3–4
  dopamine and   3
  in Parkinson's disease patients   3
Garavan, H.   10–11, 42, 129
Garland, E.L.   7
goal maintenance   82
  importance in long term   158–9
goal pursuit   58
goal selection
  factors affecting   87–8
goal setting   82
  effective   87–8
  in MI session   86
Goldstein, R.Z.   77
Gollwitzer, P.M.   125
Gordon, J.R.   21–2, 141
Grant, S.   42
Gray, J.A.   65

habit(s)
  changing   14–15
Hester, R.   129
heuristic(s)
  impact on reasoning and decision making   89–90
Higgins, S.T.   127
Higgs, S.   175
high-frequency heart-rate variability (HFHRV)   7
"high-risk situations"   21
Hiroi, N.   12
Houben, K.   111

ICD-10
  criteria for substance dependence   15
illusion(s)
  focusing   90
impaired insight
  case example   80–1
  described   77, 80

therapeutic relationship and   75–80, 78t–9t
impaired Response Inhibition and Salience Attribution (iRISA) framework   36, 37f
implementation intentions
  in motivation   125–9
implicit associations
  in implicit cognition approaches in addictive behaviour field   7
implicit cognition
  addition and   6–9
  behaviour and   56
  definitive feature of   6
implicit cognitive patterns
  educating client about   120–2
implicit denial   162–9, 169t
  case example   162–4
impulse(s)
  craving and   104–5
  managing   99–133. see also impulse control
impulse control
  AACTP in   108–10
  attentional bias and   106–8
  behavioural experiments in   123
  brain training in   112–17
  building resilience in   100–2
  CBM in   105–6
  CFT in   115
  CM interventions in   126–9
  cognitive processing in   104–5
  craving and urge report in   103–4
  DCS in   131–2
  described   102–3
  expectancy in   124–5, 124t
  implementation intentions in   125–9
  modifying implicit approach tendencies in   110–12
  neurocognitive rehabilitation approaches in   112–17

neurophysiological techniques in 129–30
neuropsychopharmacological approaches to 130–3
physical exercise in 115–16
structuring session in 99–100
tried and testing techniques in 119–25, 124*t*
"impulsive amygdala-dependent" system 29
impulsive behaviour
 pathways to 67
impulsive system 28–31, 30*t*
 described 76
impulsivity
 described 102
 goal selection related to 87
 managing 173–6
 "real-world" analogues of experimental paradigms of 120*t*
incentive salience 41
incentive theories
 of addiction 35–6
individual differences
 in addiction liability 63, 64*f*
inferior frontal gyrus 36
Ingjaldsson, J.T. 56
inhibitedness personality disorder 66
inhibition
 addiction effects on 8–9
insight
 impaired. *see* impaired insight
integrated approach to negative emotions 147–53, 151*t*
integration
 in addiction control 15–16
interpersonal
 defined 22
intervention(s)
 formulating and planning 88–90

interviewing
 motivational 77, 81–8
intrapersonal
 defined 21
iRISA framework. *see* impaired Response Inhibition and Salience Attribution (iRISA) framework
Irwin, J.E. 24

Jones, A. 119
Jonides, J. 50

Kahneman, D. 89
Kamboj, S.J. 131–2
Kastner, S. 50
Kaufman, J.N. 8
Kennerley, S.W. 38
Kiyatkin, E.A. 39
Knowlton, B.J. 37
Koban, C. 87–8
Kober, H. 124
Koch, C. 48
Kohut, H. 11
Koob, G.F. 34
Krishnan-Sarin, S. 116
Kuyken, W. 89, 101

lack of perseverance
 in impulsive behaviour 67
lack of premeditation
 in impulsive behaviour 67
Lady Windermere's Fans 64
lapse
 vs. relapse 182
Lavie, N. 59–60
Le Moal, M. 34
learning
 aberrant 41
learning mechanisms
 in addiction 36–40
Letter Number Sequencing 117
Leventhal, A.M. 6

liability
  addiction   63–73
Libet, B.   53–4
"liking"
  in clinic   41–2
Litt, M.D.   26, 27
Livesley, W.J.   66
"loss of control" accounts
  by AA members   15
"loss of control" concept
  in Twelve-Step approaches   15
Lutz, A.   168
Lynam, D.R.   66, 67

MacKillop, J.   116–17
Makris, N.   156
Marcus, B.H.   116
marijuana use
  neuropsychological findings in   10
  Stroop task for   10
Marissen, M.A.E.   107
Marlatt, G.A.   21–2, 141
Maslow, A.H.   36
MBCT. *see* mindfulness-based cognitive therapy (MBCT)
MBRP. *see* mindfulness-based relapse prevention (MBRP)
MBSR. *see* mindfulness-based stress reduction (MBSR)
McClure, S.M.   117
McGinty, J.F.   69
McLeod   106
medial orbitofrontal cortex (mOFC)   36
meditation techniques   168–9, 169*t*
memory
  autobiographical   34–5
  don't trust   180
  working   47–8, 50, 58–9, 60*f*, 61, 70, 116–17, 128–9, 133, 156, 172, 175, 178

memory bias research
  in implicit cognition approaches in addictive behaviour field   7
mental-health problems
  alcohol dependence and   137–8
N-Methyl-D-aspartate (NMDA) receptor agonist
  in impulse control   131
MFG. *see* middle frontal gyrus (MFG)
MI. *see* motivational interviewing (MI)
middle frontal gyrus (MFG)   115
Miller, G.A.   50
Miller, W.R.   81
mindfulness
  in addiction management   18
mindfulness-based cognitive therapy (MBCT)   23, 168–9
mindfulness-based relapse prevention (MBRP)   168
mindfulness-based stress reduction (MBSR)   168–9
mindfulness exercise
  Awareness of Seeing   161
Mitcheson, L.   20
Modified Stroop test   54, 108
mOFC. *see* medial orbitofrontal cortex (mOFC)
monitoring
  open   168
mood
  defined   143
  managing   135–53, 176
  reciprocal relationship between addiction and   135–7
Morrison, A.   114, 118
motivation   75–97, 173
  conflicted   81–2
  distorted   41
  implementation intentions in   125–9
  neurocognitive perspectives on   78*t*–9*t*, 83–4

motivational counselling
  systematic 87–8
motivational enhancement strategies 26
  in addiction management 18–19
motivational interviewing (MI) 77, 81–3
  agenda for 85–6
  case example 86
  FRAMES in 84–8
  in practice 84–8
motivational processes
  in addiction 33–44
  anticipation and 38–9
motivationally relevant cues
  prioritization of 48–9
Muraven, M. 119

Naqvi, N.H. 77
National Institute for Health and Clinical Excellence (NICE) 126
necessary but not sufficient (NBNS) approach 95–6
negative affect
  drug effects causing 141–5
  pathways to 136
negative emotion
  integrated approach to 147–53, 151t
negative urgency
  in impulsive behaviour 67
NEO–Personality Inventory–Revised (NEO-PI-R) 67
Nersessian, E. 43–4
neural activity
  modulation of 129–30
neurocognitive framework
  providing feedback in 166–8
neurocognitive perspective
  relapse prevention strategies from 155–61

neurocognitive rehabilitation approaches
  in impulse control 112–17
neurocognitive therapy
  future directions in 171–2
neurocognitive vulnerability 70–1
neuron(s)
  dopamine 68
neurophysiological techniques
  in impulse control 129–30
neuropsychological findings
  in addiction 9–11
neuropsychopharmacological approaches
  in impulse control 130–3
neuroticism
  in addiction liability 65
NICE. *see* National Institute for Health and Clinical Excellence (NICE)
NMDA receptor agonist
  in impulse control 131
Norman, D.A. 51–2

OFC. *see* orbitofrontal cortex (OFC)
open monitoring (OM) 168
openness
  in addiction liability 65
operant (stimulus–response) learning mechanisms
  in addictive behaviour 36–40
opiate-addicted persons
  neuropsychological findings in 9
orbitofrontal cortex (OFC) 130
Orford, J. 27
overload
  capacity and 60f, 61
Owen, A.M. 113

pain avoidance
  addiction and 33–4
  beyond 43–4

Parkinson's disease
  gambling related to   3
Pavlovian learning processes   40
Pavlovian salivation response   37
Pavlovian–instrumental transfer   40
Perkins, K.A.   72
perseverance
  lack of   67
Personal Health Questionnaire-9 (PHQ-9)   138, 142
personality
  addictive   64
personality disorders
  addiction and   66–7
  anankastic   66
  anti-social   66
  asthenic   66
  avoidance   66
personality traits
  in addiction liability   63–6
  goal selection related to   87
Persons, J.B.   92–7
Pessoa, L.   60
Petersen, S.E.   46–7
PFC. *see* prefrontal cortex (PFC)
Phillips, P.E.M.   38
PHQ-9. *see Personal Health Questionnaire-9* (PHQ-9)
physical exercise
  in impulse control   115–16
pleasure
  beyond   43–4
positive urgency
  in impulsive behaviour   67
Posner M.I.   46–7
posttraumatic stress disorder (PTSD)
  alcohol dependence and   146–7
Powell, J.   104
prefrontal cortex (PFC)   155
  dorsal   36, 37f
  dorsolateral   36, 77, 155–6, 158
  ventromedial   36, 37f

prefrontal processes
  types of   156–7
premeditation
  lack of   67
preoccupation
  cognitive cycle of   56–61, 57f, 60f
Project MATCH   26, 71
psychoanalytic perspective
  beyond pleasure and pain   43–4
PTSD. *see* posttraumatic stress disorder (PTSD)
purposeful behavior
  in absence of consciousness   53–4

rACC. *see* rostroventral anterior cingulate cortex (rACC)
RAIN
  fostering detached mindfulness of cravings in   161
rapid serial visual presentation (RSVP) paradigm   48
Reason, J.T.   52
reasoning
  heuristics impact on   89
Reflective Impulsive Model (RIM)   28
"reflective prefrontal dependent" neural system   29
reflective system   28–31, 30t
reinforcers
  secondary   43
relapse
  neurocognitive perspective on   159–61
  vs. lapse   182
relapse prevention
  mindfulness-based   168
  from neurocognitive perspective   155–8
  Six Tips in   179–83

"Relapse Prevention Skills Training" model 21
relationship as treatment view 95–6
representative heuristic 89
resilience
 building of 100–2
responsibility
 in motivation building 84
reward seeking
 addiction and 33–4
RIM. see Reflective Impulsive Model (RIM)
Robbins, T.W. 36, 40, 42
Robinson, T.E. 41–2, 44
Rogers, C. 96–7
Rose, G.S. 81
Rose, J.E. 38
rostrovental anterior cingulate cortex (rACC) 36
RSVP paradigm. see rapid serial visual presentation (RSVP) paradigm
Rugle, L. 3
Rutter, M. 136–7
Ryan, F. 13, 49, 54, 56, 58, 104, xii

safety signals 148
salience
 incentive 41
Santa Ana, J.E. 131
Schmiedek, F. 114
Schneider, W. 28
Schoenmakers, T.M. 109, 112
Schultz, W. 35
secondary reinforcers
 role of 43
Segal, Z.V. 161
self-control training 118–19
self-efficacy
 in motivation building 85
self-regulation
 components in 8

sensation seeking
 in impulsive behaviour 67
session(s)
 structuring of 99–100
Severity of Alcohol Dependence Questionnaire 54
SFG. see superior frontal gyrus (SFG)
Shallice, T. 51–2
Shiffman, S. 14, 143
Shiffrin, R.M. 28
shifting strategies
 in self-regulation 8
Sinha, R. 67–8
Six Tips
 aim of 180
 in relapse prevention 179–83
SMC. see systematic motivational counselling (SMC)
smoking
 short- and long-term consequences of resuming 124–5, 124t
S–O association
 in addictive behaviour 37–9
Social Behavioural Network Therapy 24, 26
Solms, M. 43–4
Soto, D. 58–9, 175
S–R association
 in addictive behaviour 39–40
stability
 emotional 87
Stacy, A.W. 77
stepped care
 for addiction 145–7
 described 145–7
stimulus–outcome (S–O) association
 in addictive behaviour 37–9
stimulus–response (S–R) association
 in addictive behaviour 39–40
stimulus–response learning mechanisms
 in addictive behaviour 36–40

stimulus–stimulus learning mechanisms
   in addictive behaviour   36–40
Stop Signal Reaction Time task   70–1
Stout, J.C.   10–11
Strack, F.   28
stress reduction
   mindfulness-based   168–9
Stroop task
   marijuana users performance on   10
Stroop test
   cocaine users performance on   10
Suarez, L.M.   147
substance dependence
   ICD-10 criteria for   15
substance misuse. *see also* addiction
   existing cognitive behavioural accounts of   21–31
   issues related to   92
substance use disorders
   addiction and   66–7
subtle behavioural avoidance   148
superior frontal gyrus (SFG)   115
systematic motivational counselling (SMC)   87–8

Talmi, D.   40
Tarrier, N.   93
tDCS. *see* transcranial direct current stimulation (tDCS)
therapeutic alliance
   building of   88–90
therapeutic responses
   presenting problems in   149–50
thinking
   vs. doing   181
thought(s)
   vs. actions   181
Tiffany, S.T.   49, 103
TMS. *see* transcranial magnetic stimulation (TMS)
top-down attentional strategies   47
   as automatic processes   47–8
transcranial direct current stimulation (tDCS)
   in neural activity modulation   129–30
transcranial magnetic stimulation (TMS)
   in neural activity modulation   129–30
treatment approaches
   equivalent outcomes from   25–6
Treisman, A.   48
Tsuchiya, N.   48
Tversky, A.   89
Twelve-Step approaches   26–7, 31, 161–2, 172, 179
   "loss of control" concept in   15

UKATT alcohol treatment trial   26
Ungless, M.A.   68
unified protocol (UP)
   in addressing negative emotions   147–53, 151*t*
   components of   148–9
updating strategies
   in self-regulation   8
urge
   in addictive behaviour   103–4
urgency
   negative   67
   positive   67

Vaillant, G.   156
van Veen, V.   77
ventromedial prefrontal cortex   36, 37*f*
Villarroel, N.A.   71
Vipassana   168
Volkow, N.D.   45
vulnerability factors
   in addiction   63–73

affective 67–9
BDNFs 69–70
in emotional distress 137–41
neurocognitive 70–1
from research to practice 72–3

"wanting"
in clinic 41–2
Waters, A.J. 14, 49, 108, 143
Watson, B.J. 132
Weaver, T. 137
West, R. 2–3
Whiteside, S.P. 67, 102–3
Wiers, R.W. 7, 77, 111
Wikler, A. 33–4
Wilde, O. 64

will power 118–19
as not enough 182
Willlutzki, U. 87–8
Wise, R.A. 39
within-session change 83
Witkiewitz, K. 71
working memory (WM) 47–8, 50, 58–9, 60f, 61, 70, 128–9, 133, 156, 172, 175, 178
delay discounting and 116–17

Yin, H.J. 37
Yuan, Y. 156
Yucel, M. 9

Zen 168